C000135271

Three arguments in the two causes in Chancery, on the last will of Peter Thellusson, Esq. By Francis Hargrave, ...

Francis Hargrave

ECCO

PRINT EDITIONS

Three arguments in the two causes in Chancery, on the last will of Peter Thellusson, Esq. By Francis Hargrave, ...

Hargrave, Francis
ESTCID: T113121
Reproduction from British Library
The appendix has separate pagination and register.
London : printed for G. G. and J. Robinson, 1799.
[8],182;xxivp. ; 4°

Eighteenth Century
Collections Online
Print Editions

Gale ECCO Print Editions

Relive history with *Eighteenth Century Collections Online*, now available in print for the independent historian and collector. This series includes the most significant English-language and foreign-language works printed in Great Britain during the eighteenth century, and is organized in seven different subject areas including literature and language; medicine, science, and technology; and religion and philosophy. The collection also includes thousands of important works from the Americas.

The eighteenth century has been called "The Age of Enlightenment." It was a period of rapid advance in print culture and publishing, in world exploration, and in the rapid growth of science and technology – all of which had a profound impact on the political and cultural landscape. At the end of the century the American Revolution, French Revolution and Industrial Revolution, perhaps three of the most significant events in modern history, set in motion developments that eventually dominated world political, economic, and social life.

In a groundbreaking effort, Gale initiated a revolution of its own: digitization of epic proportions to preserve these invaluable works in the largest online archive of its kind. Contributions from major world libraries constitute over 175,000 original printed works. Scanned images of the actual pages, rather than transcriptions, recreate the works *as they first appeared.*

Now for the first time, these high-quality digital scans of original works are available via print-on-demand, making them readily accessible to libraries, students, independent scholars, and readers of all ages.

For our initial release we have created seven robust collections to form one the world's most comprehensive catalogs of 18th century works.

Initial Gale ECCO Print Editions collections include:

History and Geography
Rich in titles on English life and social history, this collection spans the world as it was known to eighteenth-century historians and explorers. Titles include a wealth of travel accounts and diaries, histories of nations from throughout the world, and maps and charts of a world that was still being discovered. Students of the War of American Independence will find fascinating accounts from the British side of conflict.

Social Science

Delve into what it was like to live during the eighteenth century by reading the first-hand accounts of everyday people, including city dwellers and farmers, businessmen and bankers, artisans and merchants, artists and their patrons, politicians and their constituents. Original texts make the American, French, and Industrial revolutions vividly contemporary.

Medicine, Science and Technology

Medical theory and practice of the 1700s developed rapidly, as is evidenced by the extensive collection, which includes descriptions of diseases, their conditions, and treatments. Books on science and technology, agriculture, military technology, natural philosophy, even cookbooks, are all contained here.

Literature and Language

Western literary study flows out of eighteenth-century works by Alexander Pope, Daniel Defoe, Henry Fielding, Frances Burney, Denis Diderot, Johann Gottfried Herder, Johann Wolfgang von Goethe, and others. Experience the birth of the modern novel, or compare the development of language using dictionaries and grammar discourses.

Religion and Philosophy

The Age of Enlightenment profoundly enriched religious and philosophical understanding and continues to influence present-day thinking. Works collected here include masterpieces by David Hume, Immanuel Kant, and Jean-Jacques Rousseau, as well as religious sermons and moral debates on the issues of the day, such as the slave trade. The Age of Reason saw conflict between Protestantism and Catholicism transformed into one between faith and logic -- a debate that continues in the twenty-first century.

Law and Reference

This collection reveals the history of English common law and Empire law in a vastly changing world of British expansion. Dominating the legal field is the *Commentaries of the Law of England* by Sir William Blackstone, which first appeared in 1765. Reference works such as almanacs and catalogues continue to educate us by revealing the day-to-day workings of society.

Fine Arts

The eighteenth-century fascination with Greek and Roman antiquity followed the systematic excavation of the ruins at Pompeii and Herculaneum in southern Italy; and after 1750 a neoclassical style dominated all artistic fields. The titles here trace developments in mostly English-language works on painting, sculpture, architecture, music, theater, and other disciplines. Instructional works on musical instruments, catalogs of art objects, comic operas, and more are also included.

The BiblioLife Network

This project was made possible in part by the BiblioLife Network (BLN), a project aimed at addressing some of the huge challenges facing book preservationists around the world. The BLN includes libraries, library networks, archives, subject matter experts, online communities and library service providers. We believe every book ever published should be available as a high-quality print reproduction; printed on-demand anywhere in the world. This insures the ongoing accessibility of the content and helps generate sustainable revenue for the libraries and organizations that work to preserve these important materials.

The following book is in the "public domain" and represents an authentic reproduction of the text as printed by the original publisher. While we have attempted to accurately maintain the integrity of the original work, there are sometimes problems with the original work or the micro-film from which the books were digitized. This can result in minor errors in reproduction. Possible imperfections include missing and blurred pages, poor pictures, markings and other reproduction issues beyond our control. Because this work is culturally important, we have made it available as part of our commitment to protecting, preserving, and promoting the world's literature.

GUIDE TO FOLD-OUTS MAPS and OVERSIZED IMAGES

The book you are reading was digitized from microfilm captured over the past thirty to forty years. Years after the creation of the original microfilm, the book was converted to digital files and made available in an online database.

In an online database, page images do not need to conform to the size restrictions found in a printed book. When converting these images back into a printed bound book, the page sizes are standardized in ways that maintain the detail of the original. For large images, such as fold-out maps, the original page image is split into two or more pages

Guidelines used to determine how to split the page image follows:

• Some images are split vertically; large images require vertical and horizontal splits.
• For horizontal splits, the content is split left to right.
• For vertical splits, the content is split from top to bottom.
• For both vertical and horizontal splits, the image is processed from top left to bottom right.

Francis Hargrave.

THREE ARGUMENTS,

F. H.

IN THE

TWO CAUSES IN CHANCERY,

ON THE

LAST WILL of PETER THELLUSSON, Esq.

BY

FRANCIS HARGRAVE, Esquire,

BARRISTER AT LAW, AND RECORDER OF LIVERPOOL,
ONE OF THE COUNSEL AGAINST THE WILL.

See Report of this Case when in
House of Lords 11 Ves. Jun. 112.

————

LONDON
PRINTED FOR G. G. AND J ROBINSON, PATER-NOSTER-ROW.
M.DCC.XCIX.

THE following THREE ARGUMENTS conſtitute the firſt article of a SECOND VOLUME of JURIDICAL ARGUMENTS and COLLECTIONS; and are here publiſhed ſeparately for thoſe, who may not chuſe to purchaſe the whole of that volume.

IN the volume, to which the THREE ARGUMENTS belong, there is prefixed an ADVERTISEMENT, which relates to the Three Arguments here publiſhed ſeparately; and therefore it is deemed proper to inſert it here as an introduction to them.

ADVERTISEMENT.

THIS ſecond volume of JURIDICAL ARGUMENTS *is ſubmitted by the author of them to publick notice, with very ſerious alarm, leaſt the moſt elaborate part of the contents, inſtead of obtaining favour from his readers, ſhould attract their cenſure. When he reſolved upon hazarding a ſecond volume, which was not till cloſe of the hearing of counſel in the chancery cauſes on the laſt will of the late Mr Thelluſſon, ſome ſymptoms of temporary favourable effect, from delivery of the arguments of thoſe who ſpoke againſt the will, raiſed his mind into the hope, that at leaſt the firſt and moſt extenſive article of this volume might prove intereſting   But within theſe few days enough hath occurred to ſuppreſs his expectations in this reſpect; and to make him almoſt repentant, that he ſhould be too far committed in the preſent publication to withhold it.   Not only a ſolemn judgment hath been paſſed wholly over-ruling his Arguments in the Thelluſſon cauſes: but ſuch circumſtances have occurred, as may encourage a doubt, whether topicks, which*

the

the author deemed novel momentous and difficult, should have been so confidered, or should have been amplified upon nearly in the extent in which they are treated in his three Arguments; and more especially, whether his history of the dry subject of EXECUTORY DEVISE should not have been reserved for future and more apposite application. Some consolations, however, present themselves to the author. Whatever may have been the impression with others, the noble lord, whose office it was to adjudge the causes, and whose extraordinary endowments eminently qualify him to fulfil the duties of that office, most certainly saw the case on the will as demanding full and solemn discussion. After hearing the leading counsel against the will of the late Mr. Thellusson, his Lordship interposed to postpone the proceedings, with an explicit declaration, that the case on the will struck him as being " of GREAT IM-
" PORTANCE and SINGULAR NOVELTY;" and that he " thought, he
" could not do better than call in the assistance of two judges." It should be remembered also, that his Lordship afterwards encreased the number of his assessors, by adding his honor the master of the rolls. Nor when the judgment was given in the causes, doth his Lordship appear to have disapproved the great scope of the arguments of any of the counsel against the will: for, notwithstanding the unfavorableness of the result to their side of the causes, his Lordship, with a polished sensibility, which at least operated as discountenancing all supposition of having trespassed upon the time of the court, observed, that he
" was not surprised the case had been brought forward, and had called forth such
" great exertion of learning and ingenuity." Under the latter part of this very handsome testimony, so far as it concerns the counsel against the will, the author of this volume feels it convenient to claim some shelter. Indeed he is sensible, that very little of the praise, thus generously bestowed, can be presumed to have been intended for himself. But small as his share may be, he trusts, that it will suffice to protect him against any ill effects from remarks of a different tendency. Fortunately also for the author, there is another circumstance

of

of a very confolatory defcription. It fo happened, that the firft impreffions of the gentleman, who was leading counfel againft the will, and whofe very long experience and great profounanefs in the law and equity of the country render him oracular in the profeffion, were unfavorable to thofe for whom he was engaged to plead, and in the outfet of the bufinefs, this circumftance had cafually tranfpired. But on clofe of the Arguments now publifhed, this eminent lawyer took the opportunity, of moft explicitly and repeatedly avowing to the gentlemen of the bar prefent and to others, that he was at length fully convinced the grand truft of the will in queftion was againft law and ought to be declared invalid. It was manifeft alfo in the earneft and mafterly reply, he afterwards made, to the very able and learned arguments of the counfel for the will, that he compleated his profeffional exertions againft it, under a ftrong influence from the conviction he had recently expreffed out of court

F H

28 April 1799.

CONTENTS.

FIRST ARGUMENT. Page 1.

SECOND ARGUMENT. Page 23.

THIRD ARGUMENT. Page 126.

NOTE, that the Three Arguments (exclusive of the notes, some corrections of language, and some few passages, chiefly explanatory) are printed as they were actually delivered in Court.

APPENDIX.

No. I. Extract from a CASE and ARGUMENT on the LAST WILL of the late PETER THELLUSSON, ESQUIRE, by the Author of the Three Arguments now printed. Page i.

No. II. Mr. MORGAN's Calculation of the Accumulation under the Trusts of the late Mr. Thellusson's Will. Page xxiii.

The Reader is requested to make the following Corrections.

In *running title* of pages 26, 28, 30, and 32, for First Argument read Second
    Argument
Page 30, line 7, for (*n*) read (*nn*), and in line 1 of the Note to fame page, for (*n*)
            read (*nn*), and in the Margin, before *As to inheritance*, ftrike
            out the I
   115, laft line of the text, for (*t*) read (*uu*); and in line 1 of the Note, for (*t*)
            read (*uu*).
   117, line 4, for Fifthly read Sixthly; and line 12, for Sixthly read
            Seventhly; and line 23, for *executive* read *executory*.
   123,   21, after *happened* put a comma
   126,   5, after *charge* add *for excefs of executory devife*.
   129,   2, for *happened* read *happen*.
   136,   1 of Note, after *requires* add a comma.
   171,   18, for *ftamp* read *fave*.

THREE ARGUMENTS

IN THE

TWO CAUSES IN CHANCERY

ON THE

LAST WILL of PETER THELLUSSON, Esq.

O curas hominum ! O quantum est in rebus inane !

     Quo divitias hæc per tormenta coactas,
Cùm furor haud dubius, cùm sit manifesta phrenesis.

        Quæ reverentia legum,
Quis metus, aut pudor est, unquam properantis avari ?

       Omni
Membrorum damno major dementia, quæ nec
Noscit verba sua, uxoris nec vota, nec illos,
Quos genuit, quos eduxit. nam codice sævo
Hæredes vetat esse suos   bona tota feruntur
Nummi ad congeriem.   Tantum valet halitus auri !

[The three following ARGUMENTS were delivered, at Lincoln's-
Inn Hall, the 5th, 6th, and 7th of December 1798, before the
Right Honourable the LORD CHANCELLOR, assisted by the Right
Honourable the MASTER OF THE ROLLS, the Honourable Mr.
Justice BULLER, and the Honourable Mr. Justice LAWRENCE,
in the causes, of THELLUSSON against WOODFORD, and WOOD-
FORD against THELLUSSON.

B

It is apprehended, that enough of the facts is occasionally introduced into the Arguments, to make the force of them intelligible without the aid of a formal and regular statement But least this should not be so, there is added an Appendix, with a view to putting the reader into full possession of the particulars of the case, which is the subject of the Arguments.]

FIRST ARGUMENT

DELIVERED

THE 5th OF DECEMBER 1798.

MY LORD,

AS one of the counsel for the widow and children of the late Mr. Thelluson, I have the honour of addressing this court on the present very important and interesting occasion.—— In that character, it is my duty, to assist to the utmost, in inducing your Lordship's condemnation of a cruel and deceitful testamentary disposition : which aims, not only to overwhelm the most near, most affectionate, and most unoffending relatives, by an unnatural proscription, merely for the sake of an eccentrick and outrageous vanity ; but by an abuse of the art of will-making, to overreach the law of the country, and to pervert some of it's most wise and convenient rules for regulating the enjoyment and transmission of property, into instruments of mischief to the whole community.

LITTLE

LITTLE accuftomed to forenfick bufinefs, and by nature quite barren of thofe higher qualifications, which that fuperior line of our profeffion demands, I have ever approached the temples of juftice with fear and trembling. But though laborioufly prepared for the prefent occafion, I never before prefented myfelf under fuch a preffure of apprehenfions: for I feel, that I am now one of thofe entrufted with the vindication of valuable private rights complicated with invaluable publick interefts, and that I am pledged to take my full fhare in an argument, which, in point of fubject, will, as I conceive, be found, to involve and rifque the credit of the law, and the energies of the people of England, in the fame event, as hangs over the individuals, whofe claims are immediately at ftake.

THERE are two caufes before your Lordfhip.—One is on a bill brought by the widow of the late Mr. Thelluffon, and his three fons, and his three daughters, and the hufbands of the two who are married. Of this caufe the object is, to invalidate the trufts his laft will creates of his general real eftate and of his refiduary perfonal fortune, and to fubftitute a refulting truft for his heir and next of kin, in other words, on the ground of vice and illegality in the nature of the trufts, to have a decree in equity for the grand bulk of the property real and perfonal, diftributing it as if there was an inteftacy.—The other caufe is on a crofs bill by the acting truftees and executors of the late Mr. Thelluffon, to fubftantiate the trufts of his will, and to direct the manner of carrying them into execution.

THESE two caufes involve the right to property of immenfe value. Even in the prefent ftate of the publick funds, the property in queftion, exclufive of a landed eftate of about £4000. a year, may be confidered as above half a million fterling.

I AM very unwilling to trefpafs upon your Lordfhip's patience; which I know, by perfonal experience in a caufe of great delicacy (a) heretofore adjudged by your Lordfhip againft the party for whom I zealoufly argued, to be exemplary; and which, for that very quality, ought to be the lefs intruded upon. Coming alfo after the two very learned gentlemen, who have already applied their very powerful energies, to expofe the illegality of the teftamentary trufts in queftion, I dare not hope, that what I have to offer for the fame purpofe will be found, either to comprize any new topicks of reafoning, or very materially to conduce to the enforcement of thofe already advanced.

YET I know not, how to avoid being very full and particular in acquitting myfelf of my fhare of the argument.

THF immenfe value of the property at ftake will, I truft, be fome apology for me in this refpect.

SOME apology alfo may arife from it's being known, that I come prepared to argue in thefe caufes; after the fulleft opportunity of confidering the fubject of them; and under an expectation from thofe who have repofed profeffional confidence in me, that I fhould fubmit to your Lordfhip the full refult of my refearch and impreffion in their behalf.

BUT, as I have already hinted, I have fomewhat more than all this, to excufe me to your Lordfhip, for unbofoming myfelf on the prefent occafion. In my view of the two caufes, the unufual value of the property at ftake, the painful anxiety of the

---

(a) The caufe in Chancery here adverted to is Myddelton v Lord Kenyon and others. It is reported in 2 Vef Jun 391 The author's two Arguments in that caufe are in the volume of his Juridical Arguments and Collections publifhed in 1797.

Thelluf-

Thelluffon family about the event, and their very ftrong claim to the beft efforts of piofeffional affiftance, are almoft fecondary confiderations. I feel myfelf urged on by incitements of a higher clafs. I ought to be, and I am, zealous for the intereſts of the widow and children of the late Mr. Thelluffon, and extremely anxious to fee them extricated by the juftice of this court from the injurious effects of an unnatural will. But I am far more zealous and more anxious, for the honour of the law of England, and for the good of the community at large, than I can be for the interefts of any particular family, however intrufted I may be piofeffionally to affift, in guarding their particular rights, or in enforcing their particular pretenfions To the law of England I look up with confirmed reverence. It is not exempt from imperfections or fuperfluities. No human law is or can be fo. But our law in it's great outlines I confider as a combination of the wifeft policies. Thofe theorifts among us, who endeavour to create difefteem of our law, but who, I truft, are few, would do better, if they were grateful for the extraordinary protection it affords to all claffes of fociety I lament, when I fee the leaft approach to a depreciation of the law of England. I therefore lament, when I hear it's greateft luminaries in former times, fuch as Lord Coke and Lord Hale, adverted to otherwife than with veneration. To run down the characters of fuch great men of our profeffion is to undermine the law of England : for their adjudications and their writings are fome of it's chief depofitaries. To throw a veil over the infirmities of fuch perfons, is far more honourable, than fubfifting on the loan of their talents and wifdom and at the fame time declaiming againft their characters. But being thus anxious for the law of England, I cannot look to the nature of thefe caufes on the will of the late Mr. Thelluffon, without feeling an apprehenfion, that if they fhould be adjudged in fa-

vour

vour of the will, some advantage may be gained by those, who
wish to depreciate our law, and to encourage a disesteem of it.
Certainly the law of England abounds with excellent policies.
But I have ever understood, that one of those admired policies
is it's wisdom, in regulating the entail and transmission of property; and in steering between the extreme of enduring perpetuity of entail and the extreme of enduring no entail at all.
The policy of our system in this respect is more especially to
be seen in our doctrine of fines and recoveries, in our doctrine
of remainders and reversions, in our doctrine of uses and trusts,
and in our doctrine of executory devise. It is one of the aims
of all these doctrines, to set a just and rational boundary to entails of every description; and to set such a boundary, as may
conciliate private accommodation with public good. But unless
I greatly mistake the causes now before your Lordship, it will
depend upon the decision of them,—whether all the wisdom,
so long exerted for that important purpose, is not liable to be
baffled by three or four lines from the most ordinary convey-
ancer :—and whether a fabrick, which our most enlightened
judges have been two centuries in raising, is not so feebly constituted, as to be at the mercy of the pen of every conveyancing draughtsman throughout the kingdom :—and whether also,
in consequence of this imperfection, it is not ~~also~~ at last dis-
coverable, that by the law of England, there is *a mode of settle-*
ment, by which it is possible with CERTAINTY, *not only to make*
an entail completely unbarrable for almost a century and an half;
but during the whole of that space to render property of every spe-
cies and in every extent, unenjoyable, unexpendible, and unusable.

I BEG leave, therefore, to repeat, that the subject of the con-
test on the present occasion, is much more than the cause of
the late Mr. Thelusson's family against his testamentary dispositions.

fitions.—It is the caufe of the law of England, againſt an attempt, to defraud it's policy, to abuse it's indulgence, to degrade it's character, and to charge a long feries of our moſt admired judges with imbecillity.—It is the caufe of the judicatures, nay of the people of England, againſt an attempt to foiſt upon them such a monſtrous precedent of *truſt of accumulation grafted upon entail by executory devife*, as, being taken full advantage of, might hereafter gradually paralize the beſt faculties of the country, by converting all the property of the kingdom from a fubfiſtence and defence for the living into a meie gratification for avarice in the tomb.—In other words it is the caufe of the kingdom againſt an *experiment*, to impofe upon Englifh judicature, what, as I infiſt, was never yet endured by any law, in any country, or at any time ; and *under the ſhelter of a policy, emanating from an exercife of judicial difcretion for the fake of general convenience, to make judicature itfelf acceſſary to a moſt extravagant public mifchief.*

If fuch be the natuie of thefe caufes, theie is a ſtiong demand upon this court, to exert it's utmoſt vigilance, it's utmoſt wifdom, and it's utmoſt fortitude ; leaſt, by the working of others under the fuiface of executory devife, the boundary of that mode of entail ſhould be fo erafed, as to let in moſt of the mifchiefs fuch boundary was conſtituted to prevent, with the addition of mifchiefs ſtill more ferious. The judges .of former times had to contend, with ingenious fchemes of extending entails beyond the ufual time for fuffering common recoveries. *Perpetuity of entail* affumed various forms for that purpofe. In the reigns of Elizabeth and James the fiiſt, the form was *provifo of forfeiture* for ceſſer of eſtate in cafe of any attempt to bar entail by recovery or otherwife : and how much exeition was required to fupprefs this mode of defrauding the law of
common

common recoveries, appears in Lord Coke's report of the three great cafes of Corbet (*b*), Mildmay (*c*), and Portington (*d*). Another form affumed was *executory devife*, which from it's nature is not within the reach either of fine or recovery: and to prefcribe a boundary to the contingency on which this mode of entail depends, and to foil thofe attempting to exceed that boundary, the courts of Weftminfter Hall have been almoft continually reforted to for about two centuries. Another form for perpetuities has been *executory truft*, directing eftates for life to *unborn* children to be fo conftituted, as to make them tenants for life and to let in their iffue to the inheritance as purchafers: and this enterprize was crufhed by Lord Chancellor Cowper foon after the death of Queen Anne (*e*), in the cafe of Humberfton and Humberfton; that great judge of equity refufing to make truft the handmaid for extending the unbarrablenefs of entail, and to admit the fubftance of inheritance under the veil of fucceffive leffer eftates. A further form of eluding the policy againft perpetuities was a *power of revocation*; that is, under a truft to revoke eftates of inheritance to unborn children the moment they were born, and to fubftitute ftrict fettlement: and this fhift to accomplifh perpetuity did not receive it's final condemnation till the cafe on the will of John Duke of Marlborough at the beginning of the prefent reign(*f*). But in all thefe inftances our courts have had only to counteract fchemes for unduly prolonging entails. Yet even this was found to be a work of difficulty. Mary Portington's cafe, as Lord Coke informs us, was argued in the Common Pleas more than feven times. Moft of the other cafes I have adverted to, were alfo elaborately confidered. But, in the

---

(*b*) 1 Co. 77   (*c*) 1 Co. 175.   (*d*) 10 Co. 35.   (*e*) 1 Wms 332.
(*f*) Cafe of Lord Charles Spencer and others *v.* the prefent Duke of Marlborough in Dom. Proc. Feb. 1763. in 5 Bro Caf. in Parl. 592.

prefent

prefent inftance, your Lordfhip has to combat, with *a fcheme involving to a vaft extent both perpetuity of entail and perpetuity of accumulation:* and you have to defend the country, againft *ftopping the ufe of property,* as well as againft *ftopping the power of alienating it.* Convinced alfo though I am, that the monftrous enterprize of truft, the fate of which it is for your Lordfhip in thefe caufes to decide, falls within clear principles of judicial condemnation , yet I am not blind to the difficulties in your Lordfhip's way. You have to detect and overcome encroachments upon the boundary of executory devife in new forms ; fo contrived in fome refpects, as to have the fpecious appearance of literal conformity to the very rule meant to be fubverted ; and confequently fo contrived, as to fecure a very ftrong prejudice, that it is a kind of abufe only reftrainable and corrigible by legiflative interpofition. You have alfo *to prefcribe a boundary, where hitherto our courts have not been provoked regularly to fix one;* where hitherto the moft unfeeling avarice has not fo tampered with truft of accumulation, as to demand from this court an inveftigation of limits. The prefent cafe thus calling for the defence of the eftablifhed rule of executory devife againft new fhifts to elude it's boundary, and at the fame time calling for a boundary to truft of accumulation, I feel, that there is a demand for the beft faculties and the beft exertions in the performance of judicial duty : and as well for the fake of the country at large, as for the fake of the individuals for whom I am one of the counfel, I am heartily glad, that it devolves upon your Lordfhip to adjudge,—whether fuch extended executory devifes and fuch extravagant trufts of accumulation, as the will of Mr. Thelluffon attempts to incorporate, are not mifchiefs againft the reafon and policy of the law of England ;— and whether his compound of exceffive entail and exceffive accumulation is not equally controulable by a firm exercife of ju-

C   dicial

dicial wifdom and judicial power, with the leffer mifchief of excefs of entail only.

————————

THE great queftion in the two caufes arifes on the validity of the trufts, which the teftator Mr. Thelluffon has annexed,—to the devife in fee of his great landed property in Yorkfhire and his real eftate elfewhere, except his houfe and eftate at Plaiftow in Kent and his houfe in Philpot Lane London,—and to the bequeft of his immenfe refiduary perfonal eftate.

IT is, whether the trufts, to which he has devoted a landed property of about £4000. a year, and about half a million in perfonal eftate,—in difinherifon of his eldeft fon and heir,—and in exclufion of the widow and all the exifting iffue of him the teftator,—and in order to accumulate three vaft landed fortunes for three future male defcendants of his blood and name in at leaft the fecond, and moft probably the third or fourth, or even more remote generation, and in cafe of there being only one fuch male defcendant at the time fixed, then to confolidate the three fortunes into one huge mafs for his fingle ufe ;—are fit to be executed by an Englifh court of Equity.

IN other language the queftion is, whether from fome vice in the extent of the directed accumulation, or from fome vice in the conftitution of the beneficial interefts limited to commence when the accumulation is appointed to ceafe, all the trufts created by the late Mr. Thelluffon of the chief bulk of his fortune ought not to be condemned as void and inoperative.

On,

ON the confequences of an abfolute failure of the trufts, I fubmit, that there cannot be any doubt: for if they are void, there muft, I prefume, be a refulting truft, that is, for his eldeft fon and heir as to the *real* eftate, and for his widow and all the children as his next of kin as to the *perfonalty*.

THE fhort general point then is, whether the trufts of accumulation and thofe appointed to commence when the accumulation is limited to determine are or are not valid.

THE odioufnefs of the trufts cannot be denied. In this refpect, and as to the grand bulk of his vaft fortune, the will of the late Mr. Thelluffon is a complication of profcriptive cruelty towards all parts of his numerous exifting family.

HIS three fons had married, with his fulleft approbation, to ladies, to whom he appeared almoft as devoted as if they had been his own children.

THE three fons were upon the moft affectionate terms with him, and fo continued to his death. They were living on a liberal fcale proportioned to their fituation and natural expectancies, that is,—as perfons, who had received fome fortune from their father, and fome fortune through the ladies to whom they were married,—as perfons, who had fucceeded their father in the very great mercantile bufinefs in which his vaft fortune was acquired;—as perfons, who, feemingly to the gratification of his pride, had obtained feats in the Britifh Houfe of Commons;—as perfons, who faw their father already poffeffed of about two-thirds of a million fterling, and likely to live long enough to augment this vaft fortune by very great accumulations,—and as perfons, who, from his external kindnefs to-

C 2

wards

wards them, and from his profeffions, had every reafon to con-
fide in receiving at his death their due proportions of his immenfe wealth.   But, by the trufts created of the great bulk of
his fortune, the teftator excludes thefe his three fons wholly and
abfolutely.   Nay, he fharpens this extreme unkindnefs or rather
barbarous injuftice,—with the infulting confolation of his having provided enough for them to fecure comfort ;—with an injurious infinuation of their being too fond of fhew ;—and with a
fanctified leffon of morality againft vanity and oftentation, at
the very moment he was wantonly facrificing at their altar
above half a million of property, to the difinherifon and grief of
his unoffending iffue.   What alfo appears from the admiffion
in the pleadings in the two caufes, and, if it was neceffary, might
be regularly proved, adds to the cruelty to the three fons, is, that
upon their marriages, he made verbal promifes to the families
into which they married, to make further provifions for the fons
much exceeding the pittances his will gives to them ; and that
according to his declaration to fome relations and friends of the
family made but recently before his death, his eldeft fon and his
eldeft grandfon were to have his great Brodfworth eftate, and
he the teftator wanted to purchafe two other great eftates for
his two other younger fons.

Not content with thus infultingly difappointing his three
fons, the teftator involves in the fame fate all their exifting
iffue ; the trufts being fo conftituted, as to make it impoffible,
if the will prevails, that any male iffue of his three fons born in
the teftator's lifetime, *or born within due time after his death* [in
whatever fenfe thofe words of the teftator's will are to be un-
derftood] or any female iffue of the three fons born in the
teftator's lifetime, fhould have the leaft benefit from the immenfe property in queftion, or it's accumulations.   Nay, it is at
                                                              leaft

leaft dubious, whether this excluſion was not meant to reach even future male iſſue of the three ſons to a certain extent. The preſent reſult of this unfeeling part of the arrangement is an abſolute excluſion of ſix grandſons of the teſtator and four granddaughters. The grandſons are ſons of the teſtator's eldeſt ſon living at the date of the will, and two twin ſons born within nine months after the deceaſe of the teſtator, and a ſon of the third and youngeſt ſon of the teſtator born a few months before his death. The granddaughters are two daughters of the teſtator's eldeſt ſon, and two daughters of the teſtator's ſecond ſon. Nor is this proſcription of the teſtator's grandchildren a little aggravated by other circumſtances of the caſe. For the ſeven grandchildren, who were born before his laſt will, he ever ſhewed the moſt affectionate kindneſs. To the eldeſt of them, the one next in ſucceſſion to him after his eldeſt ſon the heir apparent of the family, this excluſion is ſcarce even credible. It appears, that the teſtator, only ten days before his death, ſent for his eldeſt ſon ; deſired him to give a private tutor to the eldeſt grandſon, obſerved upon his promiſing talents, and propheſied his becoming a great man in this country. The teſtator emphatically added, I HAVE TAKEN CARE OF HIM. According to the will, this care conſiſted of a French life annuity of 800 livres in the French funds ; which the will deſcribes as not having been paid for many years ; which there is no proſpect of ever receiving ; and which, if it could be received, would be ſcarce worth having.

THE three daughters of the teſtator are not treated with more lenity in the truſts in queſtion. On the contrary, they and their iſſue are excluded without the leaſt reſerve or exception. Not even their male iſſue are ſpared. Yet if his three ſons and their exiſting iſſue were to be proſcribed, it was natural, that the

daughters

daughters and their iffue fhould be looked to.   He had married his eldeft daughter to a gentleman born of a noble family (g) and of great perfonal merit.   The vaft fize of the teftator's fortune, and his profeffed kindnefs towards his eldeft daughter and her hufband being confidered, they might reafonably have expected a great encreafe of provifion from him, even though he had not thus excluded his fons and grandchildren.   Indepen-dently alfo of the fame exclufion, the two other daughters, who were become marriageable, and who always appeared to have a proper fhare of his parental affection, might for like reafons have been juftified in expecting a much greater fortune than he has thought fit to provide for them by his will.   How much more then might thefe three daughters have expected to be con-fidered by the teftator, in the difpofition of his immenfe fortune, if the bulk of it was to be denied to their brothers and the child-ren of the brothers !   But the teftator's natural affections were too much under the dominion of his vain and avaricious paffions, to liften to fuch a confideration of his daughters.   Inftead of being more favourable to them, becaufe his harfhnefs to their brothers and the children of their brothers, gave the opportu-nity, he is more harfh to the daughters ; his will not even ad-mitting to the fucceffion to his general fortune, either them, or their iffue of any kind or at any diftance of time.

If the trufts are viewed with a reference to the teftator's wife, to whom he ever appeared moft affectionately attached, and of whofe merits even the difpofitions of his will in other re-fpects bear fuch ample teftimony, the odioufnefs of the trufts is ftill further encreafed.—As the teftator's children and grand-children were thus profcribed, it might have been expected, that

(g) The Honourable Auguftus Phipps.

his

his wife would have been highly confidered in the trufts of his vaft refiduary eftate, and would have become a principal object of them. But fo to have fhaped the trufts, might finally in great meafure have difappointed his profcription of his children and grandchildren; for her maternal affection would naturally have been exerted to repeal the effect of the teftator's cruel difpofitions. Even therefore the wife of the teftator is wholly excluded from the poffibility of benefit under the trufts in queftion.

IT is a ftill further aggravation of this exclufion, by the teftator, of his wife, children, and grandchildren, and even of his iffue in the third generation, from the chief mafs of his fortune, that the facrifice of them is made merely to indulge the outrageous vanity of erecting three landed fortunes of a fizé unheard of in England for three future male defcendants of his three fons; and that the trufts are fo contrived, as to make it impoffible, either that his fons or his exifting grandfons fhould even have the confolation of knowing, which of their male defcendants are to be the happy poffeffors of the accumulated eftates. It is the nature of the trufts to continue the accumulation, till all the fons and exifting grandfons are dead, and in the mean time to make the future proprietors of the eftate quite uncertain.

THUS in every point of view, with reference to the family of the teftator, the trufts appear to be of the moft hateful defcription. By them, the teftator not only difinherits his exifting family; but he difinherits them from motives of a vicious caft. His wife, children, and grandchildren, are excluded from the bulk of his fortune,—not becaufe they had offended him; not becaufe they were not dear to him; not becaufe they did not

deferve

deferve to be fo, not becaufe others were more dear to him: but becaufe he thought fit to yield himfelf up a flave to the avaricious vanity of eftablifhing a long accumulation after his death, and of fo conftituting for remote male defcendants fortunes of a fize as yet unknown in Great Britain. Anger and refentment againft his family could not be the fources of his ungenerous and unfeeling difpofitions: for he and his family were all harmony and affection, and fo continued to the laft moment of his life. The real incentives to the will were avarice and vanity. *Inde faces ardent.* Thofe paffions were the real fource. So traced, the trufts in queftion are more than a difinherifon of the family of the teftator, without fo much as the colour of provocation from them; are more than a cruel difappointment of expectations encouraged by his own fatherly kindnefs and profeffions to the very moment of his death; are more than a breach of his duties and promifes to his wife and iffue, without the femblance of apology of any kind for him. I fay that his will is not only all this accumulation of the harfheft injuftice to his exifting family. It is all this,—with the aggravation of his thus facrificing the moft valuable interefts of thofe, who fhould have been, and appear to have been, the moft dear to him, wholly in order to gratify the avarice of pofthumous accumulation, and the vanity of pofthumous aggrandizement of the Thelluffon name in the perfons of future and remote male defcendants;—with the further aggravation of endeavouring to palliate his cruel difpofition by fatirical infinuations againft his three fons, at the fame time tending to injure their credit as merchants, and in fome degree to detract from the efteem of them as men,—and with the ftill further aggravation of endeavouring to win both parliament and judicature into an approbation of his ungenerous difpofitions, by an

affected

affected zeal to pay off the national debt, and by the hypocritical offer of a remote and improbable contingency in his refiduary fortune to effectuate fuch a public good.

But the teftamentary trufts, the odious nature of which it is my duty as one of the counfel againft the will to expofe, are not merely injurious to the widow, children, and grandchildren, of the late Mr. Thelluffon; are not merely in breach of his duty and profeffions as the father of a family. They are not merely vicious in a moral fenfe. They are alfo injurious politically. They are againft the intereft of the commonwealth, againft public good.——Under fhelter of the teftamentary power, it is the aim of the teftator to fufpend both fucceffion to and enjoyment of much above half a million fterling, till it fhall have accumulated into landed property of the value of millions, nay, of tens of millions. On this topic I fhall have occafion to enlarge in a fubfequent part of this argument. Here it may be fufficient to fay of fuch a precedent of accumulation, that trufts conftituted for fuch a purpofe are at leaft of a tendency highly dangerous to the publick intereft.

It may at firft feem, as if thus minutely animadverting upon the trufts in queftion was inveighing againft them with more particularity and more harfhnefs, than the real argument of the cafe requires.

But, impreffed as I am, with the prefent cafe, it appears of importance to thofe, who claim to annul the trufts, that the odious nature and pernicious tendency of them fhould be fully underftood, even in the outfet of the argument. Notwithftanding the extreme harfhnefs of the trufts towards the exifting family of the late Mr. Thelluffon, it is very far from being then

D   wifh

wifh to difturb his memory further than juftice to themfelves extorts. They are too mindful of his affectionate kindnefs whilft he was living, except in his grand teftamentary difpofition, and too mindful alfo of the benefits they derive from
him under the very will they complain of, to wifh to fee his
memory unneceffarily wounded. Nor if they had fuch a wifh,
would it become their counfel to gratify it. But in contefting
the trufts of his general refiduary eftate, his widow, fons, and
daughters, have for themfelves and the grandchildren of the
teftator, much above half a million of property at ftake; and it
is not to be expected, that they, or at leaft thofe acting to
fuftain their interefts, fhould, in a cafe of fuch vaft value, make
a facrifice of any real advantage in the argument againft the
will, from mere delicacy towards the memory of one, whofe
teftamentary difpofition of his principal fortune is fo exceedingly
cruel to his family. If his memory could be fpared, without
the moft ferious injury to thofe who conteft the chief trufts of
his will, they would rejoice at the opportunity; and would
referve their griefs and injuries for private lamentation. But it
fo happens, that the cafe againft the will is of fuch a nature, as
to render the argument of *favour* and *disfavour* to it, of fome
importance in the conteft. Confequently the odioufnefs of the
will is a topick againft it, which cannot be conveniently fpared.
We truft indeed, that there is a fufficiency of objection to the
legality of the trufts, without aid from any topick of favour to the
family of the teftator or of disfavour to the trufts of his will. Yet
it muft be confeffed, that the points raifable againft thofe trufts
are not without nicety and difficulty. Both in conftruing the
intention of the trufts, and in applying the principles by which
that intention is controulable, the argument may occafionally be
fomewhat influenced by fuch topicks of favour or disfavour.
Nay, it is poffible, that in fome pofitions of the argument,

favour

favour or disfavour towards the trusts may turn the balance for or against the validity of them. — If the words constituting the trusts shall be found to be so ambiguous and equivocal, that construed favourably, they will be within the boundary of the law of executory devises, but construed unfavourably they will exceed that boundary, the decision of a Court may be ruled by the quality of the trusts. Were they meritorious, it might be a duty to understand the words restrictively, and so to declare the trusts legal. But the trusts being odious, it may be justifiable to understand the words largely, and so to condemn the trusts as against law. — Again, if the trusts constituted shall be found of such a nature, that it shall depend on the discretion of a Court of Equity to decide, whether they are fit or proper to be assisted by the exercise of equitable jurisdiction, were the trusts meritorious, it might induce going the utmost length in favour of them. But on the other hand, if the trusts shall appear to be of an odious description morally, and of a dangerous tendency politically, a Court of Equity may feel it a duty to do all in it's power towards disappointing them; may feel itself called upon to administer it's discretion by declaring the trusts unworthy of being performed. — So again, if it shall be found, that in constituting the beneficial interests appointed to take effect when the trust of accumulation is permitted to cease, the will is so obscure in the language, as to make it very doubtful, who are meant to take primarily, and what kind of succession is meant to be constituted, were the object of the testator just and becoming, it may be the duty of a Court to strain every nerve to explore the intention; and, for the sake of facilitating it's execution, to risque adopting a construction however dubious. But if the object of the trusts shall be found nearly as odious and dangerous in their tendency, as I understand and state them to be, it may be justifiable in a Court to decline construing obscurity into intelligibility, to decline making sense of nonsense, to decline making

cer-

certainty of uncertainty; and thus it may become the duty of a Court to condemn the trusts, as being too vague and obscure to be executed.

IN these views of the case, then, the odiousness of the trusts in question may have great weight in the argument against them. Their odiousness may not only inspire judicature with a desire or rather an anxiety to disappoint them; but may actually afford the opportunity. Therefore in arguing to subvert the great trust of the late Mr. Thellusson's will, I submit that the cruelty and injustice of his chief testamentary disposition should never be lost sight of. Nor is it new in our courts of equity, or even in our courts of law, to resort to the unmeritoriousness of testamentary dispositions, in order to influence the interpretation of them. Both jurisdictions are accustomed to look to meritoriousness and unmeritoriousness in the construction of instruments of every kind, as well as in various other respects (h).

HOWEVER it cannot be contended, that the mere odiousness of the trusts in question will suffice to invalidate them. Such is the extent of the testamentary power with us in England over property both real and personal, that notwithstanding the greatest harshness, or even cruelty, in the dispositions of a will towards the family of a testator, the will may be good in law and irrelievable in equity. Amongst the Romans a will might

---

(h) For FAVOR,—to *heir*, see a series of cases at law and in equity in Viner's Abridgment *Heir* R S. T. & U *Executors*—Z 3 & *Portions* I. Comyns's Digest *Devise* N 22. and title *Chancery* 3 P 3 1 Equity Cases Abridged *Heir* C D & E. & 2 Eq Cas Abr. same title A — to *Wife and Children* and *grandchildren*, see Com Dig *Chancery* E 1 Eq. Cas Abi. 202 Grounds of Law and Eq 66.—to *Charities* see Vin. Abr *Charitable Uses* E,—and to *Creditors* see Com. Dig 3 A 3 Vin. Abr. *Creditor & Debtor* A.

be

be invalidated for undutifulnefs to near relations, efpecially to children ; and if they were difinherited or paffed over without juft caufe, there was a remedy againft the will by the *querela teftamenti inofficiofi,* that is, a complaint of the will for being made againft duty, againft moral obligation, againft the dictates of nature, *contra officium pietatis, contra naturale officium* (i). When and how this relief to difinherited children and other near relations originated, whether from a benevolent fubtlenefs of interpretation in confidering fuch unnatural difpofitions as proofs of infanity, or from pofitive conftitutions, is a difputed point amongft civilians. But certainly it was fettled law in the time of the Emperor Juftinian, and long before, that a will might be impeached for undutifulnefs. Certainly alfo the teftamentary power became circumfcribed in like manner in fome countries of modern (k) Europe. It was fo in fome provinces of (l) France. But it is not fo with us in England. By our law, the teftamentary power is in this refpect unqualified (m). Our law agrees with the twelve tables, in which according to the extract in Juftinian's Inftitutions (n), the language was, UTI LEGASSIT SUÆ REI, ITA JUS ESTO. Therefore unlefs there is fomething wrong in the trufts in queftion beyond the moral injuftice of them, to the family of the late Mr. Thelluffon ; unlefs the public inconvenience of them be of fuch a defcription as to be contradicted by fome known policy of our law, or be of fuch a magnitude as to render them

(i) See Inft. lib 2. tit. 17. 18 & 19 & Heinecc. Syntagm. Huber Prælect. and Vinn. on thofe titles.

(k) Hoppii Commentatio ad Inftit. lib. 2. tit. 18

(l) Traduct. des Inftitutes de Juftinien par M de Ferriere liv 2. titr. 18. in the Notes.

(m) See Swinb. part 5. f. 1. Cowelli Inftitutiones Jur. Anglican. lib. 2. tit. 19. Co. Litt. 13th ed. 176 b. note 6.

(n) Inftit. lib. 2. tit. 22. princip.

unfit

unfit for execution by our courts of equity, the trufts, however they may be reprobated, however thofe they exclude may be compaffionated, muft prevail in our Courts of Juftice ; and in that view nothing fhort of legiflative interpofition can annul them.

THE cafe then comes to this. Can it be fhewn, that the trufts militate with any principle, rule, or policy, of the law of England; or that they are of fuch a nature, as to be unfit for execution by an Englifh Court of Equity, or that they are otherwife unexecutable ?

THESE, I agree, are the proper fubjects of enquiry and inveftigation, and I enter upon the argument accordingly.

So looking to the cafe, I accufe the trufts of *infringing the rule introduced into our law to circumfcribe executory devifes*, nay, of fo infringing in feveral points, on any one of which, the charge, if proved, is, I contend, fufficient to nullify the trufts in queftion.

I ALSO accufe the trufts of *excefs of accumulation* ; and in that refpect, *of being fo grofsly againft public good, and fo grofsly improper, exclufive of the limits prefcribed to executory devife, as to juftify a Court of Equity in condemning them,* or rather to require fuch a condemnation.

FURTHER I impute to the trufts, that they are *fo vague, fo obfcure, and fo uncertain, in the defcription of the primary beneficial devifees and legatees, as to be rejectable on the ground of unintelligibility* and impracticablenefs.

SUCH

Such are the *three points of view*, therefore, in which I propofe to examine the trufts, to put them to a teft, and to impeach their validity.

SECOND DAY'S ARGUMENT.

DELIVERED

THE 7th OF DECEMBER, 1798.

MY LORD,

ANCIENTLY I had obligations to your Lordfhip for perfonal attentions; which were of no flight importance to me in the younger part of life, when all attentions, from one of your Lordfhip's defcription, were peculiarly gratifying and valuable. Of thofe attentions I fhould have been proud, even in times the moft profperous; fuch as I never reached, nor am ever likely to gain an approach to. It was my ill fortune, to fee thofe attentions intermitted, from caufes : which, neither on your part proved pride, enmity, inconftancy, or infenfibility; nor on mine were, for a moment, even in the leaft degree incompatible with high refpeét, great admiration, or fincere gratitude. My own feelings have ever teftified for me in this point. Your Lordfhip's conduét to me on feveral occafions heretofore has convinced me, that, however unpropitious fome appearances might be, fubftantially your difpofition towards me, though checked by circumftances, was moft honourably juft, nay, was even liberal. But had all other proofs been

wanting,

wanting, this would have fufficiently appeared from your Lordfhip's generous indulgence to me yefterday, at a moment highly
diftreffing to one : who, though a veteran in the ftudy of Englifh law, and in that retired practice, which is only to be feen
in the gloomy folitude, of chamber-confultation, and of cham-
ber-application to juridical bufinefs and juridical ftudies, is not
only a novitiate in the forums of juftice ; but a novitiate, the
moft nervous, the moft unprotected, and a novitiate fo defcribed, with the further drawback of being in the wane of
a life never fortunate, fometimes imminently the reverfe. Nor,
I am perfuaded, will any liberal perfon of the fame honourable profeffion with myfelf murmur, at fuch an occafional
indulgence to one of my age and under my circumftances, as
the option your Lordfhip fo kindly gave me yefterday. I mean
the option of wholly poftponing my long argument, in caufes,
in point of fubject uncommonly novel, arduous, and important,
to a fecond day, or of dividing my argument between two
days.

THE boon, which I thus acknowledge, and which I eagerly
took advantage of, was a great affiftance to me, a great relief to
my apprehenfions. I truft alfo, that it will at the fame time be
found an arrangement, not ill calculated to promote the important purpofe of more deliberately at leaft exploring,—what is the
real juftice of the two great caufes now in judgment before your
Lordfhip ;—and whether in deciding on the will of the late Mr.
Thelluffon, the honour of the law of England, and the interefts
of the country, are really implicated in the extenfive way I
yefterday took the liberty of reprefenting to your Lordfhip.
Had it not been for the confiderate attention to my fituation in
thefe caufes, I know not, how without danger of difgufting
your Lordfhip and the reverend judges who are affeffors to you,

or

or even without difguft to myfelf, I could have difcharged my profefsional duty, nearly in the full extent of the matter I have gathered and digefted for the occafion. If my labours had been the moft perfect fecret to all but myfelf, it was not to be fuppofed, that the fcience, acutenefs, learning, zeal, and eloquence, of the two learned gentlemen I have the honour of following, would have left the great fubject of *executory devife*, and the great fubject of *truft of accumulation*, which are the chief topicks of thefe caufes, with much ground untrodden. But it fo happens, that to ferve the interefts of the family, for which I am one of the counfel, and to fhorten the labour of fuperior perfons, my imprefsions were communicated for common ufe. Had I therefore been prefsed yefterday, to follow my two learned leaders in thefe caufes, with any thing beyond mere introduction, I fhould have been in a very diftrefsed fituation. My operofe details, after their fpirited comprefsions of the fame topicks, would have been fcarce endurable, even by your Lordfhip's patience, highly polifhed and difciplined as it is. So inftantaneous a fuccefsion, of the flow productions of the lamp, to the quick flafhes of forenfick eloquence, might have been like a great and long faft fucceeding a fhort but luxurious feaft. But the interval, which has been allowed, may leffen the difadvantage I am under, from exhibiting at length, what has been already ftated to the Court, not only more briefly, more agreeably, and more imprefsively, but with accefsions of more value than any materials originating from me.

I r would indeed be of little confequence, if there was little more to be derived from the interval I mention, than my perfonal accommodation But I flatter myfelf, that much more important effects may be expected from the ar-

E   rangement

rangement your Lordſhip thus indulged to myſelf. Though, as I have already hinted to your Lordſhip, I am individually the moſt ſtrongly impreſſed with the untenableneſs of the will of the late Mr. Thelluſſon, both from *exceſs of executory deviſe*, and from *exceſs of accumulation*; and though I am even very ſerriouſly ſtruck with the objection to his beneficial truſts for *uncertainty of deſcription*; yet I am aware of the difficulties and delicacies, which belong to the caſe. More particularly I am aware of a ſtrong prejudice, which has ſomehow or other almoſt unaccountably reached ſome of the moſt reſpectable members of our profeſſion, and may perhaps have aſcended ſtill higher, that the calamitous publick miſchiefs, which are confeſſedly incident to the eſtabliſhment of ſuch a precedent of *artificial extenſion of executory deviſe and truſt of accumulation combined,* as Mr. Thelluſſon's will comprizes, can only be effectually obviated by an act of parliament. I am aware alſo, that this prejudice is very much aſſiſted in one very important branch of the preſent caſe, by the great authority of a recent but unrepealed certificate of the King's Bench to your Lordſhip in the caſe of Long and Blackall. To encounter prejudice thus powerfully in ſome degree aſſiſted; and to ſubdue the difficulties which otherwiſe belong to the preſent caſe; a full expreſſion of arguments and a full reference to caſes and authorities, however tireſome and unpleaſant, may be not only uſeful in a ſubſidiary way, but even neceſſary. The two learned advocates, whom I have the honour of following, having inſpected the rough materials I was able to furniſh by digging at the mine, have ſeparated the finer and better parts of the ore I drew forth for their ſervice; and by a proper application of them, have exhibited an impreſſive though ſhort picture. But fine pictures are ſometimes compoſed, with colours very ſplendid, but very tranſient

and

and fading; and it is for those, to whom the appreciation of the value of the picture is entrusted, to examine the quality of the colours, and to require evidence of their firmness. Accordingly to enable such an examination in the present instance, it may be expected, that I should actually produce enough of the rough materials extracted by me for the service of the present case, to shew, that the picture, Mr. Mansfield and Mr. Grant have so ably drawn, is both a genuine and a lasting portrait. Indeed I feel this to be a justice more especially due to the family, for which I am counsel; because I have reason to believe, that those two learned gentlemen, from a generous sensibility towards me, have actually forborn to enlarge upon many topicks, for which they knew me to be copiously and laboriously prepared. Under such circumstances, if I was to keep back what I have extracted and digested, it might injure the cause it is both my duty and my anxious wish to sustain.

NOTWITHSTANDING therefore the masterly anticipation of the arguments, which I have prepared to offer to your Lordship in the great points of these causes, I shall venture to address you and the reverend Judges by whom you are afsisted, with the same fullness, as if I was not under the disadvantage of any anticipation whatever.

THE FIRST ground, upon which I have undertaken to argue against the trusts in question, namely, their *infringement of the boundary of executory devise*, depends upon the policy, by which our law limits and regulates executory devises,

First, general ground against the trusts, namely, *infringement of the boundary of executory devise.*

E 2

vifes, and fpringing ufes and executory trufts of a fimilar nature.

IF the grand trufts of the late Mr. Thelluffon's will are fupportable, it muft be, becaufe they are fhelteied under the iule of entail by executory devife and by tiuft of the fame natuie : for, except under that protection, theie is no pofsibility of enforcing the trufts.

IN arguing the piefent cafe, therefore, it may be very mateiial to know, when, and how, and by what authority, and undei what qualifications, the doctrine of executory devife became incorpoiated into our fyftem of law and equity.

ACCORDINGLY, with your Lordfhip's leave, I fhall heie attempt fomewhat in that way. Such a refeaich, indeed, is not only dry and difficult ; but extenfive. To make it inteiefting will, I fear, be much beyond my ftiength. But it is within my power to reftrain myfelf in the enquiry : and with that view, I fhall endeavour to be as fhort, as the purpofe of the prefent cafe in my impiefsion of it fhall allow.

Origin and progrefs of Executoiy Devife.

EXECUTORY devifes have chiefly fprung up fince the ftatute of ufes in the 27th of Henıy the Eighth, and the ftatutes of the 32d and 34th of the fame ieıgn, enabling the devife of lands *at the fiee will and pleafuie* of the ownei. Some glimpfe, howevei, theie is of executory devife in much cailier times; and it is pofsible, that undei the cuftom of devifing land, as it prevailed in London and other places, fomething of the

5   kind

kind might be occasionally at least attempted. Accordingly
it has been asserted by judges of high authority, that executory devises, determining the fee in one person on a contingency, and raising the fee up in another, have always in some
respect prevailed. This assertion, which came from the bench
in Pell v. Brown, in the 18th of James the First, as appears
by Judge Coke's report in that case, might be true in a small
degree, under the power of devising land by custom. In
favor of the assertion so restrictively understood, our Year-books
furnish some little evidence. Gowdchep's case in 49 Edw. 3.
fol. 16. which is of a devise, under the custom of London,
that executors should sell land to make distribution for the
soul of the testator, seems to be of that description; the fee
till sale descending to the heir, but afterwards passing to the
vendee. The case put in the Year-book of 11. Hen. 6.
fol 13. b. of a devise of land in London under the custom,
that the executors should sell to pay debts, and the case put
in the same Year-book of a devise under the power by custom
to issue *en ventre sa mere*, are all instances. But even the
industry of Lord Coke's time was not sufficient to glean more
than these few examples of executory devise of land in the
times previous to the reign of Henry the Eighth, and it may
be doubted, whether these precedents alone should be deemed
precedents sufficient to prove the law, even as to the power of
devising by custom and even though executory devise should be
proved to have thus existed in a small degree, it should be considered, that in very ancient times the tendency to perpetuity,
which is a grand objection to unlimited executory devise, and
which, after the establishment of common recoveries, became
so important a consideration, was not then of so much consequence. Certainly also the undoubted rule of the common
law against creating a freehold *de futuro*, as it is stated in
                                                    Barwick's

Barwick's cafe, 5. Co. 94. b. and is in part ingenioufly accounted for in the introduction to the Manufcript treatife by Lord Chief Baron Gilbert on Remainders, which I furnifhed for the new edition of Bacon's Abridgment, made it impoffible to create fuch executory interefts in the freehold and inheritance of land, by grant or any common law conveyance (*n*): and fo Lord Coke obferves in Matthew Manning's cafe, in the eighth report 95.

To make the inquiry concerning the origin and progrefs of executory devife more fimple and intelligible, I will confider the fubject under three diftinct heads; namely, firft as to *inheritance*, next as to *terms of years*, and then as to *chattels perfonal*.

As to In-
heritance

FOR many years after the beginning of the fixteenth century, executory devifes of the *inheritance* feem to have been little known, and as little fanctioned. According to the cafe of the prior and convent of St. Bartholomew Weft Smithfield, which is in Dyer fol. 33. a. pl. 12. and arofe on an executory devife of the inheritance of land under the cuftom of London, the judges Fitzherbert and Baldwin, in the 28th. and 29th. of Henry the eighth, held it not allowable to limit a fee upon a fee. Indeed, as that cafe was, the contingency for the rifing of the fecondary fee was fuch, as might have happened at any time however diftant. Therefore, even upon the doctrine

(*n*) 5 Bac Abridg Ed by Mr Gwillim, 716   The reafon affigned is the tendency of a grant of the freehold in futuro, to make the tenant of the freehold in the mean time regardlefs of the fervices due to the Lord   But this feems only a fubfidiary reafon; for it is to be remembered, that the rifing up of future and executory eftates of freehold, on the happening of the particular contingency, would not have been confiftent, with the folemnity and notoriety required by our law for the paffing of freehold and inheritance, and would have materially affected the ufe of real actions

of executory devifes, as afterwards received and now eftablifhed under reftriction, the executory devife could not have
been fupported. But Lord Chief Juftice Vaughan, in his
report of the cafe of Sheldon and Gardiner, which was adjudged in the 23d of Charles the fecond, infers from the
before mentioned cafe in Dyer of the 28th. and 29th. of
Hen. 8. that the clear opinion of the judges Fitzherbert and
Baldwin, whom Lord Vaughan ftiles the greateft lawyers of
the age, was againft executory devifes as a thing unknown
to our law; and moft probably, notwithftanding the cafes
I have before cited from the year books of 49. Edw. 3. & 11.
Hen. 6. this might be the real ftate of the matter. However
it may be collected from the cafe in Dyer fol. 124. a. pl. 38.
that executory devifes of the inheritance became in fome degree countenanced in the reign of Philip and Mary; for fuch
a devife, on the contingency of *the death of the teftator's fon
and heir under twenty-four,* was held not to prevent the defcent
to him, in refpect that he had attained that age, which rather
implies, that, if he had died before, the devife might have
operated. That inheritance fhould thus begin to be fubject
to executory devife, may be accounted for, *from the progrefs
of ufes and trufts after the ftatute of ufes* 27. *Hen.* 8. *and from the
effect produced by the power of devifing land under the ftatutes
of* 32d. *and* 34. *of the fame reign*; fpringing ufes of the
inheritance and frechold furnifhing a precedent for like executory eftates in the form of executory devife, and the conftruction of the ftatutory power of devifing at the *free will and
pleafure* of the teftator affording to the judges an opportunity of exerting a difcretion in favour of executory devife accordingly. The further countenance to executory
devife of inheritance early in the reign of Elizabeth feems
inferrable from Boulton's Cafe of 6. and 7. Eliz. as cited

in

in 2. Ro. Rep. 217. and Palmer 132. it being ſtated to have
been in that caſe agreed, on a deviſe to teſtator's wife till his
ſon ſhould attain 21, and then to him and his heirs or to
him for ever, and in caſe of his dying without iſſue within the
age of 21 years to the teſtator's daughter, that, if the
ſon had not attained 21, the deviſe to the daughter would
have been good.   However Rolle in his report obſerves, that
there was a difference in the reports of this caſe of Boulton;
and at all events it was no more than an extrajudicial
opinion.   During the remainder of the reign of Elizabeth,
executory deviſes of inheritance gained ſome further ground.
Of this the caſes of Hinde v. Lyon reported in 2. Leon. 11.
and almoſt in the ſame words in 3. Leon. 64. and 70. Ful-
merſton v. Steward cited and ſtated in Palm. 135. and
Cro. Jam. 592. and Wellock v. Hammond Cro. Eliz. 204.
are ſufficient proof.   But in the firſt of theſe three caſes the
contingency of the executory deviſe depended on a *ſingle
life* ; in the ſecond the contingency was *almoſt immediate* ; and
in the third the contingency was confined to *two years*.   That
Lord Coke, early in the following reign, joined in ſanction-
ing ſuch executory deviſes, appears from Matthew Manning's
caſe, which was in 7 Jam. 1. and is in the 8th report: for
though this latter caſe was an executory deviſe of a term
of years, yet Lord Coke, then chief juſtice of the Common Pleas, argued in ſupport of the deviſe over of the
term after an eſtate for life, from the ſufficiency of an
executory deviſe of the fee.   A few years after Matthew
Manning's caſe, namely, in the 18th of James, there occurred
the caſe of Pell. v. Brown.   It is reported fully in Cro. Jam.
Palm. and 2 Ro. Rep. and ſhortly in Godb and the margin
of Dyer, ed. of 1688 fol. 354, a. and it was adjudged by the
King's Bench recently after Lord Coke's being angrily re-
                                                     moved

moved by King James. It was a devife to a younger Son and his heirs for ever, and if he died *without iffue living his elder brother*, then to him and his heirs. This limitation over was folemnly adjudged to be a good executory devife by all the judges of the King's Bench. All of them, alfo, except Judge Doderidge, held it not barrable by a common recovery of the firft devifee. It appears, that Doderidge, in fo differing from the other judges, was in fome meafure influenced by an apprehenfion of having perpetuity revived under the fhelter of executory devife; and if it was not for the difcretion exercifed by the Courts, in prefcribing a time for the contingency of executory devifes, fuch might be the confequence of holding them out of the reach of a common recovery. This cafe is generally looked to as the pole-ftar for direction in executory devife of inheritance; or, to ufe the nervous expreffion of the prefent chief juftice of the King's Bench in Bradley v. Porter 3. Durnf. and Eaft, is deemed the foundation and as it were the magna charta of this branch of our law. Sometimes alfo it is referred to, as if the eftablifhment of executory devifes of the fee originated from this cafe. But certainly they had at leaft been countenanced by much earlier decifions, as the before mentioned cafes, of the reigns of Philip and Mary and of Elizabeth, and in the early part of James's reign, feem to fhew. Certainly alfo the cafe is filent as to executory devife of chattels, and goes but a little way towards afcertaining the boundary of executory devife for inheritance. Therefore with great deference to others, I beg leave to fay, that I do not feel this cafe as furnifhing very much of the code of executory devife. However this cafe of Pell v. Brown may be properly faid to have fixed, that in refpect of the executory devifee's having only a poffibility, his intereft was not within the recompenfe

F   of

of a common recovery, and therefore not within the reafon of
it's barring; and notwithftanding the almoft unreachable
fubtlety of the reafoning, yet, ever fince, executory devifes
of inheritance have been held unbarrable by the common
recovery of thofe having the prefent eftate. It muft be
allowed too, that this cafe afsifts in afcertaining when limitations over, on failure of iffue, after a devife to one and
his heirs, fhould operate by executory devife, and when
by remainder. Further it muft be confeffed, that this cafe
finally fixed the legality of executory devifes for inheritance,
under the circumftance of the contingency's *not exceeding a
life*; though I do not obferve in any report of the cafe, that the
judges, who differed from Doderidge on the point of recovery,
were very explicit in ftating, how far they were influenced
by the fhortnefs of the contingency. Chief Baron Montagu,
indeed, in 3. Cha. Caf. 19. in the great cafe of the Duke of
Norfolk, or as it is fometimes called the cafe of perpetuities,
which was firft adjudged in 1681, and of which I fhall foon
have occafion to make more particular mention, almoft reprefents Pell and Brown, as if it was queftionable. For this
purpofe he refers to the report of Gay *v.* Gay or Jay *v.* Jay
in Style 258. and 274. and to the argument of Latch, who
in that cafe afferts, that after deciding Pell and Brown the
court was divided upon the point; that in the ferjeant's cafe
21 James it was made a flat query, whether an executory
devife of the freehold was good; that ever fince it had been
difputable; and that Pell and Brown was oppofed by a folemn
judgment of the Common Pleas, in a cafe, which however is
given without the name and even with the omifsion of the
reign. Yet neither Lord Chief Baron Montagu, nor the two
chief juftices Pemberton and North, who joined with him
againft Lord Chancellor Nottingham in the Duke of Norfolk's

cafe, ventured abfolutely to deny the legality of an executory devife of inheritance: and Lord Chancellor Nottingham well obferved, that queries for exercifing the wits of ferjeants were not governing opinions to decide the law by. Upon the whole then it may be affumed with tolerable accuracy, that executory devifes of inheritance were at leaft fanctioned fome years before the cafe of Pell and Brown in the 17th of James the firft; and that from the time of that cafe their validity, where the contingency did not exceed *one life*, became unqueftionable.—*From one life*, our courts gradually proceeded to *feveral lives wearing out at the fame time*, what paffed as to executory devifes and trufts of terms of years afsifting this enlargement; and at length the allowance of time for the contingency reached *lives in being and twenty-one years after, with an allowance of the time of geftation for a pofthumous child.*—But this progrefs was not without ftruggle. In Snow and Cutler, which occurred almoft immediately after the reftoration, a devife to the heirs of the body of the teftator's wife, if they fhould attain *the age of fourteen*, was warmly contefted, on the ground of it's being an executory devife to a perfon not *in effe*, and of there being a contingency on a contingency, namely, the birth of a child and the child's attaining fourteen years. But I do not obferve, that the mere circumftance of the fourteen years beyond a life was much objected to. The cafe is in 1. Lev. 135. T. Raym. 162. 1. Keb. 752. 800. 851. 2. Keb. 11. 145. 296. and in 1. Sid. 153. It was feveral times argued. It ended with the court's being equally divided. But according to Levinz's report all agreed with Pell and Brown, that executory devife might be on *one life*; and that it was not barrable by recovery. Thus the doctrine as to the compafs of time for executory devifes of the fee appears to have

refted

refted 'till the cafe of Taylor *v.* Bydal, which is in 2. Mod. 289. 1. Fieem. 243. and Cart. 182. and appears from the account of the record of this cafe in Mr. Forrefter's Reports 231. to have been adjudged in the Common Pleas Hil. 29. and 30. Cha. 2. This cafe was confidered by the King's Bench, whilft Lord Hardwicke was chief juftice, as a clear adjudication for extending the contingency of executory devife of inheritance *to twenty-one years beyond lives in being.* But it was a decifion by the Common Pleas, whilft Lord North was chief juftice, and he concurred in it; and I know not, how entirely to reconcile it, with the ftrong part he afterwards took againft the executory truft of a term of years in the great cafe of the Duke of Norfolk, except that diftinctions between inheritance and terms of years were relied upon in a great degree. However, be this as it may, even the extenfion of *one year* beyond co-exifting lives was contefted foon after the revolution; nay, in the firft inftance even with fuccefs. The cafe I mean is that of Lloyd and others *v.* Carew, which in effect was an executory limitation of the ufe of lands in fee in a marriage fettlement, to the heirs of the wife, *on the contingency of a failure of iffue of the hufband and her at the death of the furvivor and payment by the wife's heir of £4,000. to the hufband's heir within twelve months, after fuch furvivor's deceafe.* Here the contingency extended to *two lives in being and one year beyond ·* and a bill in Chancery was brought by the wife's co-heirs againft the hufband's heir to have benefit of the limitation on payment of the £4,000. The only report of the cafe is in Show. Parl. Caf. 137. and according to the account there, the court affifted by the chief juftice of the Common Pleas and judge Rookeby difmiffed the bill, and as it fhould feem, becaufe the contingency was too remote. But the plaintiffs appealed to the

Lords.

Lords. Before them the great point was, whether ONE YEAR *beyond lives in being* was not an excefs of the time for an executory devife of the fee, or for a contingent limitation or fpringing ufe of the fame nature; it being contended for the refpondent, that the life of one or more perfons in being was the *ne plus ultra* of executory devife. The cafe ended with a reverfal of the decree, and confequently a precedent for *one year beyond two lives in being.* Yet foon afterwards, that is, 9. W. 3. in the cafe of Luddington *v.* Kime, which is in 1. Lord Raym. 203. and various other books, it was contended before the Court of Common Pleas, that the contingency for an executory devife of inheritance could not be extended beyond *a life in being,* even for a *pofthumous child,* though the time for that is fhort of a year. The cafe went off without any decifion of this point; for the whole court held, that the limitation was a contingent remainder in fee. However both Lord Chief Juftice Treby and Judge Powell declared themfelves on the point; Judge Powell holding, that for SO SHORT A TIME *as the birth of a pofthumous child* a life in being might be exceeded, but Lord Chief Juftice Treby protefting againft going an iota beyond *the life of* ONE PERSON *in being,* and relying upon what paffed in the before-mentioned cafe of Snow *v.* Cutler. About three years after this cafe of Luddington and Kime, the fubject of executory devifes was difcourfed upon, with a fulnefs and particularity even exceeding the difcuffion in the great cafe of the Duke of Norfolk, which I fhall have occafion to mention when I come to executory devifes of terms for years. The cafe I now allude to is Scattergood *v.* Edge. It is in 2. Salk. 229. 12. Mod. 277. and in the fupplement to the edition of 11. Mod. publifhed in 1781. The latter book includes the record, and contains far the largeft report, and is from a manufcript of Mr. Lutwiche, who was one of the ar-

guing

guing counfel when the cafe was carried by writ of error into
the King's Bench. It was firft adjudged by the Common Pleas
Hil. 12. W. 3. On error the King's Bench affirmed the judgment. The arguments of the judges of the Common Pleas
are fully reported, more particularly by Mr. Lutwiche. But
I do not find any report of the arguments of the judges in the
King's Bench. The manner, in which the judges of the
Common Pleas are ftated to have expreffed themfelves, *againft
enlarging the limits of executory devife*, deferves minute attention in fome points of view. But the cafe was of a very
mixed and complicated nature; and fo far as it concerns the
hiftory of executory devife of inheritance, the chief thing to
be collected from it is, that, notwithftanding fome of the
prior cafes, the judges confidered *lives in being* as the *ultima-
tum* of contingency in remotenefs. As late as the year 1722,
it was ftrongly argued, that this time fhould not be exceeded,
even to include a child *en ventre fa mere*; and therefore that
an executory devife of inheritance to the fon of one being a
batchelor was too remote. So it was argued by Mr. Serjeant
Bootle in Gore and Gore before the King's Bench 6. Geo. 2.
as reported in 2. W. Kel. 204; and Mr. Peere Williams, according to his report of his own argument on the fame fide
in the fame cafe, though he occupied other grounds, infifted
on the benefit of that point; and the firft certificate of the
King's Bench, namely, by Lord Chief Juftice Pratt, and the
judges Eyre, Powis and Fortefcue Aland in 1722, was according to the report in 2. Stra. againft the executory devife
on that very ground. But the fecond certificate of the King's
Bench to Chancery in Gore and Gore, which was by Lord
Hardwicke and the judges Page Probyn and Lee, was for
the executory devife; and even the firft certificate, though,
againft the executory devife as too remote, was according to
                                                          the

the report in 9. Mod. 4. founded on the circumstance of a
precedent term of 500$^{d.}$ years.   Yet still it was doubted, whether, on an executory devise of the fee, the addition of *twenty-
one years* to *lives in being* should be allowed.   At length, however, there was a complete judgment for extending executory devise of inheritance to *lives in being and twenty-one years
after, with the allowance of the proper time for a posthumous child.*
But this was not accomplished till so lately as the year 1736.
The case, which so settled the point, is Stephens *v.* Stephens
sent out of Chancery by Lord Chancellor King.   It is stated
in Forrest. 228. with a copy of the certificate by Lord Hardwicke and the three other judges of the King's Bench.
The report of the arguments at law is in 2. Barnadist. 375.
and 2. W. Kel. 168.   The certificate of the four judges is
expressed with great care and explicitness.   It acknowledges,
that they could not find any case, wherein the executory devise of a freehold had been held good, where the vesting of
the estate was suspended until a son unborn should attain
twenty-one, except the before-mentioned case of Taylor and
Bydal.   But they represent the record of that case to agree
in the material part with the printed report in 2. Modern
Reports.   Therefore they say, that, however unwilling they
may be to extend executory devises beyond the rules generally laid down by their predecessors, yet upon the authority
of that judgment and its conformity to several late deter-
minations *in cases of terms for years,* and considering that the
*power of alienation would not be restrained longer than the law
would restrain it,* namely, during the infancy of the first taker,
which could not be reasonably said to extend to a perpetuity,
they were of opinion, that the devise in question might be
good by way of executory devise.   Ever since this decision,
executory devises of inheritance, to the extent of lives in be-

ing

ing and 21 years after, so as to include a posthumous child,
appears to have been allowed without the least controversy, and
as it seems upon an understanding, that the boundary of executory devise is universally the same, that is, the same for
inheritance as for terms of years and chattels personal. Accordingly Lord Kenyon in the late case of Long and Blackall
7. Durnf. and East. 100. which was on the executory devise
of a term of years, so states the limits for executory devise
generally. I presume also, that your Lordship's sending this
last-mentioned case for the opinion of the King's Bench did
not proceed from a doubt, whether the boundary of executory devise was established to the extent I have just stated.
The case, I can guess, had a very different object in view,
though from the report of the manner in which the case was
spoken to in the King's Bench both by the court and counsel, to me at least it seems, as if that object was not quite per-
ceived. From the circumstances of the executory devise then
in question, it's validity could not be supported without an allowance *twice over* of the time for a posthumous child, and
in the first instance an allowance *of the life of the posthumous
child besides*. In effect it was an executory devise of a chattel
lease, in trust for a son of the testator EN VENTRE SA MERE
*at the date of the will and not born till after the testator's decease,
and after the decease of such son in trust for such issue male or the
descendant of such issue male of such son as at his death should be
his heir at law*, with a limitation over, which was the devise in
question, if at the death of such son there should be no such
issue male or descendant of issue male then living, or if the
child *en ventre sa mere* should not be a son. Therefore I apprehend the objection to have been, that to begin with a
devise to a posthumous child for his life, and to graft upon it
a limitation over on failure of heirs male of his body at his

death,

death, which of courfe would include an heir male then *en
ventre fa mere,* was *to begin with allowance for a pofthumous
child,* then *to comprehend fuch child's whole life,* and afterwards to have the allowance for a pofthumous child *again*; and
confequently to claim having fuch allowance twice over with
the life of the pofthumous child in the firft inftance intermedi-
ately, and fo to enlarge the *nine* or *ten* months for a pofthumous child beyond lives in being and twenty-one years after to
eighteen or *twenty* months, with the whole life of a pofthumous
child into the bargain.   Such an enlargement of the boundary of executory devife was, I prefume, the great point,
upon which it was intended to have the opinion of the King's
Bench.   But from the turn this cafe, of which hereafter I
fhall have occafion to fpeak in a very particular manner,
took there, it feems at leaft doubtful, whether if fuch was the
point, it ought to be confidered as fully adjudged.

IN refpect to executory devifes of *terms for years,* the older
cafes are exprefs againft devifing over a term after a devife of
it to one for life.   The cafe of 6. Edw. 6. Dy. 74. b. is a
judgment to that effect; and there Lord Chief Juftice Montagu and Judge Hales ftate the point to have been fo ruled
by all the Judges, whilft Lord Rich, who had recently re-
figned the great feal, was Lord Chancellor.   There is, indeed, a cafe of 28. Hen. 8. in Dy. fol. 7. a. in which
Judge Englefielde thought a devife over of a term, even after
a devife to one and the heirs of his body, allowable.   But he
was overruled by the Judges Baldwin and Shelly; and thefe
latter faid, that it was as contrary to law to limit a term in
remainder, as it was to limit fuch a remainder of a perfonal
chattel.   However, in the latter end of the cafe, Baldwin
rather appears to admit, that the executory devife would have

As to terms
of years.

G   been

been good, if the first devife had been for life.   But this was
extra-judicial ; and it was adjudged to the contrary in the
before-mentioned cafe of 6 Edw. 6.   The reafons, however,
againft devifing a term over after an eftate for life were very
artificial ; for they appear to have been no better, than the
exility or fmall confideration of a term, an eftate for life
being legally a greater intereft than the largeft term, and the
now exploded notion of our law's not allowing a pofsibility
upon a pofsibility, which the limitation of a term after an
eftate for life is, one contingency being furviving the firft
taker, the other being the firft taker's outliving the term.
In the reign of Elizabeth, the Judges, under a nice diftinction between devifing *the term itfelf* and devifing only *the ufe
of it,* relaxed from this ftrictnefs as to a term, where the
devife over was after an eftate for life, as appears by the cafe
of 10. Eliz. Dy. 277. b. the cafe of Weleden *v.* Elkington
19 Eliz. Dy. 358. b. and Plowd. 519. and the cafe of Para-
mour *v.* Yardley Plowd. 539.   But the executory devife of a
term for years was not confidered as quite fafe, againft fale by
an executor or adminiftrator under colour of their not being
affets to pay debts ; and the cafe of Handall *v.* Brown 1 Jam.
Mo. 748. proves, that fuch danger was not imaginary.   This
danger, which muft ever belong to the devife of a term of
years, with fome doubtfulnefs, which ftill prevailed as to the
fufficiency of the later authorities to overrule the old doctrine againft limiting over terms of years, carried executory
devifes of terms into Chancery, to obtain, as well fecurity
againft alienation of the term, as the fhelter of truft ; and
there relief was given accordingly, of which the cafe of Cole
v. Moore in Chan. 5 Jam. Mo. 806. is a precedent.   About
the fame time the Courts of common law became lefs fubtle
and more firm in fupporting the executory devife of a term ;

for in Matthew Manning's cafe 7. Jam. 8. Co. it was in vain
infifted, that a term or could not in his life grant his term
over to one for life, with remainder to another, and therefore
could not fo devife; and Lord Coke and four other judges
refolved in favour of the executory devife, and alfo overruled
the diftinction between devifing a term of years and devifing
the ufe of the term. Lampet's cafe 10. Jam. in 10. Co. gave
new ftrength to the decifion in Matthew Manning's cafe.
Then one fhould have thought the queftion as to executory
devife of a term of years at reft. But ftill the judges were fo
jealous of and fo averfe to executory devifes, that Lord Coke
was fcarce removed from the King's Bench, when the controverfy as for terms of years in a manner revived. This
appears from the cafe of Child v. Baily 20. Jam. in W. Jo. 2.
Ro Rep. and Palm. for according to the report in Sir William
Jones, ten judges againft two condemned the executory
devife of a term to one fon, with a limitation over to another
fon, *if the former died without iffue in the lifetime of the latter.*
Abfolutely revoking the decifion in Manning's cafe and
Lampett's cafe was not avowed by the ten judges. But they
openly declared *againft going a ftep further*; and it was relied
upon, that the devife in this cafe of Child and Baily
was *equivalent to a devife to one and the heirs of his body* with
limitation over, and therefore differed from the cafes of
Manning and Lampett. Indeed in that point of view, though
the confining of the contingency of the limitation over to
a failure of iffue during a life in being, and the circumftance
of there being no exprefs devife of the term to the heirs
of the body of the firft devifee, furnifhed a ftrong anfwer to
the objection of its being a devife over of a term after an
eftate to the firft devifee and his iffue: yet there was not
wanting the color of reafon to fupport the decifion in this

G 2   cafe

cafe of Child and Baily ; for an unqualified executory devife
of a term, after a devife to one and the heirs of his body, is
on the contingency of a general failure of iffue, and fo leads
to a palpable perpetuity ; and as the judges, however
wrongly, confidered the cafe, the devife was conftructively
tantamount.   In that point of view alfo, that is, as the devife of a term after a prior devife to one and the heirs of his
body, Child and Baily was a proper reprobation of the
executory devife of a term.   There are many early cafes to
the fame effect.   Thofe at law are Saunders v. Cornifh
7. Cha. 1. Cro. Cha. 279 and 1. Ro. Abr. 612 and Leventhorp
and Afhby 11. Cha. 1. Wm. Jo. 15.   After the Reftoration
the illegality of limiting terms or trufts of them after an
eftate tail or a general failure of iffue was feveral times
confirmed, as appears, by Aprice v. Flower in 13. Cha. 2.
reported in Pollexf. 27. 1. Cha. Rep. 175. and Lord Nottingham's manufcript Prolegomena of Equity, Pearce v. Reeve,
alfo 13. Cha. 2. reported in Pollexf. 29. and the fame manufcript, Backhoufe v. Bellingham 16. Cha. 2. in Pollexf. 33.
and the fame manufcript, Burgefs v. Burgefs May 1674 in
Pollexf. 40. 1. Mod. 14. Reports temp. Finch 91. 1. Cha. Caf.
229. and Lord Nottingham's Mfs. Rep. and his Mfs. Prolegomena, Love v. Windham 22. Cha. 2. Knight v. Knight
28. Cha. 2. and 1. Mod. 50. 1. Lev. 290. Pollexf. 42. and
both of the manufcripts laft mentioned, Warman v. Warman
July 1672 in Pollexf. 112 to 123. and the fame two manufcripts alfo, and Ofgood v. Ofgood May 1674, which is in
Lord Nottingham's manufcript Prolegomena and there only.
It is obfervable on the certificate in one of thefe cafes,
namely, Pearce v. Reeve, the certificate in which is given
at length in Pollexfen, that Hide Twifden and Brown, the
three judges who certified to Lord Clarendon, were not content

tent with declaring the limitation over of the truft of a term, after failure of heirs of the body or of iffue underftood in the fame large fenfe, void; but in fome degree revived the old objection of its being a pofsibility on a pofsibility, the hufband and wife to whom the term was firft limited, not having had any child in effe at the creation of the truft; and actually ftated fuch a double pofsibility to be againft law. It is alfo obfervable, that though in the fame certificate the three judges allow, that it was not fit to call in queftion the judgment in Matthew Manning's cafe; yet they declared, *they did not think it fafe to ftretch the law againft its ordinary rules further than it had been done in that cafe.* This feemed like reverting, to the doctrine of confining the devife over of a term to one life, and to requiring that life to be in effe. Even the cafe of Warman v. Seaman, in which Lord Nottingham himfelf yielded to holding the limitation over void, if not carefully attended to, may feem to favour the fame notions: for the limitation over was to *children* and not to *iffue.* But Lord Nottingham's own account fhews, that in the firft opinion he gave he confidered the word *children* in the ftrict fenfe; and that in the decifion he finally made, he acquiefced in an opinion of all the judges, partly upon the confideration of underftanding the word *children* as equivalent under all the circumftances of the cafe to *heirs of the body.* Therefore he only meant to concede, that the limitation over of the truft of a term where *unqualifiedly* made after an intereft in the nature of an eftate tail, could not be fupported · which was a doctrine he never appears to have denied, and which he moft exprefsly approves both in his Prolegomena and in his judgment in the great cafe of Howard and the Duke of Norfolk. But where the devife over of a term was only after an eftate for life, it was more than adjudged good foon

after

after the Reftoration. The doctrine was a little further extended : for the limitation over of the trufts of a term **was** allowed *after two co-exifting lives.* This was decreed by Lord Chancellor Clarendon 14. Cha. 2. on the joint opinion of the chief juftices Forfter and Bridgman and of Hale chief baron, in the cafe of Goring v. Bickerftaffe and Althorp and others ; Lord Clarendon upon a rehearing reverfing the firft decree. The cafe is in Pollexf. 31. 1. Cha. Caf. 4. and 2. Freem. 163. and in the four volumes I have of Lord Bridgman's manufcript Reports of Judgments whilft he prefided over the Common Pleas, there is his own report of the cafe by the name of Althorp's Cafe ; and it is alfo reported in Lord Nottingham's manufcript Prolegomena. According to Lord Nottingham's report, it was refolved " that the limitation " of a term to SEVERAL PERSONS IN REMAINDER ONE AFTER " ANOTHER, *if they be all in being and alive together*, is good ; " and doth in no fort tend to the perpetuity of a chattel, " efpecially where each remainder is but for life, and *fo all* " *the candles are as it were lighted together*. but OTHERWISE " IT MIGHT BE, *if a remainder was limited to a perfon not in* " *effe.*" Lord Bridgman's report of the cafe confirms this account, except that he reprefents the opinion as coming from himfelf and Lord Hale, and Lord Forfter as only not gainfaying it. The phrafe, *that the candles are all lighted at once*, which has been current ever fince, Lord Bridgman gives as Lord Hale's words. But even this adjudication of Althorp's cafe, fo ex-tending the executory devife or truft of a term, from one to *feveral lives, of perfons* IN REMAINDER ONE AFTER ANOTHER, did not quite fettle the matter as to terms of years. On the contrary, in the latter end of the reign of Charles the fecond, the controverfy was refumed with great heat ; and the battle of executory devife for terms of years was completey re-
fought.

fought. This revival of the attack upon executory devise
of a term was in the great cafe of Howard and the Duke of
Norfolk, which I have already had occafion to refer to, and
which as I have before-mentioned is fometimes called the
cafe of perpetuities. The cafe is in 3 Cha. Caf. 1. 2. Cha·
Rep. 229. 2. Freem. 72. and 80. and Pollexf. 223. and
Lord Chancellor Nottingham in his manufcript Chancery
Reports gives his own argument on delivery of his judgment
after hearing the three chiefs from whom he differed. In this
famous cafe, Mr. Howard, a younger brother of the Duke of
Norfolk, claimed againft the Duke the benefit of the trufts of
a term of 200 years in the barony of Greyftock, under fettlements made in 1647 and as it was underftood with the advice
and approbation of Lord-keeper Bridgman, then a practifing
counfel. The language of the truft was particular and was
thus. By one deed the barony was limited to the Earl of
Arundel the Duke's father for life, remainder to the Duke's
mother for life, remainder to truftees for a term of 200 years,
remainder to Thomas Lord Maltravers the Earl's eldeft fon,
being infane and unmarried, in tail male, remainder to the
Duke then Henry Howard who was the fecond fon of the
Earl in tail male alfo. By another deed of the fame date,
the term was declared to be *in truft to attend the inheritance
fo long as Thomas Lord Maltravers the lunatic or any iffue male
of his body fhould live* (which to fimplify the cafe and clear
it from the opening for objection from the words *iffue male of
the body,* Lord Nottingham faid was confequently only during
his life, becaufe he was never likely to marry) but if he
fhould *die without iffue in the life-time of his brother* Henry
Howard afterwards Duke of Norfolk and the defendant in the
caufe, not leaving a wife *privement enfient* with a fon; or
which feems to have been intended as another way of exprefsing

preſsing the ſame thing, if, after the death of Lord Maltravers without iſſue male, the earldom of Arundel ſhould deſcend on his brother Henry afterwards Duke of Norfolk, then in truſt for the plaintiff Charles Howard. As was expected, Lord Maltravers the lunatic died a batchelor; and then the Duke having become tenant in tail male ſubject to the term of 200 years, his brother Charles claimed the truſt of the term. Whether the limitation over, under which he claimed was too remote, was the principal queſtion, though not the only one. Lord Nottingham called in to his aſſiſtance the chief juſtices Pemberton and North, and the chief baron Montagu. *The three chiefs were all againſt the legality of the truſt, under which Mr. Charles Howard claimed. But notwithſtanding this, Lord Nottingham decreed for him.* The great ſtrength of the caſe againſt the truſt was, that the truſt to attend the inheritance whilſt Lord Maltravers or any of his iſſue male was living might be deemed equivalent to a limitation over in truſt for him in tail, and ſo became in the nature of a limitation over after a veſted remainder in tail, and therefore after a failure of iſſue generally. Had the three chiefs been content with that mode of reaſoning, Lord Chancellor Nottingham would have had leſs opportunity of objecting fallacy to their reaſoning; and in that conſideration of the caſe various authorities, particularly Child and Baily, which the three chiefs greatly relied upon, ſeemed to preſs hard againſt the Lord Chancellor. But the three chiefs took a larger ſcope; and from their diſlike of the doctrine of executory deviſe and their zeal to ſtop its progreſs, they declaimed at large againſt executory deviſes as leading to perpetuities; and though they did not abſolutely deny the legality of executory deviſes of inheritance, yet they inſiſted upon ſome grounds, which ſeemed to amount to excluding their

influence

influence over terms of years, and confequently tended to impeach the cafes of Manning and Lampett, and to revive the doctrine which thofe cafes had in great meafure exploded. This gave great advantage to Lord Nottingham; and he availed himfelf of it. On the one hand, he treated the cafe, as in effect only the executory truft of a term on the contingency of a life in being, that is, the death of Lord Maltravers without leaving iffue in the life-time of his brother the Duke : and fo, as if the previous truft of attendancy on the eftate tail of Lord Maltravers was no material part of the cafe, he did not dwell upon it ; for exclufive of his particular obfervations againft the cafe of Child and Baily, which was mainly relied upon as authority againft him, he fcarce more than hinted, that Lord Maltravers's infanity delivered the cafe from the objection of a previous eftate tail. On the other hand, in every other branch of the argument, that is, in anfwering all other objections to the trufts of the term, fuch as the exility of eftate, its being a double contingency, the fuppofition of perpetuity when clearly the contingency was only the fingle life of Lord Maltravers and the time for the birth of a pofthumous fon to him, and the apprehenfion of danger on that account, he was full and convincing. He argued as a man; who clearly faw the weaknefs of the grounds to which his opponents had reforted to affert their opinion ; and who faw alfo, that, independent of the objection from the refemblance of the previous truft of attendancy on a vefted remainder in tail male to fuch a previous remainder itfelf (which I conceive however was the real pinch of the cafe) both the reafon of the thing and the ftrength of authorities were with him. Accordingly Lord Nottingham, *notwithftanding the united opinion of the three chiefs his affeffors to the contrary*, made a decree fuftaining the trufts of the term for Mr. Charles Howard. This

H   decree

decree was made in June 1682.   But after Lord Nottingham's
death, which was in the November following, there was a bill
of review; and Lord North, being then Lord-keeper, reverfed
Lord Nottingham's decree.   However upon an appeal to the
Houfe of Lords, they in June 1685 reverfed Lord North's
decree and affirmed that of Lord Nottingham ; Lord Jeffries
being underftood to have acceded to Lord Nottingham's opinion, and to have been active in fupporting it.   By this final
affirmance of Lord Nottingham's decree, the great point of
controverfy, as to the liability of terms for years to executory
devifes and to trufts of the fame nature, was confidered as
clofed : for the principle of the decree was, that they were
equally fubject with inheritance.   It was alfo thought to be
within the principle of the decree, that fo long as the ftrict
fettlement of any fpecies of property, by executory devife or
by trufts of the fame nature, did not exceed the ordinary time
for barring a regular entail by eftates for life with remainder
in tail to an unborn child, which was when fuch child
fhould attain twenty-one, it would be confidered as allowable.
This led to a general practice, of fettling terms of years, and of
providing portions for children under the trufts of fuch terms,
to the extent of lives in being and 21 years after : and at
length, as I have already fhewn, fuch practice was made a
chief ground, whilft Lord Hardwicke prefided over the King's
Bench, of extending executory devife of inheritance in like
manner ; the practice for terms of years thus afsifting the
extenfion of executory devife of inheritance, as the precedents for inheritance had before afsifted to eftablifh executory
devife for terms of years.   But Lord Chancellor Nottingham
forefaw the pofsibility of future abufe of executory devife ;
and having fupported it to a certain extent, by an exercife of
judicial difcretion on the principle of *convenience*, he took
                                                                care

care in his eloquent judgment in the Duke of Norfolk's cafe to have it well underftood, that there was referved to the Courts a right by a like exercife of judicial difcretion to prevent *inconvenience*. His language on this topic is of importance to be remembered, more efpecially in the prefent cafe, which in fome views of it may very much depend on an exercife of the power of controul thus referved. As the manufcript of his own reports ftates his words, they were as follow. " It has been urged at the bar, where will you ftop, if you " do not ftop at Child and Baily's cafe? I anfwer, I will ftop " EVERY WHERE WHEN ANY INCONVENIENCE APPEARS; " *no where before*. It is not yet refolved, what are the utmoft " bounds of limiting a contingent fee upon a fee; and it is " not neceffary to declare, what are the utmoft bounds to " the fpringing trufts of a term. *Whenfoever the bounds of* REA- " SON *or* CONVENIENCE *are exceeded, the law will quickly be* " *known*."

As to *chattels perfonal*, the controverfy about executory de- As to chattels perfonal vife of them in fome degree continued, even after clofe of the difpute about terms of years. The doctrine of ancient times made a fubtle diftinction, between devifing a chattel itfelf and devifing the ufe or occupation of it. If the gift or devife was of *the chattel itfelf* only for an hour, it operated for ever, and wholly paffed the property to the donee or legatee, fo that he might give fell or difpofe of it, and any limitation over was void. But if a devife was *of the ufe or occupation of a chattel* to one for life, and if he died within the term to another, the executor affenting to the legacy, it was faid, that the firft taker had only fuch ufe and occupation, and after his death the other had the property. This diftinction is ftated by Lord Chief Juftice Brooke in his Abridge-

ment

ment title Devife pl. 13. and he reprefents it as agreed in the times of Hen. 8. and Edw. 6. to be good law, he at the fame time referring to the year book of 37. Hen. 6. 30. and abridging from it a cafe containing the very fame diftinction. How this diftinction became over-ruled as to chattels real, appears from the hiftory I have given of executory devife as to terms for years. But the diftinction feems to have furvived fome time longer for chattels perfonal. Mr. Peere Williams's Reports, it is obfervable, begin with an equity cafe on this fubject of as late date as Eafter 1695. The cafe is Hyde v. Parratt in 1. Wms. 1. and 2. Vern. 331. It arofe on a devife of houfehold goods to one for life, with limitation over to another. Mr. Peere Williams gives a full report of his own argument againft the devife over; and in it the old reafoning and authorities againft executory devifes of chattels are referred to. He allowed the law to be at length fixed as to terms for years: but he infifted, that chattels perfonal were diftinguifhable both in reafon and authority; in the former, from their being in the moft part expofed to the cafualties of lofs and perifhablenefs; in the latter, from the want of thofe decifions which ruled terms for years. The caufe was firft heard before Mr. Baron Powell fitting for Lord Somers; and the former treated the point fo ferioufly as to referve it for his Lordfhip. Even the latter took time to confider the point. But at length he held the devife over good; and from that time the liability of perfonal chattels, to executory devife, in the like manner as chattels real, feems to have been treated as fully fettled. In that way Lord Macclesfield in the cafes of Tiffin v. Tiffin and Upwell v. Halfey, both of which are in Mr. Peere Williams's firft volume, feems to advert to the doctrine as not longer queftionable. Accordingly alfo in Sabbarton v. Sabbarton; which Lord Chancellor Talbot fent to

the

the King's Bench on a mixed devise of inheritance and of stocks; and which therefore left an opening for doubt, whether the latter should not follow the entail of the former; the case, as appears from the report of it in Andrews, was argued in the King's Bench as an executory devise depending on the extent of the rule for the trusts of a term of years.

THUS at length a great though partial victory appears to have been gained, for executory devises, and for limitations and trusts of the same nature, over every species of property in England: that is, over freehold and inheritance; over real chattels; and over chattels personal.—Thus neither the feudal strictness of conveyance in the first of those three kinds of estates, especially against creating a freehold in futuro; nor the exility and meanness of interest in the second; nor the moveableness casualness and perishableness of quality in the third; nor the doctrine against possibility on possibility, with the danger of perpetuity and of abuse in other respects as to all three; finally availed to accomplish the absolute exclusion of executory devise. all these objections being so successively encountered and so successively subdued, that at the utmost they have only contributed to reduce executory devise within regulation and circumscription.

Short result of the preceding history of executory devise.

BUT from the preceding history of the rise progress and final establishment of executory devise, which for the purpose of the present case I have laboriously extracted out of an indigested mass of materials frequently obscure and almost always dry even to the most professional practiser, it appears, that the struggles against executory devise were long and obstinate, and were sanctioned by judges and lawyers of the first eminence.

Inferences.

NOTWITH-

NOTWITHSTANDING alſo the imperfection of my hiſtorical deduction (for in many points of view, though I tiuſt not very much in thoſe more immediately connected with the preſent argument, I feel it to be imperfect) there is I conceive enough to found very important inferences; not only ſuch as evince the light of our Courts of juſtice to check the exceſs and over extenſion of executory deviſe, and to prevent an abuſive application of the indulgence it grants; but ſuch, as may moie particularly be made to bear upon the tiuſts now in judgment before your Lordſhip.

PROBABLY thoſe, who, with profoundneſs in this bianch of oui juiidical ſyſtem unite a vigorous penetrancy, would in this reſpect eaſily and quickly perform that duty for the purpoſe of the pieſent caſe. But I have found a ſerious pauſe requiſite. After, however, cloſe and induſtiious attention to the ſubject, I feel myſelf juſtified, and by the nature of the pieſent caſe called upon, to offer the following inferences from the hiſtoiy of executory deviſe, as ſubſidiary and introductory foundations of argument againſt the truſts now in queſtion; the other inferences, which that hiſtoiy may furniſh to the pieſent caſe, being reſeived for application, in the argument of the paiticular points, into which I propoſe breaking the caſe.

Firſt inference. IN the FIRST place I ſubmit, that executory deviſe appears to be, not a genuine ancient branch of our law, but *an indulged ſupei induction to it*; not a *iegulai pioduction of our geneial ſyſtem*, but an *eicreſcence*; not a *ſtrictly regulai ſpecies of entail*, but a *permitted irregular mode of ſettlement*; not a *legitimate offspring of our common law*, but a *privilege gradually inſinuated into our juriſpiudence*. It operates, by creating future eſtates and intereſts

of

of every kind, freehold as well as chattel, in a way not endured by our common law ;—in a way quite inconfiftent with the folemnity of it's forms as to freehold ;—in a way, which, without the rules the Courts of Weftminfter Hall have by an exercife of difcretion introduced to circumfcribe this mode of creating eftates, would have afforded the opportunity, of making inheritance and freehold and chattel almoft ever unceftain precarious and determinable, and confequently of making property almoft eternally unalienable. The rule, againft creating a freehold *de futuro*, makes it impracticable fo to create a freehold by any common law conveyance ; and as for any leffer eftate, terms of years were anciently rather contracts than eftates; and even now future interefts in the nature of remainders *cannot* be created in chattels real and perfonal, except through the medium of ufes trufts and executory devife. Nay, executory devife is ftill fo confidered as a privilege, and fo much disfavour is ftill fhewn to it, that a rule has prevailed ever fince it's introduction, againft conftruing any eftate as operating by executory devife, where it can take effect by remainder. This rule is particularly mentioned by Lord Hale in Purefoy and Rogers in 2. Saund. 388. and has been fince acted upon in an abundance of cafes, of which fome of the principal are enumerated in the beginning of Mr. Fearne's excellent Treatife on Executory Devifes. Even Lord Manffield, who was not indifpofed to emancipate the conftruction of wills from every thing like technical reftraint, confeffed, in the cafe of Goodtitle and Billington in Mr. Douglafs's Reports, that fuch clearly was the rule ; and the prefent chief juftice of the King's Bench, in the cafe of Doe and Morgan 3. Durnf. and Eaft 763. goes the length of faying, that if ever there was a rule concerning executory devifes, which has uniformly prevailed without any exception, it is what
Lord

Lord Hale lays down againſt reſorting to executory deviſe, where remainder can operate. As I have already explained in the hiſtory of executory deviſe, it is upon the whole an irregular ſpecies of entail, little countenanced till ſome years after the death of Henry the eighth, and not thoroughly fixed even for inheritance till the caſe of Pell v. Brown in the 17th of James the firſt; and this account of the matter doth not much differ from the notion of Lord Kenyon in 3. Durnf. and Eaſt 765, where he ſtates executory deviſes as eſtabliſhed in the reign of Charles the firſt. Whilſt alſo this priority or precedence of remainder continues, ſo long there will exiſt a badge, not only of the juniority of executory deviſe, but of the disfavour of our law towards it, and of its being an indulgence.

Second infe-
rence.

IN the NEXT place I ſubmit, that this indulgence of executory deviſe appears to have originated, from *an exerciſe of diſ- cretion by our judges* FOR THE SAKE OF GENERAL CONVENI- ENCE. The ſtatute of 27. Hen. 8. for annexing the poſſeſ- ſion or legal eſtate of land to the truſt or uſe, or, as we uſu- ally term it, for transferring uſes into poſſeſsion, together with the ſtatutes of the 32d and 34th of the ſame reign giving the power to deviſe lands, might indeed lead to executory de- viſes. But the eſtabliſhment of them ſeems to be more pro- perly referrable to the judges themſelves. At the utmoſt, the ſtatutes, I have juſt mentioned, can I think only be con- ſidered, as affording to the judges a better opportunity of permitting executory deviſe; for certainly there is not any thing in thoſe or any other ſtatutes profeſſedly introductive of executory deviſes, and ſtill leſs is there in them any re- gulation of them. Nor is this manner of ſtating the orga- nization of executory deviſe ſubſtantially novel. It is in

effect

effect exactly Lord Kenyon's notion of it as reported in the cafe of Doe on the demife of Muffel againft Morgan in 3. Durnf. and Eaft: for there his lordfhip is ftated to have faid, that " it was fome time before executory devifes were *permitted* " *by the courts of law;* but being found of *general utility,* they " were eftablifhed in the time of Charles the Firft." The fame notion may be traced in the reports of Scattergood and Edge, which I have before mentioned as a famous cafe on the fubject of executory devife fome few years after the revolution. It may be traced alfo into the great cafe of the Duke of Norfolk in the reign of Charles the Second, upon which I have before fo much enlaiged; or rather into the cafes of the prior reigns of the firft James and Charles.

FURTHER I beg leave to affert, that ALL THE RULES, by Third inference *which executory devifes and limitations and trufts of the fame nature are* CIRCUMSCRIBED, appear alfo to have ORIGINATED IN THE DISCRETION OF THE JUDGES, and to have been *from time to time made by them, as occafion demanded upon the principle of preventing public inconvenience* from the permiffion thus indulged. Executory devife was, as I have fhewn, not regularly admitted till about two centuries ago. The rules for circumfcribing it are confequently not of earlier date, and there are not any ftatutes for the purpofe. It is impoffible, therefore, that the rules fhould be derived from any other fouice than the difcretion of the judges. *For general utility and public convenience they permitted executory devife.* But it was feen, that if executory devife or ufe or truft of a fimilar nature was permitted without fome reftrictions, great abufes might be generated. It was foon fettled by the courts of law, that executory devife could not be barred by common recovery, that is, as early as the cafe of Pell and Brown in the 17th of James the Fiift.

I   Afterwards,

Afterwards, though not without much conteſt, it was further ſettled, that executory deviſe might be ſo ſhaped, as to make the deviſee uncertain (o) till the very inſtant appointed for riſing of the executoy eſtate. But executory deviſe, thus unbarrable by recovery or otherwiſe, and thus uncertain as to the perſon of the deviſee till the moment of taking effect, if ſome limit had not been preſcribed, would have been a ſhelter for perpetuity. To prevent ſuch an abuſe, the judges limited the time for the contingency, on which an executory deviſe was to operate; holding, that unleſs the contingency was ſuch, that if it ever happened, it would neceſſarily happen within a limited ſpace of time, the executory deviſe ſhould be deemed illegal, and conſidered as a nullity. Thus, as for the ſake of geneial utility the judges exerciſed a diſcretion in permitting executory deviſe to be introduced; ſo to prevent public inconvenience, they limited the time for the contingency, and proſcribed all contingencies exceeding that time as too remote and therefore againſt law. The courts of equity followed the courts of law in this, and circumſcribed truſts of the nature of executory deviſe in like manner. Hence GRADUALLY aroſe the boundary, which now circumſcribes executory deviſes, and limitations and truſts of the ſame nature; namely, the rule confining the contingency for the ſpringing up of future and executory eſtates to the compaſs of a life or lives in being and 21 years after, including a ſufficient number of months for the birth of a child *en ventre ſa mere.*

Fourth in ference. STILL FURTHER as I conceive, it appears, that this limitation of time, for the contingency of executory deviſe, was a boundary, which the diſcretion of the courts of Weſtminſter

(o) See caſe of Snow *v*. Cutler, before page 35.

Hall

Hall eftablifhed, *with reference to the fpace of time, during* *which, according to the courfe of an ordinary entail, of land by* *eftates for life with remainders to unborn fons and daughters in* *tail, inheritance may be kept unalienable.* Under this latter and direct and regular fpecies of entail, inheritance may be fo fettled, as to render barring of the entail impracticable, till the tenant for life has had iffue, and fuch iffue has attained twenty-one, and fo becomes qualified to fuffer a common recovery or to levy a fine according to the nature of the cafe : or, by making the parent tenant for a long term of years if he fhall fo long live, and vefting the freehold in truftees during his life to pre-ferve contingent remainders, may be fo fettled, as to protract a compleat bar of the entail till both the child's attaining twenty one and the death of the parent. The rule, therefore, as to the boundary of executory devifes, was a reftriction introduced by the courts of Weftminfter Hall to prevent entail by executory devife from going further than entail by remainders. It was much the fame, as if the judges had faid, " It is required by " general convenience, that we fhould permit entail by exe-" cutory devife and by limitations of a like defcription. For " *inheritance,* it would be hard to difappoint fuch a mode of " fettlement, though for *that* the regular mode might be re-" forted to. For *chattels* both real and perfonal, it would be " ftill harder not to permit executory devife and limitations by " truft of the fame defcription, becaufe otherwife the fettle-" ment of terms of years and of perfonal chattels, for fe-" curing portions of younger children, and for other family " and neceffary purpofes, would be in a manner imprac-" ticable. We therefore indulge this irregular kind of entail " and fettlement. But we muft take care not to indulge it, fo " as to protract it's duration beyond the period allowed to the " antient and regular mode of entail by remainder. As too

" fines

" fines or common recoveries will not apply for barring entail
" by executory devise, we muſt ſubſtitute ſome other mode of
" circumſciibing it's duration. For that purpoſe we will con-
" ſtitute ſuch limits for executory deviſe, as ſhall prevent it's
" operating one iota beyond the uſual time for ſuffering a com-
" mon recovery in the caſe of a family ſettlement by remain-
" ders. Accordingly we declare, that, when executory deviſe
" is preceded by giving ſuch an intereſt as is equivalent to an
" eſtate tail; or when without giving ſuch a preceding equi-
" valent intereſt the executory deviſe limits a future eſtate on a
" contingency, which may happen after the expiration of lives
" in being and 21 years beyond, that is, may happen beyond
" the uſual time for a common recovery to bar an ordinary en-
" tail on an exiſting perſon for life with remainder to his un-
" born iſſue in tail; in either caſe the executory deviſe ſhall be
" void for remoteneſs of contingency and have no effect."

IN thus explaining the principle, upon which our courts of
law have erected a boundary for executory deviſe, and our courts
of equity have done the ſame thing for limitations of the ſame
nature by truſts, I only expreſs what many years ago I ſtated
on this ſubject, firſt at the end of a note in my part of the new
edition of Coke upon Littleton (*p*), and ſome years afterwards
in my argument in Wicker and Mitford (*q*), which is in the volume of Law Tracts I publiſhed in 1788.

MY note in the Coke upon Littleton was as follows:
" Here *two* things ſeem eſſential to an entail within the ſtatute
" *de donis*. One requiſite is, that the *ſubject* be land or ſome
" other thing of a *real* nature. The other requiſite is, that

(*p*) Co. Litt. 13th fol 20. a note (5).   (*q*) Haigrave's Law Tracts, p. 518.

the

" the *estate* in it be an *inheritance*. Therefore, neither
" estates *pur autre vie* in lands, though limited to the grantee
" and his heirs during the life of *cestui que vie*, nor *terms*
" *for years*, are entailable any more than *personal chattels :* be-
" cause as the latter, not being either interests in things *real*
" or of *inheritance*, want *both* requisites ; so the two former,
" though interests in things *real*, yet not being also of *inheri-*
" *tance*, are deficient in *one* requisite. However, estates *pur*
" *autre vie*, terms for years, and personal chattels, may be so
" settled, as to answer the purposes of an entail, and be ren-
" dered unalienable almost for as long a time, as if they were
" entailable in the strict sense of the word. Thus estates *pur*
" *autre vie* may be devised or limited in strict settlement by
" way of *remainder* like estates of inheritance ; and such, as have
" interests in the nature of estates tail, may bar their issue and
" all remainders over by *alienation* of the estate *pur autre vie*,
" as those, who are strictly speaking tenants in tail, may do by
" *fine* and *recovery* ; but then the having of issue is not an essen-
" tial preliminary to the power of alienation in the case of an
" estate *pur autre vie* limited to one and the heirs of his body,
" as it is in the case of a conditional fee, from which the mode
" of barring by alienation was evidently borrowed. The man-
" ner of settling terms for years and personal chattels is different ;
" for in them no *remainders* can be limited: but they may be
" entailed by *executory devise* or by deed of *trust*, as effectually
" as estates of inheritance, if it is not attempted to render them
" unalienable beyond the duration of lives in being and 21
" years after, and perhaps in the case of a posthumous child a
" few months more ; a limitation of time, not *arbitrarily* pre-
" scribed by our courts of justice, but wisely and reasonably
" adopted in analogy to the case of freeholds of inheritance,
" which cannot be so limited by way of remainder as to post-
                                                    " pone

" pone a complete bar of the entail by fine or recovery for a
" longer fpace.   It is alfo proper to obferve, that in the cafe
" of terms of years and perfonal chattels, the *vefting* of an in-
" tereft, which in reality would be an eftate tail, bars the iffue
" and all the fubfequent limitations, as effectually as fine and
" recovery in the cafe of eftates entailable within the ftatute *de*
" *donis*, or a fimple alienation in the cafe of conditional fees
" and eftates *pur autre vie*; and further, that if the executory
" limitations of perfonalty are on contingencies too remote,
" the whole property is in the firft taker. Upon the whole,
" by a feries of decifions within the laft two centuries, and
" after many ftruggles in refpect to perfonalty, it is at length
" fettled, that every fpecies of property is in *fubftance* equally
" capable of being fettled in the way of entail; and though the
" modes vary according to the nature of the fubject, yet they
" tend to the fame point, and the duration of the entail is cir-
" cumfcribed *almoft* as nearly within the fame limits, as the
" difference of property will allow."

My remark in the Law Tracts was in thefe words :

" When executory devifes were firft permitted, it was fore-
" feen, that entails made in that form could not be barred by
" fines or recoveries.—If they were of *real* eftate, the executory
" devife could not be barred by fine, becaufe the title of the exe-
" cutory devifee is not *through,* or as *privy* to the immediate
" taker, but quite independent of him : nor could the execu-
" tory devifee be affected by a recovery, it being foon fettled,
" that the recompence, which in the fuppofition of law is the
" ground of barring the iffue in tail and thofe in remainder
" and reverfion, doth not extend to an executory devifee (*r*).

(*r*) Pell v Brown, Cro. Jam. 590. Pig. on Recov 129.

" —If

" —If they were of *perfonal* eftate, whether chattels real or
" perfonal, from the nature of the property they could not
" be the fubject of either fine or recovery.—Entails by exe-
" cutory devife being thus exempt from any legal mode of
" barring them, it became neceffary to prefcribe bounds and
" limits to this new fpecies of fettlement, left otherwife en-
" tails fhould obtain a longer duration through the irregular
" and barely permitted medium of executory devife, than the
" law endures, where the entail commences in the regular way,
" by creating eftates for life and eftates tail with remainders over.
" Hence originated the rule both at law and in equity, that
" the contingency, on which executory devifes depend, fhould
" be confined to a ftated period ; and by analogy to the cafe
" of ftrict entails, which cannot be protected from fines and
" recoveries, longer than the life of the tenant for life in pof-
" feffion and the attainment of 21 by the firft iffue in tail, it
" was at length fettled, that the longeft period for vefting of
" an executory devife fhould be *any life or lives in being and* 21
" *years after* ; to which may be added *a few months more for the*
" *cafe of a pofthumous child.* Therefore every contingency, which
" is not fuch, that if it ever happens, it muft neceffarily be within
" the period fo defcribed, is too remote for an executory de-
" vife. The confequence of thus circumfcribing the limits of an
" executory devife is, that it is not lawful to limit an executory
" devife on a *general and indefinite failure of iffue* ; namely, a
" failure of iffue of the perfon named whenever it happens, be
" the time of the event ever fo diftant. It is equally a confe-
" quence of the rule, that if the failure of iffue is reftrained
" to the death of any perfon or perfons actually living, or to
" any period not beyond a life and lives in being and 21
" years with a few months beyond, then the contingency is
" good, and the executory devife has it's full effect. Per-
" haps

" haps if the doctrine of executory devifes was *res integra*, and
" was now to be fettled, it might be thought a fufficient and
" more juft check of them to hold, that they fhould be good
" as far as the given period, whether the contingency was too
" largely and widely expreffed or not. But our anceftors have
" not left us a choice; it having been long a fixed rule, that,
" if the contingency is too remote, the executory devife de-
" pendent upon it fhall not be merely void fo far as it exceeds
" the line prefcribed, but fhall wholly fail."

Now too, I have the fatisfaction of knowing, that a great
living judge, who is peculiarly converfant in the law of real
property, confiders the principle of the boundary to executory
devife in the fame way : for fo it appears from the cafe of Long
and Blackhall, which I had occafion to cite from 7. Durnf. and
Eaft in the preceding hiftory of executory devife, and which
was adjudged as recently as Hilary term laft year. The words
of Lord Kenyon are thefe : " The rules refpecting executory
" devifes have conformed to the rules laid down in the con-
" ftruction of legal limitations ; and the courts faid, that *the eftate*
" *fhall not be unalienable by executory devifes for a longer term,*
" *than is allowed by the limitations of a common law conveyance.*
" In marriage fettlements the eftate may be limited to the firft
" and other fons of the marriage in tail ; and until the perfon,
" to whom the laft remainder is limited, is of age, the eftate
" is unalienable. In conformity to that rule, the court have
" faid, so FAR we will allow executory devifes to be good."

Fifth infe-
rence

THE NEXT inference which I make from the hiftory of executory devife is, that, as to prevent all material inconvenience
from permitting the executory devife of property, our courts
have already exerted a difcretion in laying down certain rules ;

fo it is apparent, that *there is referved to them a right of further exercifing their difcretion for the fame purpofe, whenever cafes pregnant with any great evil fhall provoke it.* The principle, which, as I have fhewn, firft generated the introduction and fanction of executory devife, and afterwards limited and controuled it, was *general convenience;* or to ufe Lord Kenyon's words, *general utility.* Such a principle imports, that to apply the permiffion of executory devife *againft general convenience, againft general utility,* is an abufe of the permiffion. It imports alfo, that executory devife muft continue fubject to the controul of the courts: for otherwife the principle might become dormant, and the courts would not be adequate to prevent new abufes, and only thofe which have already occurred would be checked. To prevent abufe effectually, it is as neceffary, that the courts fhould be armed with authority to ftop new abufes in their career, as that the courts fhould continue the prevention of old abufes. Lord Chancellor Nottingham, the great patron of executory devife, appears in the Duke of Norfolk's cafe to have fo confidered the difcretion of the courts of Weftminfter Hall: for this is the amount of his anfwer to thofe who afked, where executory devife was to ftop; his anfwer being, as I have already ftated at length from his manufcript reports, that it was to ftop where inconvenience begins. Alfo the practice of the Courts from the firft introduction of executory devife imports, that their difcretion for controuling them was of a *continuing* nature. The prefent boundary was not the effect of one exercife of difcretion; was not the work of one fet or of two fets of judges. The limits were from time to time enlarged and contracted, as the cafes, which called for judgment and public convenience and public inconvenience refpectively demanded: and it is moft evident, that the boundary, fo far as it has yet proceeded, required much above a

K century

century in the forming (*s*).   Hitherto, indeed, the inconvenience, againſt which our Courts have been called upon to
guard, has been the inconvenience of *perpetuity* of entail,
the inconvenience of making property *unalienable* for a longer
time than our law endures.   But there may be *other inconveniences*, even thoſe of a ſtill higher order, thoſe of even
ſtopping *the uſe and enjoyment of property :* and when ſuch
inconveniences become the ſubjeĉt of judicial examination,
there may be, at leaſt as great a demand upon the courts
to prevent executory deviſe from being made a ſhelter for ſuch
abuſes, as there ever was a demand to prevent the ſhelter of
perpetuity of entail.   How far the preſent caſe may fall within
the compaſs of this remark, will be the ſubjeĉt of conſideration,
when I have made further advance in the argument.   Here I
only inſiſt, that the whole hiſtory of executory deviſes implies
a continuing diſcretion in judicature to prevent the abuſe of
them ; and that the very principle of executory deviſes, which
is *general utility*, preſumes the exiſtence of an aĉtive power
ſufficient to prevent *general inconvenience*.

Sixth and   I HAVE ONE OTHER inference to offer.   It is, that during
laſt infe-
rence

(*s*) In a manuſcript report I have of the caſe of Gore and Gore in 1733, when it
was for the laſt time argued in the King's Bench, Lord Hardwicke, then chief juſtice,
even went the length of making out executory deviſe to be a ſubjeĉt, over which the
courts had ſo much diſcretion, as to be entitled to *retreat* or *advance* as publick convenience or publick inconvenience ſhould require.   His words are thus given.—Indeed
" the deviſe is in favour of a perſon not born at the time of the deviſe made.   *Yet
" poſthumous children have the ſame right to a proviſion that other children have*, and deſerve
" the ſame favour from courts of juſtice.   *None but Treby ever ſaid the time of executory
" deviſe was fixed.*   Holt held otherwiſe   And ſo it appears from many reſolutions,
" *where the judges have taken a latitude to execute the will of the dead, according to the
" circumſtances of the caſe, not confining themſelves within any determinate bounds, but* AD-
" VANCING FORWARD *or* RETREATING, JUST AS THEY FOUND IT DANGEROUS OR CON-
" VENIENT."   Lord Hardwicke, according to the note I have, followed this with a
citation of various caſes to prove this doĉtrine.

the

the progress of executory devise from it's infant state to maturity, there has prevailed amongst some of our greatest judges and lawyers a vast jealousy of the liability of executory devise to an abusive application, and a vast averfion to extending it's limits.—In the case of Pell and Brown, which in the 18th of James the First so operated to fix executory devise of inheritance, judge Doderidge inveighed zealously against executory devise as a very dangerous invention, and endeavoured to stop it's progress by making it barrable by common recovery, and called forth his deepest learning and his utmost acuteness for the purpose; and his reasoning in this respect will be found fully given in the report of the case by Rolle and Palmer.—In the case of Child and Baily, which came close upon Pell and Brown, being only two years after, the same court of King's Bench, as had but recently allowed executory devise for inheritance, refused it *unâ voce* for a term of years, though the contingency of the limitation over was not more restrained in the one case than in the other, and words of inheritance were equally used in both. Upon error in the Exchequer chamber, their judgment was confirmed by lord Hobart and six other judges out of seven from the Common Pleas and Exchequer. The manner, in which Sir Jeffrey Palmer reports this affirmation, strikingly shews, how very great the apprehension was, that some vast inconveniences would be generated by the allowance of executory devise; for they did not merely condemn the devise in question on account of the extent of the contingency of the limitation over, but expressed themselves, as if there was a repentance of going the length of Lampett's case and Matthew Manning's case and other such cases, which allowed the limitation over of a term after a mere devise for life, observing, that " time had discovered the incon-" venience, which such limitations introduce in the common-

K 2   " wealth."

" wealth." The fame thing in effect is expreffed in Sir William
Jones's report, for he ftates, that he and the fix other judges of
the Exchequer chamber, who joined in affirming the judgment
of the King's Bench, faid, " that they would not queftion Lam-
" pett's cafe and Manning's cafe ; nor would they extend them
" to any other cafe, which varied fiom them, nor give any la-
" titude to thofe cafes."—Strong language alfo againft the extenfion of executory devife came from the judges in fubfequent
times. Lord Bridgman, whilft chief juftice of the Common
Pleas, is reprefented in Grigg v. Hopkins 1. Sid. 37 to have expreffed himfelf, as if he doubted, whether if Matthew Manning's
cafe was to be adjudged again, fuch a judgment would have
been given, adding, that the judges would not extend their re-
folutions more favourably to fuch devifes.—Language to the
fame effect, as I have before ftated, makes part of the certificate of the three judges, Hyde Twifden and Brown, to Lord
Chancellor Clarendon in Pearce v. Reeve 13th of Charles the
Second.—In Snow and Cutler in the King's Bench 18 Ch. 2.
lord chief juftice Kelynge and judge Windham, according to
the Report in 2 Keb. 11. faid, " they conceived, that execu-
" tory devifes had gone far enough, and it will be dangerous to
" go farther." Something of a fimilar tendency is attributed to
judge Windham in a further ftage of the fame cafe in 2 Keb.
297.—So anxious were the three chief juftices, who affifted
Lord Nottingham in the Duke of Norfolk's cafe, to prevent
the extenfion of executory devife, that they refufed to terms for
years, what they could not deny to have been fettled for inheritance. Even Lord Chancellor Nottingham did not claim more
for the former than was allowed to the latter.—Nor did the
Courts of Weftminfter Hall, after the revolution, ceafe to declare againft the extenfion of executory devife. In Scattergood
and Edge, lord chief juftice Treby and judge Powell were
                                                              loud

loud against extenfion. None I believe have avowed being favourable to it. Lord Hardwicke himfelf, and the judges of the
King's Bench who joined him in the certificate finally extending the twenty-one years beyond lives in being to the contingency of executory devife of inheritance, expreffed themfelves
on the occafion, as if they thought themfelves bound to difavow
all intention of extending executory devife. Your Lordfhip
alfo, in the very recent cafe of Long and Blackhall, thought fit
to fhew your jealoufy, leaft executory devife fhould be extended
beyond the eftablifhed limits; and therefore you would not decree the allowance of time for a pofthumous child, where the executory devife began with a child *en ventre fa mere* and comprized
the whole life of fuch child when born, and might in favour of
fuch child's iffue have ended as it began, without firft having the
opinion of a court of law, whether fuch double allowance for a
pofthumous child including his life in the firft inftance was
allowable; a point which, however, feems at this moment not
to have been fully difcuffed, and if fo not fully adjudged.

SUCH are the inferences, which I make from my own hiftory
of executory devife, imperfect as, notwithftanding the labour of
extracting it, I feel it to be. Without the fatigue of fo journey-
ing to the remote fprings of executory devife, and thence purfuing
it's courfe through fome of it's principal channels, and fo gradually reaching it's prefent extenfion, I fhould not perhaps have
been either able or warranted to make fuch inferences. But
I looked for the proper fources of argument againft the abufe
of executory devife; and I was aware, that I could not find
them, without in great meafure maftering it's hiftory: and this
muft be my apology for fo large a view, of a moft dry, though,
in refpect of the effect it produces upon the fettlement and enjoyment

joyment of property in England, a moſt intereſting ſubject to
Engliſh juriſprudence.

Facts, on
which, the
firſt gene-
ral head of
arguments
againſt the
truſts de-
pends, ex-
plained.

I NOW come to my firſt general head of imputation, againſt
the truſts, to which the late Mr. Thelluſſon's will devotes the
grand bulk of his magnificent fortune.

My accuſation againſt the will of the late Mr. Thelluſſon in
this branch of the argument is, that the beneficial truſts, which
the teſtator appoints to begin when his previous truſt of accumulation is reluctantly permitted to ceaſe, and for the ſake of
protracting which that truſt is ſo anxiouſly conſtituted by him,
are upon a contingency, with too much of remoteneſs and latitude for the rule of executory deviſe.

EXCEPT in the ſingle inſtance of a will; which came from
the hands of an eminent conveyancing lawyer; whoſe apathy in
the cloſe of life preferred engendering a project of accumulation
for forenſick exerciſe to a juſt and honourable diſtribution of his
fortune amongſt his relations and friends; but whoſe vain and
fanciful production ſhrunk into nullity under the manly and in-
ſtantaneous reprobation of Lord Chancellor Thurlow : never I
believe was there an example, of ſo ſtudied a deſign of experi-
menting upon the latitude of executory deviſe, as appears in the
will now in queſtion.

I SPEAK with the exception of the late Mr. Bradley's will;
becauſe I conſider him as aiming to be the founder of the art of.

extended

extended pofthumous accumulation, and his will as meant to be the chef-d'œuvre of precedent in that way. But with that fingle exception, thus unfuccefsful in the event, fuch a deliberate tampering with the law of truft and executory devife, in order to combine accumulated with executory devife, to make them commenfurate, and to render both fubfervient to a protracted exclufion of all ufe of property beyond adding to it's own bulk, as the will of the late Mr. Thelluffon amounts to, is not, fo far as I am able to learn, to be paralleled in the records of Englifh judicature.

Not content with making it impoffible to afcertain the firft beneficial devifees of his immenfe refiduary fortune, until the very moment of the happening of the contingency, upon which the trufts for them are to begin to operate,—not content with conftituting a truft of accumulation to exclude all enjoyment of the huge mafs of his property in the mean time;—Mr. Thelluffon, artificially to protract the accumulation, and confequently the executory devifes, which are not to commence until the accumulation ceafes, felects, not one or two lives, not one or two claffes of lives, but a great variety of exifting lives, a great variety of claffes of lives, and in a manner, which fhews, that if he had not been deterred by the fear of outraging the judicatures for executory devife, and perhaps by the prudent difcouragement of his profeffional affiftants in the drawing of his will, he would probably have rifqued going greater lengths.

Thus impelled by the phrenzy of pofthumous avarice, the teftator Mr. Thelluffon grafps no lefs than *feven claffes of lives, for the duration of his accumulating project, and confequently for poftponement of the executory devifes, which are permitted to commence when the accumulation ceafes.*

THE

THE lives selected for this extraordinary purpose are thus arranged by the testator.   That is, he appoints his trust of accumulation to continue during the lives of the following persons, namely,—1. Of his three sons Mr. Peter Isaac Thelluson, Mr. George Woodford Thelluson, and Mr. Charles Thelluson.—2. Of his grandson John Thelluson, the eldest son of Mr. Peter Isaac Thelluson.—3. Of such other sons, as Mr. Peter Isaac Thelluson had or might have, he having at the time of the will two other sons, who are still living.—4. Of such issue, as testator's same grandson John Thelluson might have.—5. Of such issue, as any other sons of testator's son Mr Peter Isaac Thelluson might have.—6. Of such sons, as testator's sons Mr. George Woodford Thelluson and Mr. Charles Thelluson might have.—and 7. Of such issue, as such sons might have ; the testator adding at the end of this seventh and last class of persons these restrictive words, " AS SHALL BE LIVING AT THE TIME " OF MY DECEASE OR BORN IN DUE TIME AFTER."

NAY, the testator is not satisfied with the lives of all this variety of persons, and the lives and life of the survivors and survivor of them.—He is not satisfied with the variety of classes; thus furnishing six existing lives ; and in respect of the testator's being in perfect health at the date of his will and likely to live many years, and of his having three sons married to ladies likely to bear many children, also promising such a successive supply of young lives, as on the supposition of his living only ten years longer might have encreased the six existing lives to twenty or to a much greater number.—He is not satisfied with thus including the lives of persons *in the womb at his death*, or as the words *born in due time after his decease* were probably meant, the lives of all such issue as should be born to his three sons or their sons during *twenty-one years after*, that being the time, which con-

stitutes

ftitutes the ultimate allowance beyond lives in being for the contingency of executory devife, and which probably the teftator thought fit to confider as the due time for gaining a frefh fupply of lives.——Eager therefore to catch at the means of ftill further protraction to his trufts of accumulation and confequently to the vefting of his executory devifes, the teftator cunningly takes the chance of a further protraction beyond the laft of the exifting and expectant lives fo anxioufly collected to gratify his avaricious ambition. Accordingly the will contains a provifion, the aim of which, from the equivocalnefs of the language, feems to poftpone the vefting, until the *actual partition* amongft the three lineal male defcendants. The will alfo contains a provifion, which, after reciting that the truftees of the will might not be able immediately to find convenient purchafes of land, directs the truftees in fuch cafes to lay out his vaft refiduary perfonal eftate and the money from the accumulations of his refiduary eftate both real and perfonal upon real fecurities or in the public ftocks; but then inftead of ordering, that the intereft and dividends fhould be applied as the rents and profits of the lands if purchafed would be applicable, flily requires an *accumulation* of the intereft and dividends, in the fame manner and for the fame purpofe as the rents and profits of the lands to be purchafed under the trufts are directed to accumulate. This latter provifion, I contend, amounts to abfolutely forbidding, to the executory devifees, all enjoyment of the income of the refiduary perfonal eftate and of the accumulations from that and the general landed fortune of the teftator, till lands fhall be actually purchafed.

HAVING thus analyfed this compound of contrivances, to try the extremes of executory devife, and fo to pervert an in-

L   dulgence

dulgence for general utility into a source of general inconvenience, I shall now specify,—wherein the beneficial trusts in question appear to me challengeable, for excess of the limits prescribed to the contingency of executory devise by the wise policy of the courts of Westminster Hall.

Six distinct excesses of executory devise imputed to the will.

IN this respect, I impute, to the beneficial trusts in question, excess of contingency in six different ways.

FIRST, I charge against the will, that the contingency, till the happening of which the beneficial trusts are prevented from beginning, *is partly on a general failure of issue,* or at least includes the lives of *unborn grandchildren of the testator indefinitely.*

SECONDLY, I insist, that the contingency of the beneficial trusts covertly attempts to add, to lives in being, the lives of all such issue of future sons of the testator's two younger sons, as shall be born *at any time within twenty-one years from his decease.*

THIRDLY, I impute to the will, that the commencement of the beneficial trusts is so managed and postponed, as to add to lives in being, *issue in the womb* at the death of the testator, *for a purpose not allowed* by the rule of executory devise, and also in an extent in several respects exceeding the boundary of that rule.

FOURTHLY, I insist, that the will nominates lives for the contingency of the beneficial trusts *in an extent and in a manner not consistent with the true spirit of the rule of executory devise.*

FIFTHLY, I charge it as an excess, that, *in point of effect,* the will continues accumulation, till the lands to be purchased with

the

the refiduary perfonal eftate *fhall be actually purchafed*, whether the lives fo anxioufly chofen for poftponing commencement of the beneficial trufts *are or are not expired*.

SIXTHLY, I contend, that the will aims to protract the vefting of the executory trufts for the three eldeft lineal male defcendants of the three fons, till the moment of *actual partition* amongft them.

THESE fix charges of trefpafs upon the limits of executory devife I fhall confider feparately.

———————————

THE firft excefs of the boundary of executory devife, which I impute to the will of the late Mr. Thelluffon, depends upon the conftruction of the reftrictive words in the conclufion of his enumeration of the lives for the accumulative truft his will creates.

Firft excefs, namely, in fome degree comprehending the lives of future iffue generally.

As I have juft explained, the will fixes upon feven claffes of lives, for protracting the trufts of accumulation and confequently the vefting of the primary beneficial trufts. Of thefe claffes the fixth is made to confift of fuch fons, as the teftator's two younger fons Mr. George Woodford Thelluffon and Mr. Charles Thelluffon might have; and then the teftator makes the feventh clafs to be " of fuch iffue as fuch fons may have" adding, " AS SHALL BE LIVING AT THE TIME OF MY DECEASE OR BORN IN DUE TIME AFTERWARDS."

Now if thefe added reftrictive words are conftrued, as applying-

L 2   ing

ing merely to the feventh clafs of perfons to which the words
are immediately fubjoined, it will leave the *four* immediately
preceding claffes, unqualified and unguarded in point of time,
that is, will let in the lives of unborn fons of teftator's eldeft
fon, the lives of the iffue of teftator's grandfon John Thelluffon,
and the lives of the iffue of the unborn fons of teftator's eldeft
fon, and alfo the lives of the future fons of teftator's two younger
fons, indefinitely and without reftriction of any kind whatever. I
fay it will leave thus unguarded the *four* claffes immediately preceding the feventh clafs; becaufe as to the firft and fecond of the
feven claffes, confifting of the teftator's three fons and of the teftator's grandfon John Thelluffon, and indeed as to fo much of the
third clafs as confifts of living younger fons of the teftator's eldeft
fon, thefe being of exifting lives, no reftriction was neceffary for
them.

HERE therefore the point, which I make againft the will, is,
that it leaves the *third, fourth, fifth, and fixth* claffes of lives, or
at leaft the *third* clafs in which are included Mr. Peter Ifaac
Thelluffon's future fons, without any limitation in point of time,
and fo makes the beneficial trufts, which are to fucceed the
truft of accumulation, dependent upon a contingency beyond
the boundary of executory devife, and on that account illegal
and void.

THAT if the words of reftriction at the end of the feventh
clafs of lives are to be confined to that clafs only, the third,
fourth, fifth, and fixth claffes of lives will become too indefinite
for executory devife, cannot I prefume be denied: becaufe then
the beneficial trufts will be an executory devife after determination of the lives of future fons of the teftator's eldeft fon Mr.
Peter Ifaac Thelluffon at whatever time born, of the lives of all
                                                                    iffue

iffue of the teftator's infant grandfon John Thelluffon, and of the lives of future fons of the teftator's two younger fons.

Nor can it I prefume be denied, that if *any one* of the third fourth fifth and fixth claffes fhall be conftrued as not reached by the reftrictive words at the end of the feventh clafs, the beneficial trufts in queftion will depend on a contingency too remote to be valid: for then the third clafs will take in the lives of fons not in being, and fo will the fixth clafs; and as to the fourth and fifth claffes, they will then include the lives of iffue generally.

The matter to be confidered, therefore, in this branch of the cafe is, whether the reftrictive words fubjoined to the feventh and laft clafs of lives fhould be applied to that clafs only, or fhould be extended fo as to cover the four preceding claffes. And it is my duty, on behalf of the family of the late Mr. Thelluffon, to contend, that *only the feventh* clafs of lives is within the reftriction, or at leaft that the THIRD clafs confifting of Mr. Peter Ifaac Thelluffon's future fons is not included.

In raifing this point againft the trufts, I am not unaware of the difficulties, which belong to maintaining, that the reftrictive words do not give fhelter to fuch of the claffes of lives preceding the feventh clafs as have occafion for it. Nor will I conceal, that I do not myfelf think it perfectly clear what was the precife extent, in which the teftator intended to apply the reftrictive words. But, according to my impreffion, there is more reafon to attribute the intention of excluding at leaft fome of the material claffes of lives from the reftriction, than there is to fuppofe the contrary. Befides, as I fee the cafe, to make it doubtful, whether the teftator did not intend fome degree of

trefpafs

trefpafs and irregularity, is at leaft to endanger the validity of the
will: for what favourable interpretation can be expected for
teftamentary difpofitions fo harfhly and unnaturally eccentric,
that the teftator himfelf deemed it neceffary to deprecate the
legiflature againft annulling them?

UNDER this explanation, I fhall contend, that the reftrictive words added to the feventh and laft claffes of lives fhould
fhould not be conftrued, as intended by the teftator to apply to
the four claffes immediately preceding the feventh clafs, and
more efpecially fhould not be conftrued to apply to the third
clafs, which includes the lives of future fons of Mr. Peter Ifaac
Thelluffon.

IN the FIRST place I infift, that the ftrict rule of conftruction is with confining the reftrictive words to the feventh and
laft clafs of lives, which the reftriction immediately follows,
namely, to the lives of the iffue of the teftator's two younger
fons Mr. George Woodford Thelluffon and Mr. Charles Thelluffon. The feven claffes of lives, affumed by the teftator for
his truft of accumulation, are fo many diftinct members of the
fame fentence. All of the claffes before the feventh are in
themfelves without words of reftriction. Then comes the
feventh clafs with reftrictive words; and thefe are of fuch a
kind, that they are not in the leaft neceffary to make fenfe of
the fix preceding claffes of lives. Applying the reftrictive
words to the lives of the feventh clafs only amounts to faying,
that during the fix firft claffes of lives the accumulation fhall
operate abfolutely and at all events, but that the accumulation
fhall not be affected by the feventh and laft clafs of lives except
conditionally, and under certain circumftances. It is, therefore,
as to the fix preceding claffes, a cafe exactly falling within the
rule,

rule, that words fhall relate to the laft antecedent, unlefs it im-
pedes or obftructs the fenfe. *Proximo antecedenti fiat relatio* is
not merely a rule of grammar. It is a rule alfo of legal conftruction. The Courts of Weftminfter Hall have affifted themfelves with the rule from very early times. In the year book
of 9th Hen. 6. fol. 2⊗. the rule is appealed to in argument, as
if the ufe was familiar: and what is remarkable enough, the
rule is there given with its proper qualification; for the words
of the book are *ad proximum antecedens fiat relatio nifi impe-
diatur fententia.* Judge Brown, according to Plowden 127.
cited the rule in a cafe of the reign of Philip and Mary. Sir
Henry Finch in the reign of James the Firft tranfcribes the rule
into the early part of his profound difcourfe on law, and il-
luftrates it by cafes extracted from the year books. Attorney
General Noy, in his Maxims of Law, which was written in
the reign of Charles the Firft, gives the rule and exemplifies
the application in like manner. The fame thing is done by
Wingate in his book of Maxims, which was publifhed juft before the reftoration. As to the inftances, in which our Courts
have acted upon the rule, the cafe of *indictment* in 9 Edw. 4.
fol. 48. a. the cafe of reftrictive words in a *grant* of tithes in
Cro. Jam. 48. the cafe of covenants in Littleton's Reports 80.
and the cafe on *return to a mandamus* in Rep. temp. Holt 449.
are all precedents of an application of the rule. If it was neceffary, many more inftances might I apprehend be collected.
But the exiftence of the rule under the qualification I have ftated
will fcarce be queftioned. The objection I prefume will be to
applying the rule to the prefent cafe.

IN the SECOND place I infift, that the language of the will
is not fuch, as even to afford the opportunity of applying the
reftrictive words at the end of the feventh and laft clafs of lives

to

to the firſt and ſecond claſſes, namely, thoſe compoſed of the
lives of the teſtator's three ſons and of the life of his eldeſt
grandſon.   The reſtrictive words are, " AS SHALL BE LIVING
" AT THE TIME OF MY DECEASE OR BORN IN DUE TIME
" AFTERWARDS." To expreſs, that the lives of exiſting perſons ſhould not be lives for the truſt of accumulation, unleſs
thoſe perſons ſhould ſurvive the teſtator, was *unneceſſary*: for
unleſs they ſurvived him, their lives could not be ſo applied.
To expreſs, that the lives of exiſting perſons ſhould not be
counted, unleſs thoſe perſons ſhould be born within due time
after the teſtator's deceaſe, would be *nonſenſe*. Therefore as
to the firſt and ſecond claſſes of lives, one part of the reſtrictive
words is nugatory; and it is not poſſible to apply the other part.
Beſides, in the deſcription of the two firſt claſſes of lives, there
is not any word leading to a connection with the reſtrictive
words added to the ſeventh claſs.   Each of the five claſſes after
the firſt and ſecond is with the word SUCH in the deſcription.
Thus the third claſs is " of SUCH other ſons AS my ſaid ſon
" Peter Iſaac Thelluſſon now has or may have." The ſucceed-
ing five claſſes are with the word SUCH in like manner.   And
though the word AS not only ſatisfies the word SUCH without
reſorting to the reſtrictive words, but even renders the application of SUCH to AS a ſecond time in the reſtrictive words at leaſt
ſomewhat more than the idiom of our language ſeems to admit; yet I confeſs, it gives the opportunity of connecting the
reſtrictive words at the end of the laſt claſs with the prior
claſſes, if the preſumption from the ſtrict rule of *proximo ante-*
cedenti fiat relatio is really overcome by the clear ſenſe of the
whole paſſage.   But the word SUCH being omitted in the firſt
and ſecond claſſes, there is almoſt a negative againſt connecting
it with the words of reſtriction at the end of the laſt claſs; the
omiſſion of SUCH amounting to a diſconnection.   However all
                                                        the

the ufe I am entitled to make of this difconnection of the firft and fecond claffes from the reftrictive words is, that it makes it more natural to underftand the teftator, as not meaning to extend the reftrictive words beyond the clafs to which they are fubjoined. If two of the fix preceding claffes were intended to be excluded from the reftriction, it leads in fome degree to the fuppofition, that the other four were intended to be excluded alfo. The rule of *proximo antecedenti fit relatio* being admitted to apply to two out of the fix prior claffes, it is in itfelf in fome degree a reafon for not exempting the other four : becaufe in one and the fame fentence to decide, that the rule of relation doth apply and doth not apply, at leaft demands fome fpecial ground to juftify the difcrimination.

In the THIRD place, I infift, that there is barely the opportunity of applying the reftrictive words at the end of the feventh clafs of lives to the third clafs : and that the *letter* of the will is confiderably againft fuch an application, and the *fpirit* of the will is ftill more fo. The words of the will in defcribing the third clafs are, " and of SUCH other fons as my faid fon " Peter Ifaac Thelluffon now has or may have." Here the word SUCH in point of ftructure of language is fatisfied by the word AS in the fame defcription : and fo the defcription is compleat in itfelf. Confequently there is no neceffity of looking further in the fentence on account of the word SUCH. At the fame time I admit, that there is a poffibility of applying AS to SUCH a fecond time, though not quite according to the idiom of our language without an intermediate conjunction. For inftance, if the teftator had in his will exprefsly appointed his truft of accumulation to endure " during the lives of SUCH fons " AS his eldeft fon had or might have and AS fhould be living " at the teftator's death," I fhould fay, that the language was

M   ftrictly

ftrictly correct. But if the words were " during the lives of
" such fons as his eldeft fon had or might have, as fhould be
" living at the teftator's death," I fay, that thus applying the
word as, a fecond time to such without the conjunction *and*
intervening, at leaft approaches to bad Englifh. However in
conftruing the will, this would not be the leaft objection to
giving effect to the fecond application of the word as. The
objection would be to the propriety of the expreffion, not to
the efficacy of it. Therefore if the reftrictive words in queftion were literally fubjoined by the teftator to the third clafs as
they certainly are to the feventh, I fhould be forced to concede,
that they muft operate as far as they can. By fo fubjoining the
reftrictive words to the third clafs of lives, it would ftand thus
defcribed in the will. It would be " of such fons as my faid
" fon Peter Ifaac Thelluffon now has or may have, and as *fhall*
" *be living at the time of my deceafe or born in due time after-*
" *wards.*" Then alfo I fhould be forced to apply the rule of
fingula reddendo fingulis, and I fhould accordingly apply the
firft part of the reftrictive words to the exifting fons of Mr.
Peter Ifaac Thelluffon at the time of the will, and both parts
to the future fons. But as the will really ftands, the cafe is
widely different. The third clafs is without the reftrictive
words fubjoined; and between the third clafs and them there
are three other claffes, and even each of thefe is fo compleat, as
to prevent in point of language all neceffity of applying the reftriction at the end of the feventh clafs to them. The procefs of
conftruction, therefore, to extend the reftrictive words at the
end of the feventh clafs to the defcription of the third clafs, becomes very complicated. The difficulties to be furmounted are
three-fold. The prefumption from the rule of grammar and
of law *proximo antecedenti fiat relatio* is firft to be overcome.
When that is accomplifhed, the difficulty of fhewing, that the
reftrictive

reftrictive words at the end of the feventh clafs fhould not be applied to fome of the fix preceding claffes in the fame fentence, and yet fhould be applied to others, that is, fhould fkip over two claffes and then attach upon three, next prefents itfelf, and muft be encountered with. Then comes the difficulty, from the double contents of the third clafs of lives, and from the double contents of the reftrictive words; for it is not poffible to apply more than one half of the entire reftrictive words to one half of the entire third clafs, in refpect that fuch of the reftrictive words at the end of the feventh clafs, as confine the lives to perfons born in due time after the teftator's deceafe, are quite incapable of application to fo much of the defcription of the perfons in the third clafs, as confifts of fons *in effe* at the date of teftator's will, and fo it becomes neceffary to divide what according to the language is entire both in the third clafs and in the reftric- tive words, and for that purpofe to cut the knot by the rule of *fingula reddendo fingulis,* and through that medium of conftruc- tion to effectuate an application of one moiety of the entire re- ftrictive words to one moiety of the entire third clafs. Such an operation in the conftruction of the will is at leaft multifarioufly refined It is not, therefore, of courfe to have the benefit of fuch an elaborate and metamorphofing interpretation. To be entitled to it, very decifive evidence, that it is demanded by the actual intention of the teftator, fhould be extracted from the other contents of the will. But the language of the other parts of the will is I apprehend by no means calculated to give affift- ance in this refpect, and as to the *fpirit* of the will, fo far as the trufts of accumulation and the beneficial trufts commence- able when the accumulation is made to determine are con- cerned, it is from beginning to end, as I have before explained, a complication of cruel experiments, facrificing the teftator's whole exifting family of wife fons daughters and grandchil-

dren, and even iffue in the third generation, to an unfeeling and
abfurd vanity, and for that purpofe tampering with the extremes
of the rule of executory devife and ftriving to abufe it's indulgence.   With the fpirit of fuch a will it is more congenial, to
impute to the teftator an intention of covertly trefpaffing on the
boundary of executory devife, and to fuppofe him betrayed
by his avaricious vanity into an excefs of that boundary, than to
fuppofe him nicely obfervant of a boundary fo obftructive of
his general defign.   At leaft, a teftator ;—who fo anxioufly tampers with the law of executory devife ;—and who for that purpofe
in a way not paralleled in the records of teftamentary law, in a
way not even attempted by the learned effayift in applying
executory devife to accumulation fo as to make the latter commenfurate with the former, the profound Mr. Bradley himfelf,
takes feven claffes of lives to work upon ;—and who appears alfo
to be reftrained from taking a much larger compafs, only by
the fear of provoking the rejection of his fcheme ;—may, I
conceive, be more eafily prefumed to intend irregularity than
to intend the contrary.   Againft fuch a teftator as the late
Mr. Thelluffon I fay, in the language of a maxim of our
law as expreffed by Lord Bacon, *verba fortius accipiantur
contra proferentem.*   In truth the fpirit of the will is to apply
the means of ftretching the law of executory devife.   Therefore the fpirit of the will, fo far from affifting to extricate it from
the ftrict rules of interpretation, tends to provoke the moft
rigid obfervance of thofe rules.   When alfo there is fuperadded
the cruelty of the will towards the family of the teftator ; with
the aggravation of his appearing affectionately devoted to them
to the laft moment of his life ; and with the further aggravation
of excluding every body dear to him for the fake of an uncertain perfon, of a generation after his death and probably very
long after, for the fake as it were of nobody, for the fake only

of

of gratifying an infanity of avaricious ambition ; all this being
confidered, if there is a doubt about his intention, furely it will
be much more becoming to refolve that doubt by difappointing
his plan of devoting his great refiduary fortune to an unnatural
and cruel excefs of vanity (which without going further into the
cafe muft be the inevitable confequence of not extending the
reftrictive words to the third clafs of lives) than by fubftantiat-
ing fuch a plan to the difinherifon of his deceived and injured
family.

In the FOURTH place, I contend, that even as to the fourth
fifth and fixth claffes of lives, there is not enough to induce a
relaxation, from the ftrict rule of referring to the laft antecedent,
and of fo confining the reftrictive words at the end of the
feventh clafs to that clafs only.   But I have dwelt fo long upon
exempting the third clafs of lives from the operation of the reftrictive words fubjoined to the feventh clafs, and the argument
for that purpofe is fo inclufive of the argument againft extending the reftrictive words to the fourth fifth and fix claffes, that
no more is neceffary for the latter, than to point out wherein
the argument for them differs.   I make two differences.   One
of them is, that the fourth fifth and fixth claffes of lives are
nearer to the feventh clafs, and confequently nearer to the reftrictive words added to it.   But this is of fmall confideration.
The other difference is of greater weight.   It is, that all the
reftrictive words are fuch, as may be properly applied to the
fourth fifth and fixth claffes, if fuch was the intention of the
teftator : for they all confift of unborn iffue, namely, of fuch
iffue as the teftator's eldeft grandfon might have, of fuch iffue
as any other fons of teftator's eldeft fon might have, and of fuch
fons as teftator's two younger fons might have, and confe-
                                                    quently,

quently, it is neither nugatory, nor infenfible, to confine thofe three claffes to perfons living at the teftator's death or born in due time after.   In refpect of thefe two differences, efpecially the latter of them, there muft be a proportional deduction from the arguments I have ufed againft extending the reftrictive words to the third clafs.   But that deduction being made, the remainder of thofe arguments is fully applicable to the fourth fifth and fixth claffes, and I refer to them accordingly.   Indeed, as I am at prefent ftruck, a more particular confideration of the fourth fifth and fixth claffes is the lefs neceffary : becaufe, as on the one hand, if the arguments againft including the third clafs in the operation of the reftrictive words are inadequate to prevent it, a part of the fame arguments cannot be expected to produce that effect for the fourth fifth and fixth claffes ; fo on the other hand, if there is enough in the arguments to exclude the third clafs from the operation of the reftrictive words, there is a clear excefs of the boundary of executory devife, and therefore enough to make illegal and annul the whole of the trufts of accumulation and of the fubfequent beneficial trufts, without looking to any other clafs whatever, or indeed to any other branch of the cafe.

Such are the arguments, which occur to me, againft applying the reftrictive words at the end of the feventh and laft clafs of lives to any of the preceding claffes.

If they are well founded to the extent of excluding from the reftriction all the claffes prior to the feventh clafs, then four out of fix claffes, namely, the third fourth fifth and fixth, all of which require reftriction to keep them within the boundary of executory devife, will become unguarded ; and the trufts in
queftion

queſtion will be void, not only for conſtituting executory deviſes on lives *not in being*, but for ſo conſtituting them *on a general failure of iſſue*.

BUT it is not eſſential to the overturning of the truſts, on the ground of the inſufficiency of the reſtrictive words at the end of the ſeventh claſs of lives, to unguard all ſuch of the ſix prior claſſes, as without protection from the reſtrictive words will let in lives too remote for executory deviſe. For that puɪpoſe it is ſufficient to unguard only the thɪrd claſs of lives, and ſo to let in the unborn future ſons of Mr. Peter Iſaac Thelluſſon indefi-nitely. Whatever alſo may be the inſufficiency of the argu-ments to unguard the fourth fifth and ſixth claſſes of lives, I am ſo ſtruck with the cogency of the ɪeaſons againſt extendɪng the protection of the reſtrictive words to the thɪɪd claſs of lives ; and now that I have thus minutely laboured this branch of the argument, I ſo ſee both the letter and the ſpɪrɪt of the will to be againſt ſuch an extenſion ; that I very much doubt the propriety of my ɪntroducing this firſt charge of treſpaſs upon the rule of executory deviſe with any thɪng like a dɪſtɪuſt of being able to pɪove the imputation.

THE argument, on my ſecond charge of exceſs of the boun-dary of executory deviſe, lies ɪn a narɪow compaſs.

IN ſubſtance the charge is, that the teſtator *coveɪ tly* attempts to extend his truſt of accumulation, to the lives of *iſſue born at any time wɪthɪn twenty one years after hɪs own deceaſe.*

Second ex-ceſs of exe-cutory de-vɪſe, nɪmely, including lɪves of peɪ-ſonɪ boɪn at a-ny time with-ɪn 2ɪ years af-teɪ teſtator's deceaſe.

THIS

THIS charge arifes from the manner, in which the teftator has expreffed the latter part of the reftrictive words added to the feventh and laft clafs of lives for his truft of accumulation, that is, to the clafs comprehending the iffue of his two younger fons.

BUT to underftand the meaning of the feventh and laft clafs of lives, it may be convenient here to ftate the words of the fixth clafs, as well as thofe of the feventh, the latter referring in fome degree to the former.

THE words of the defcription of the fixth and feventh claffes of lives, including the reftrictive words at the end of the feventh clafs, are, " and of fuch *fons*, as my faid fons George Wood-" ford Thelluffon and Charles Thelluffon may have ; and *of fuch* " *iffue as fuch fons may have, as fhall be living at my deceafe,* OR " BORN IN DUE TIME AFTERWARDS"

Now the queftion I make is on the fenfe, in which the teftator meant to ufe the concluding words BORN IN DUE TIME AFTERWARDS.

IF the teftator intended by thefe words, merely to include fuch iffue of future fons of his two younger fons, as fhould be *in the womb at his death*, then the objection of extending the *lives* to fuch iffue of future fons of his two younger fons as fhould be born at any time *within twenty-one years after his death* cannot arife.

BUT it fhould be recollected, that the boundary of executory devife, as finally extended, and as now underftood to be fettled, is lives in being and *twenty-one years after*. Hence it is natural to confider the *twenty-one years* as the *due time* after lives in being :

being: and in difcourfing on executory devife it is, I believe, quite current to refer to the twenty-one years as the due time after a life or lives in being in that fenfe.

THIS leads to the confideration, whether the teftator in the prefent cafe did not really mean to augment his collection of lives for protraction of his truft of accumulation, and confequently of the commencement of the fubfequent beneficial trufts, by including the lives of all iffue of future fons of his two younger fons born within twenty-one years after his own deceafe.—If fuch was his meaning, I conceive it to be beyond doubt, that his intention amounts to an excefs of executory devife; and fo vitiates all the trufts in queftion for though the rule, as for many years paft it has been enlarged, allows twenty-one years beyond lives in being, yet it doth not allow *the twenty-one years as a time for multiplying lives to extend executory devife upon.*

MY grounds, for imputing to the teftator, an intention of taking the twenty-one years as a fpace for accumulating new lives to protract his executory devife, are thefe.

THE teftator cannot be fuppofed to have had any reafon to refer to the birth of the iffue of future fons of any of his fons within due time after his own deceafe, except *with a view to the boundary of executory devife,* and thereby to give fome further extenfion to his truft of accumulation. The reference could not be, with a view to the due time for the birth of a pofthumous child in refpect of *legitimacy* for the reference is to the birth of the children of others; and as to the legitimacy of fuch children, whether they were born within nine or ten months after his deceafe, or at the remoteft time poffible,

N   was

was perfectly immaterial. Nor could the reference be *with a view to the* BENEFIT *of iffue born to future fons of any of his fons in due time after his deceafe*; becaufe it is the profeffed purpofe of the reference to fuch iffue, that the truft of accumulation fhould be extended to *their exclufion*. It being then the teftator's object, in making the reference, to extend the truft of accumulation, and through that the beneficial trufts neceffarily allowed to commence when that expired, it was natural, that he fhould look to the twenty-one years allowed to exe-cutory devife beyond lives in being. His anxiety was apparently to gain a new fucceffion of lives for his abforbing truft of accumulation. From the beginning to the end, his truft of accumulation is an experimental tampering with the rule of executory devife, in order to elude the real principle of its limits, without incurring the penalty of exceeding them. In fuch an enterprize, to convert the *letter* of the doctrine of executory devife into a fhelter for *abufe of its real fpirit*, the infertion of words, merely to fecure the lives of children in the womb at the teftator's death, was fcarce an object large enough for fuch a teftator. Befides if pofthumous children may be made ufe of, for the mere purpofe of extending execu-tory devife during the *life* of a child in the womb at a tefta-tor's death (which thofe looking no further than the *letter* and *furface* of executory devife may be apt to fuppofe, but which is a latitude I cannot concur in) it was unneceffary to mention the pofthumous iffue of future grandfons. If poft-humous children may be fo introduced into an executory de-vife, which I fhall prefently controvert, no fpecial words were requifite; for where the pofthumous child is admiffible under an executory devife, he comes in as a child *in effe* by the conftruction of law. But if the teftator meant to take the benefit of the twenty-one years after lives in being, which

is the due time beyond such lives, special words for that
purpose were required: and it was natural, that a testator so
eager, as the late Mr. Thellusson was, to protract his trust of
accumulation and his succeeding executory devises, should
not only grasp at taking benefit of the twenty-one years in
the most extensive way; but should be betrayed,—into an excefs in the *manner* of applying the twenty-one years;—into the
excefs of taking the twenty-one years for the generation of
new lives and for protraction of the contingency of executory
devise, instead of merely adding the twenty-one years to existing lives. It is also to be considered, that, without understanding the late Mr. Thellusson by the words *born within due
time after his death* to mean the *twenty-one years*, it is scarce to
be accounted for, that he should extend his comprehension of
issue born in due time after his death to the issue of his *future
grandchildren* · for it was at least very extravagant, more especially in a person so conversant in calculating lives as the late
Mr. Thellusson was, to suppose, that a man of above sixty
years of age should live long enough, not only to see future
grandsons married and having issue, but to see such issue of
future grandsons also married and parents of children.

TAKING therefore into consideration,—that the testator was
tampering with the law of executory devise to stretch its
limits to the utmost, in order to serve his vain and odious project
of sacrificing all his existing family to a trust of accumulation
for raising monstrous fortunes for future male descendants ·—
that he was seeking to grasp at as many lives to protract such
his proud trust of accumulation, as could be collected, without
a gross avowal of meaning to abuse the indulgence of executory devise:—that it was natural for such a testator to take
the fullest advantage of the twenty-one years allowed to executory devise beyond lives in being:—that unless he is under-

N 2   stood

ftood to point at twenty-one years after his death, he has taken no
advantage of the twenty-one years beyond lives in being :—that
it is ufual to look to fuch *twenty-one years* as the due time for extending executory devife beyond exifting lives :—that unlefs he
is underftood by the words *born in due time after his deceafe* to point
at *twenty-one years*, he not only has omitted to take any advantage of that latter link in the chain of executory devife ; but,
though above fixty years of age, muft be underftood to fuppofe he fhould live to fee the iffue of future grandfons married
and having iffue in the womb :—taking, I fay, all this into
confideration, I fubmit, that the teftator fhould be conftrued,
to comprehend, within his multifarious claffes of lives, *the
lives of iffue born within twenty-one years after his deceafe* ; and
that in confequence of fuch an extenfion of his truft of
accumulation, all the fubfequent and dependent executory
devifes become an excefs of the limits of executory devife,
and on that account the whole is againft law.

I ALLOW, that the excefs thus imputed is merely conftructive.
I allow alfo, that in the cafe of wills in general it might be
too much, thus argumentatively to impute an illegal intention
to a teftator, to impute it upon grounds which however probable are not quite decifive : and that on the contrary it is
in general the office of judicature, to labour at faving an
executory-devife by the moft favourable conftruction.   But
the prefent cafe arifes on a devife, which,—from its unnatural
harfhnefs to the whole exifting family of the teftator,—and
from the monftroufnefs of the teftator's project of facrificing
every body for the fake of nobody, and of conftituting a precedent of accumulating at leaft of the moft injurious tendency to the interefts of the commonwealth,—ought to be
conftrued by judicature in a manner the moft unfavourable to
the views of the teftator ; ought to be confidered with every

                                                                pre-

presumption against those views; and ought to be as singularly and harshly construed, as it is singularly and harshly fabricated.

———————————————

My THIRD charge, against the trusts, for excess of the boundary of executory devise, is on the supposition, that the late Mr. Thellusson, in comprehending for his trust of accumulation the lives of *issue born to the persons described by him in due time after his decease*, did not mean, as I have contended, *twenty-one years afterwards*, but merely meant *issue in the womb at his death*. In this latter sense of the words, by which the testator includes the lives of issue born to *other persons in due time after his own decease*, my objection to his including such lives is, both to the *nature of his purpose* and to the *extent* of it.

Third excess of executory devise, namely, one, by so managing, as to have the nine or ten months, for posthumous children twice over, and in the first instance the lives of such children besides

With respect to the *nature of the purpose*, for which the late Mr. Thellusson includes issue in the womb at his death, I have already had occasion to state, that the extension of the contingency for executory devise, from a life in being to the further time allowable for birth of a posthumous child, was disputed some years after the revolution; and not only that such an extension was denied by Lord Chief Justice Treby, in Luddington (*t*) and Kime 10. W. 3 and about two

O1

————

(*t*) The case of Luddington v Kime as stated in 1 Lord Raym 203 was on devise of land to Evers Armyn for life without impeachment of waste, and in case that he should have any issue male, then to such issue male and his heirs for ever, and if he should die without issue male, then to Sir Thomas Barnardiston remainder to the devisor and his heirs. The words of Lord Raymond, where he states the opposite opinions of Judge Powell and Lord Chief Justice Treby on the point of executory devise made in that case, are as follow

' Objection It was objected at the bar, that it was the devisor's intent, that " every issue male of Evers Armyn should take. *But if the court construe it a fee-*

or three years after in Scattergood v Edge ; but that the extenſion, coupled with the time for the unborn child's attaining
21, was not quite ſettled 'till the year 1733 by the certificate

" chaſe in the iſſue male, then a poſthumous ſon of Evers Armyn cannot take   for if he could
" take, it muſt be either by way of contingent remainder, or of executory deviſe.
" Not the firſt, becauſe the remainder will not veſt before the particular eſtate de-
" termines, viz before the death of Evers Armyn   And *executory deviſe it cannot be*
" *to ſuch a poſthumous ſon, becauſe it will not happen within the uſual time allowed for ex-*
" *ecutory deviſes to take effect, which is but the ſpace of the life of one man then* IN ESSE ;
" but this would be too long a time being after the death of Evers Armyn .
"   Anſwer   But to this objection *Powell* juſtice ſaid, that there were two ſorts of
" executory deviſes   The one, where the entire eſtate paſſes out of the deviſor, as
" 2. Cro 590 Pell and Brown's caſe 2 Ro Rep 217 (which *Treby* chief juſtice
" ſaid was properly the executory deviſe)   The ſecond ſort is a ſort of future de-
" viſe, in which in the mean while the lands deſcend to the heir of the deviſor, as
" Hainſworth and Prety's caſe 3 Cro. 319 and the time allowed for ſuch to take
" effect was *no more than one life then* IN ESSE.   But Powell ſaid, *if this had been a de-*
" *viſe to Evers Armyn for life, and if after his death he ſhould have a poſthumous ſon born*
" *by his wife then to ſuch ſon and his heirs,* and if not, then *to Sir Thomas Barnadſton*
" *in fee,* he was of opinion, that if *Evers Armyn in ſuch caſe ſhould have a poſthumous ſon,*
" *he would have taken by way of executory deviſe for though this would not happen within*
" *the life of Evers Armyn, yet,* HAPPENING SO SHORT A TIME AFTER THE DEATH
" *of Evers Armyn,* AS IT MUST BE to be the ſon of Evers Armyn, he was of *opinion,*
" *that this would have been a good executory deviſe*   But Treby chief juſtice *doubted*
" *much of that, and was of opinion, that* THE TIME ALLOWED FOR EXECUTORY DE-
" VISES TO TAKE EFFECT OUGHT NOT TO BE LONGER THAN THE LIFE OF ONE
" PERSON THEN IN ESSE. and ſo it was held in Snow and Cutler's caſe.   But in this
" caſe the whole court was of opinion, that this was a contingent remainder to the
" iſſue of Evers Armyn in fee, and therefore a poſthumous ſon could never take for
" want of a particular eſtate to ſupport the remainder* UNTIL HE CAME *in eſſe*
" And if the limitation had been to the firſt ſon, it had been the ſame thing, FOR
" A POSTHUMOUS CHILD THERE COULD NOT HAVE TAKEN; and though the in-
" tent of the teſtator might be otherwiſe, yet his intent could not controul a rule of
" law ſo ſtrongly eſtabliſhed, that a contingent remainder ought to veſt during the
" particular eſtate, or eo inſtante it determines.   And for theſe reaſons all the court
" held, that Evers Armyn took an eſtate for life, by this deviſe, remainder contin-
" gent to his iſſue male in fee."

     * This was about two years before the ſtatute of 10 and 11. W. 3 providing for ſuch a caſe.

FH
MVSEVM
BRITANNICVM

of

of the King's Bench in Stephens v Stephens. However I
agree, that since the year 1733 the point has been so far at
rest, as to leave no room for now arguing against adding,
either the twenty one years beyond lives in being, or the proper and legal time for the birth of a child *en ventre sa mere*.
But then I contend, that this addition of the time for birth
of a posthumous child is only allowable, to give effect to a
devise in favour of such child, or at least to give effect to a
devise to some other person in the event of his being born or
of his not being born. In general this extension of the indulgence of executory devise to a child in the womb and to a
child unborn generally has been for the sake of the child
himself. So it was for a child unborn in that very case of
Stephens and Stephens. So it was for a child *in the womb* in
Snow and Cutler soon after the restoration, as appears by Levinz and the other reports of that case. So it was for a child
unborn in Gore and Gore before the King's Bench in 1722 and
1733. If there be any cases, in which the extension of executory devise, either to a *child in the womb*, or to an unborn
child of a living person generally, has been allowed for the
benefit of third persons, it is for the gentlemen on the other
side to collect and cite such authorities. I will only say, that
I protest against considering the case of Gulliver and Wicket
in 1. Wils. 105. as being an adjudication to that effect, for in
that case no posthumous child was born. But I will suppose,
that the extension may be applied to effectuate a provision for
some other person; as where the executory devise is to A, but
in case of his A's dying without a child living at his death or
born to him in due time after, then to B. At least I will not
now assert the contrary. For the present, therefore, I will
suppose, that exceeding lives in being and twenty one years
after, by addition of the time for birth of a posthumous child,

is allowable, that is, that the extension of the birth of a
posthumous child may be applied to effectuate a provision
either for such child or for some other person   But the purpose, for which the late Mr. Thellusson comprehends issue in
the womb at his death, is quite of another kind.   It is not
to make provision for the posthumous child.   Nor is it to
make provision for any other person in the event of there being such a child or in the contrary event.   But the intent of
the testator is, *to exclude the posthumous child from enjoyment of
the devised property, and also to prolong the exclusion of every other
person from such enjoyment* ; and his purpose merely is to prolong the term of accumulation, and so as to eke it out beyond lives in being.   In other words, it is merely to enlarge
the trust negativing all beneficial enjoyment of the property,
and so to postpone both the executory devises themselves and
the ascertainment of the persons intended to take under them.
But I beg leave to say, that this is *an abuse of the extension of
the contingency for executory devise as to the time for birth of a
posthumous child*; and I beg leave to say, that *extension of executory devise to the time for birth of a posthumous child was not
conceded for such a purpose, was not conceded to make a posthumous child an instrument of posthumous accumulation*, and consequently is not applicable to such a purpose.   Therefore
though the late Mr. Thellusson had merely introduced a posthumous child, under the qualification of only adding, to the
term of his trusts of accumulation, nine or ten months beyond
lives in being, I should insist, that for such a purpose the extension is not allowable to him.   In this instance of the time
for birth of a posthumous child, as indeed in the whole system
of executory devise, the indulgence was granted in the way
of general accommodation for purposes of general convenience : and to apply such an indulgence for the mere gratification

tification of a pofthumous felfifh vanity and the confequential exclufion of all beneficial enjoyment of the devifed property, is to convert an enlargement of the time for keeping property unalienable into an enlargement for making it unufable.

But I do not merely object to the *nature* of the purpofe for which the late Mr. Thelluffon introduces pofthumous children. I object alfo to the *extent* of that purpofe; to the extent in which he makes ufe of pofthumous children.

The extenfion, allowed by the Courts to the cafe of a pofthumous child, proceeds on the fuppofition of only adding *nine or ten months* after a life in being as a laft or further link to the chain of executory devife, that is, the time allowed by law for a woman's going with child after her hufband's deceafe. To that effect is the language of Lord Kenyon in the cafe of Long v. Blackall and others, which I have before cited from 7. Durnf and Eaft 100. for his words are, " it is an eftablifhed " rule, that an executory devife is good, if it muft neceffarily " happen within a life or lives in being and 21 years, and *the* " *fraction of another year allowing for the time of geftation.*" But the late Mr. Thelluffon is not content with the *fraction of a year* for the birth of a pofthumous child. *He firft takes that fraction; and then he fuperadds the life of the pofthumous child,* as a new life for prolongation of his truft of accumulation and confequently of his executory devifes. In other words, firft he takes lives in being; next he takes the nine or ten months after his own death for the birth of a pofthumous child; *and then he takes the life of the child fo born after his own deceafe.* Even this is not the full extent of the cunning of the teftator. This fuppofes the gain of the life of one pofthumous child only, that is, one pofthumous life, or in cafe of twins two

O

pofthumous

posthumous lives. But, unless the restrictive words of the
will, confining the lives of unborn issue to persons living at
the testator's decease or born in due time afterwards, are to
be considered, as guarding all such of his seven classes of lives
of accumulation as require to be within protection of the restrictive words, namely, all the classes after the first and second, the trust of accumulation and all the subsequent beneficial trusts must fall to the ground for excess of the due
boundary of executory devise, independent of the particular
objection of including posthumous children. Here consequently, I have a right to argue upon the will, as intended to
comprehend the posthumous children of all of the various
persons described in the third and four following classes of
lives. But such a comprehension tends wonderfully to mul-
tiply the lives through the medium of posthumous issue. In
that construction of the will, the testator must be understood
to aim at *gaining posthumous lives, for prolongation of his trust
of accumulation, and consequently for postponement of the dependent executory devises, not from one person only; not merely from
two or three persons; but from three existing sons and three existing
grandsons, and also from all such issue of any of the same sons
and grandsons as should have issue in the womb at his decease,*
without any other limitation, than what necessarily arises
from the making nine or ten months after his death the ulti-
matum of the time for lives of posthumous issue. In this
way, then, the indulgence of nine or ten months, for the
gestation of posthumous issue of one person, would not only
become extended into the further allowance of such one person's posthumous issue; but such extended allowance would
become multiplied into an allowance of the lives of posthumous issue from six existing persons, and also from an indefinite number of persons not existing but possible to have been

born

born and to have had iffue in the womb at the death of the testator. To such a monstrous latitude would it lead, if the late Mr. Thelluffon was intitled, fo to protract his truft of accumulation, by fuperadding the lives of pofthumous perfons!

Thus ftating the extraordinary purpofe, for which the late Mr. Thelluffon's will calls pofthumous perfons in aid of his truft of accumulation; and that fuch purpofe is, not to admit either them or any others, into the beneficial enjoyment of his property, but to make the pofthumous perfons mere inftruments for lengthening the period of exclufion of all mankind from fuch enjoyment: and thus ftating alfo, that the extent of that purpofe goes the length, of not merely including the nine or ten months for geftation of a pofthumous child, but of adding the whole life of fuch child, nay, of adding the lives of pofthumous children from fix different perfons and from iffue of thofe fame perfons: I really cannot conceive, how it is pofsible, that either the unmeritorious purpofe of the teftator in reforting to the birth of pofthumous iffue can be brought within the reafon of the extenfion of executory devife 'till the birth of a pofthumous child; or that even for a meritorious purpofe, fo adding to lives in being the lives of the pofthumous iffue of one perfon, and much lefs the lives of the pofthumous iffue of many perfons, can be fhewn to be within the meaning of that allowance.

But not even all this is quite the extent of the ufe the late Mr. Thelluffon makes of pofthumous iffue · for his will is fo conftructed in his executory devife, as notwithftanding it's extravagant purpofe to have the allowance of the time for birth of pofthumous children *twice over*. This will appear from attending to the artful manner of the will in this

refpect.

respect. His truft of accumulation is fo formed upon the
bafis of his feven claffes of lives, as to begin with the benefit of
the nine or ten months for geftation of pofthumous children;
for, in order to add to lives in being at his death the lives
of a new generation, he comprehends fuch iffue of the
various perfons he means to defcribe, as fhould be born within
due time after his death. Confequently, he begins with
taking benefit of the nine or ten months for the birth
of a pofthumous child. Nor is this all. He begins his fo,
taking the nine or ten months; with a reference to the pofthumous iffue, not of one perfon or of two perfons, but, as I
have already explained, of fix exifting perfons, and of an indefinite number of additional perfons pofsible both to be born
and to have iffue between the date of his will and the day of
his death; and alfo with a view to gain a new fucceffion of
lives, for protracting his truft of accumulation and inclufively
his executory devifes. The teftator doth not indeed exprefsly claim the benefit of the nine or ten months for the
birth of pofthumous iffue, after the determination of the laft
of the numerous lives, which he felects to poftpone actual
enjoyment of the devifed property. But the fubftance of the
cafe is the fame, as if he had exprefsly made fuch a claim. It
required no language from the teftator to let in the pofthumous iffue, being male defcendants of his three fons at expiration of the truft of accumulation. The rule in favour
of pofthumous children operates of courfe, that is, lets in the
child *en ventre fa mere*, more efpecially, if there is no other
child to take. Accordingly Lord Chancellor Thurlow in
Clarke v. Ball 2. Bro. Cha. Caf. 320, fo confidered the doctrine; though in that cafe there were other children, and the
queftion was only, whether the pofthumous child fhould take
with the others; and though alfo the bequeft was to children
                                                      living

living at the death of the testator. Indeed the opinion of Lord Kenyon in Cooper v. Forbes in 2. Bro. Cha. Caf. 63, feems to the contrary, where fpecial words confining the legacy to perfons living at the death of the perfon named are ufed. But, even with fuch fpecial language, it appears to be now fettled by the cafe of Doe on the demife of Clarke v. Clarke and others 2. Hen. Blackft. 399. that the children en ventre fa mere when born fhall be permitted to fhare with children living when the devife takes effect. The prefent cafe then is tantamount to taking advantage of the time for birth of a pofthumous child, both *at the beginning* of the time for the contingency of the executory devife, and *at the end* of it. On the one hand, to increafe the late Mr. Thelluffon's ftock of lives for feeding his truft of accumulation, his will expresfly affumes the time for birth of pofthumous children in the outfet. On the other hand, his will conftructively gains the fame time at the expiration of the laft of the lives, that is, the law allows to the will to let in children in the womb, if there fhould be no perfons ready to take as male defcendants of the three fons.

In this branch of the argument, then, it becomes a queftion in the prefent cafe, whether the teftator, by grafping at the nine or ten months for a pofthumous child at the beginning of his truft of accumulation, in order *to gain a new flock of lives* and *to double the nine or ten months*, which it is of courfe to allow at the end of the fame trufts, has not trefpaffed upon the rule of executory devife.

Now as to this point of adding the allowance for birth of pofthumous children, to lives in being twice over, even upon the fuppofition of it's being the naked cafe of an executory-devife, beginning with a pofthumous child, and ending with

one,

one, I fhould contend, that thus taking the time for birth of
a pofthumous child twice over was a clear excefs of the
fettled boundary of executory devife.   Ever fince the cafe of
Stephens and Stephens adjudged, as I have before ftated by
the King's Bench in 1733, the boundary of executory devife has been univerfally defcribed as a life or lives in being
and 21 years after, with the further allowance of due
time for birth of a pofthumous child, that is, nine or ten
months.   So, as I have already mentioned, Lord Kenyon
defcribed the boundary of executory devife in the late cafe
of Long and Blackall.   This is indeed fo univerfally underftood, as to be part of the decantatum of the rule.   But if the
time for a pofthumous child is to be allowed, firft at the
beginning of the contingency for executory devife, and then
a fecond time at the end of it, the *nine or ten months*
will be increafed to *nineteen or twenty months*.   In other words
a new link to the chain of executory devife will be gained.   It
is to be confidered alfo, that even the fmalleft extenfion
of the boundary may be of dangerous confequence : for if the
9 or 10 months may be made nineteen or twenty, it will
be a precedent for a ftill further exceeding, and there will be
no faying what is the boundary.   Nor fhould it be forgotten,
that indeed the courts are in a manner pledged not to admit
any further enlargement of the rule.   Accordingly I obferve,
that Lord Mansfield in the cafe of Goodman v. Goodright,
which was before the King's Bench in Mich. Term in the
33d year of the prefent King, but is not in print, pointedly
declared, that he fo confidered the matter.   I fay this, upon
the authority of a note, taken of the argument in that cafe,
by a diftinguifhed lawyer of the prefent age, though greatly
to the lofs of his country, one long retired from all practice.
It is almoft unneceffary to fay, that I mean Mr. Francis
                                                    Filmer.

Filmer. According to his note of Goodman v. Blackman.
which was a cafe involving a point of executory devife, Sir
Fletcher Norton, in arguing againft the validity of the limitations of the will in that point of view, obferved, that it was
going further than the cafe of Stephens and Stephens ; and
that in that cafe executory devife was extended *to the
utmoft*, and that it was with reluctance the King's Bench
certified in that cafe conformably to the cafe of Taylor and
Biddal. In *this* part of the argument Lord Mansfield inter-
pofed with thefe ftriking words: " That point is well fettled ;
" and a life and twenty-one years after is the *utmoft extent* for
" an executory devife; and is no more than the common law
" allows in legal limitations, which reftrains the heir from
" aliening till twenty-one." This paffage, from that enlightened and moft eloquent Judge, Lord Mansfield, is, I conceive, applicable againft extending the 9 or 10 months to 19
or 20 months. It fhews, that fuch an extenfion, though
only of a few months, is not to be tolerated ; becaufe it is
beyond that, which is the utmoft extent for executory devife.
At the fame time it fignificantly refers to the principle, on
which that utmoft extent is made the extreme of the boundary, namely, that to go further would be allowing to the
irregular and indulged mode of entail by executory devife,
what cannot be accomplifhed in a regular courfe of fettlement
by remainders.

Under thefe views of the manner, in which the will of the
late Mr. Thelluffon applies iffue in the womb to protract his
plan of executory devife and the concomitant accumulation,
I fubmit to your Lordfhip, that in this inftance alone there is
a complication of fin by him againft the rule of executory
devife.—I fubmit, that he abufes the indulgence of the rule
by

by applying that time, which our courts granted beyond a
life in being for the benefit of a posthumous child, to the exclusion and disinherison of him.—I submit, that he aggravates
this abuse of the indulgence of the rule, by so offending
against it, not for the sake of any predilection for, or to let
in others, but for the unfeeling purpose of extending his plan
of accumulation, in exclusion of all the world from the least
use of the devised property.—I submit, that he complicates
this aggravated abuse, by involving in its destructive purpose,
not merely the child in the womb to one person or two persons of his own blood, but children in the womb to many
persons being his own issue, to sons, to grandsons, nay, even
to issue of grandsons.—I submit also, that he adds, to the
abuse thus complicated and aggravated, a gross violation of
the rule, by converting an allowance of 9 or 10 months for
the birth of a posthumous child, into an allowance for the
whole life of such child.—I submit too, that he complicates this
excess also by grasping, not merely at the life of a child or
children in the womb of the wife of one person, but at the
lives of children in the wombs of the wives of many persons,
of the wives of his sons and grandsons, and even of their
issue.—Further I submit, that to complete this aggregate of
excess of the rule, he takes the chance of having, at the end
of the lives of his stock of unborn persons, that allowance for
the birth of posthumous children, which, as the rule is settled, belongs of course, in the close of executory devise, in
favor of issue of the persons on whose death the particular
executory devise is made to begin.

Case of Long
v Blackall
considered,
and question-
ed

BUT here I must expect to be reminded of the late case of
Long v. Blackall, which, as I have before mentioned, was
sent by your Lordship for the opinion of the King's Bench,
                                   2   and

and is reported both in 7. Durnford and Eaſt, and in Mr. Veſey's third volume. I muſt at the ſame time expect to be told, that the certificate of the King's Bench, in that caſe, ſanctions Mr. Thelluſſon's will in treating children in the womb at the teſtator's death as lives in being within the rule of executory deviſe, and alſo in taking the allowance for poſthumous children twice over.

THIS caſe of Long and Blackall, I do confeſs, very much claſhes with my manner of arguing againſt Mr. Thelluſſon's preſſing the lives of iſſue in the womb, at his death, into the ſervice of his executory deviſe. It is, I acknowledge, a very ſerious drawback upon me; one, which, in reſpect of the high authority of the adjudication, and in reſpect of the ſincere reverence I have for the Judges of the King's Bench, and in reſpect alſo of the little weight one of my vaſt inferiority can expect to have in queſtioning what has been done by perſons of ſo high a deſcription, puts me into a ſituation very diſtreſſing; more eſpecially as I am now ſpeaking before, and your Lordſhip is now aſſiſted by, one of the very learned Judges, who joined in deciding for the executory deviſe in Long and Blackall.

BUT though I ſeverely feel the immenſe diſadvantage, with which I have thus to contend in this very material part of the argument; and though I lament this, not only on my own account, but for the ſake of the great intereſts, publick as well as private, which, as I conceive, are at ſtake in theſe cauſes on the will of Mr. Thelluſſon: yet I am at the ſame time moſt ſtrongly impreſſed, both that *the deciſion in Long and Blackall is open to a variety of the moſt ſerious objections*; and that *even on the ſuppoſition of its being above all exception, it*

will

will not nearly reach the extensive complication of tampering with issue in the womb, as practised to protract the executory devise now in question. In other words, my duty as an advocate upon the present occasion extorts from me the most explicit avowal, as far as the homage, due from one destined to continue a mere nobody in our profession towards those who are elevated into almost the pinnacle of judicature, will permit me to declare myself, that, according to my humble apprehension of the subject, after repeated study of it, *the adjudication in Long and Blackall ought not to rule the present case, either in point of* AUTHORITY *or in point of* APPLICABILITY.

THE case of Long and Blackall arose on the will of a Mr. Blackall. The devise in effect was of a lease for years to trustees, in trust for testator's son, Thomas Blackall, for his life; and after his decease, in trust for such issue male of him, or descendants of his issue male, as at the time of his death should be his heir; and if at the time of Thomas's death there should be no such issue male, or descendants of issue male, then living, then in trust for testator's son, George Sawbridge Blackall, for his life; and after his decease in trust for such issue male of him, or descendants of his issue male, as at his death should be his heir: and if at the time of his death there should be no such issue male, or descendants of issue male, then living, then in trust for the child with which testator's wife was then *enseint,* if the child should be a son, during his life; and after his decease, in trust for such issue male, or descendants of his issue male, as at the time of his death should be his heir; and if at the time of the death of such child, there should be no such issue male, or descendant of such issue male, then living, or if such child in the womb should not be a son, then in trust for such persons as should then be testator's legal repre-
                                                                    sentatives.

fentatives. The child in the womb at the time of the will was born after the teftator's deceafe, and was a fon. The two fons, living when the will was made and when Mr. Blackall the teftator died, and alfo the third and pofthumous fon, died without leaving iffue. Then two queftions arofe. One was, whether the limitation over to fuch perfons as were the teftator's legal reprefentatives was good. The other was, who were entitled under that limitation. On thefe queftions your Lordfhip faw fo much of objection to the remotenefs of the ultimate limitation, in refpect of the intervening life of the pofthumous fon, that you thought fit to fend it as a queftion for the opinion of the Court of King's Bench. The refult was a certificate of the King's Bench, that, in the events that had happened, the ultimate limitation or truft was a good executory devife. In confequence alfo of this certificate, your Lordfhip found it neceffary to decide upon the fecondary and confequential queftion, namely, who were meant to take under the defcription of perfons being the teftator's legal reprefentatives when all the preceding trufts determined: and after much argument, your Lordfhip held the next of kin, according to the ftatute of diftribution, to be the perfons intended.

Such having been the cafe upon which the Court of King's Bench certified in Long v. Blackall, I do agree, that it is natural to confider their certificate as a decifion, that the time for a pofthumous child is allowable on executory devife, both in the beginning of the contingency and at the clofe of it, and for adding the life of a perfon in the womb at the death of a teftator to a life in being: for otherwife the ultimate truft of the leafe for years, devifed by the will in that cafe, moft undoubtedly could not have been fupported as a good

execu-

executory devife.   But fince publication of the printed Report
of the argument on the cafe in the King's Bench, I have
very much doubted, whether the point did receive a full and
complete decifion.   If the point was determined, the effect
is to increafe the allowance of *nine or ten months* beyond a life
to *nineteen* or *twenty* months, that is, to nine or ten months
before the beginning of the life, and nine or ten months after
its expiration: and to try that very point was, as I underftand, the real object of fending the cafe to the King's Bench
for their opinion.   But from the printed report of the argument in the King's Bench, it feems as if fome how or other
the effect of beginning executory devife with the life of a
perfon in the womb (which is not only doubling the allowance
of the nine or ten months for birth of a pofthumous child, by
exprefsly taking that time at the beginning of the contingency of the life named, which conftructively is allowed at
the clofe of the fame life; *but is liable to the objection of adding*
the life of a perfon in the womb, at the death of the teftator, to
the life of an exifting perfon) had efcaped attention.   At leaft
fuch an effect is not adverted to by the counfel.   So far alfo
was Lord Kenyon, in giving his opinion, from exprefsing himfelf as if he was giving the allowance of nine or ten months
for a pofthumous child twice over, that is, as extending the
nine or ten months to *nineteen* or *twenty months,* and inclufively adding the lives of pofthumous perfons to the lives of
perfons exifting, that he concludes with ftating it to be the
eftablifhed rule, to limit executory devife to a " life or lives
" *in being,* and 21 years, and *a fraction of another year* allow-
" ing for the time of geftation."

WITH refpect to the effect of the cafe of Long v. Blackall,
if it is to be confidered as an adjudication reaching the whole
length

length of the point upon which your Lordſhip meant to be adviſed by a Court of Law; if it is to be looked upon as any thing more than a deciſion affirming the allowance of the legal time for the birth of a poſthumous child beyond a life or lives to executory deviſe, I beg leave to controvert the grounds of the deciſion. I do this with leſs ſcrupuloſity; becauſe your Lordſhip was ſo ſtruck with doubts on the caſe, as to require the aſſiſtance of the Judges of the King's Bench. I am the leſs ſcrupulous alſo, becauſe, notwithſtanding the caſe's coming for argument under ſuch high ſanction, it ſome how or other happened, that the Court, after hearing the argument of the very learned Counſel for the executory deviſe, ſo declared in favor of it, before hearing what could be ſaid on the other ſide, as to induce the Counſel againſt the executory deviſe, notwithſtanding his acknowledged talents and extenſive knowledge, to decline the argument, under an impreſſion, which was very natural in a modeſt advocate, that he ſhould not be able to change the opinion thus early avowed by the Court.

My objections to the authority of this caſe of Long v. Blackall, conſidered as deciding the points meant to be referred, are various.

FIRST, I humbly contend, that the deciſion adds *nine* or *ten months to the boundary of executory deviſe*, as it is commonly ſtated. It is quite a decantatum, not only of our writers on the law of executory deviſe, but of our Courts, ever ſince extending executory deviſe to 21 years beyond lives in being, that it muſt be within lives in being and 21 years, including the *fraction of a year*, as the legal time for birth of a poſthumous child. But the executory deviſe, upon which your

Lord-

Lordſhip thus ſought the opinion of the King's Bench, began with expreſsly taking this fraction of a year; and the rule allowing a like fraction and for the like purpoſe at the end of the life named, to let in the tenant for life's iſſue, the executory deviſe could not, I conceive, be good, without holding that the fraction of the year was allowable *twice over*, that is, without enlarging the *nine* or *ten* months into above a *year and an half.* Allow me, my Lord, to ſay, that thus converting two into one, operates upon my mind, not by conviction, but magically. Allow me to ſay that I feel it, not as plainly conſtruing the rule of executory deviſes, but as indulging a fiction upon it; a fiction which, though allowable in certain ſpecial caſes, *to prevent the excluſion of poſthumous children contrary to the intent of a teſtator*, or *to effectuate ſome other good purpoſes*, ſhould not, I humbly conceive, be allowed merely to protract executory deviſe beyond the plain boundary fixed by the Judges themſelves (*u*). Beſides, my Lord, I aſk for the autho-

(*u*) The fiction of conſidering children *in the womb*, as children *in being*, for ſome ſpecial purpoſes, and more particularly *for their benefit*, may be traced into the Roman law as promulged by Juſtinian. It is expreſſed in the following paſſages extracted from his *Corpus Juris Civilis.*

DIGEST. LIB I. TIT. V. DE STATU HOMINIS L 5 MARCIANUS *lib.* 1 *Inſtitutionum.*

S. 2. *Ingenui ſunt, qui ex matre libera nati ſunt ſufficit en m liberam eo tempore quo naſcitur, licet ancilla concepit; et è contrario,* SI LIBERA CONCEPERIT, DEINDE ANCILLA PARIAT, PLACUIT, EUM, QUI NASCITUR, LIBERUM NASCI *Nec intereſt juſtis nuptiis concepit, an vulgo, quia non debet calamitas matris nocere ei, qui* IN VENTRE EST—S. 3 *Ex hoc quæſitum, ſi ancilla* PRÆGNANS MANUMISSA SIT, *deinde ancilla poſtea facta, aut expulſa civitate, pepererit,* LIBERUM AN SERVUM PARIAT? *Et tamen rectius probatum eſt,* LIBERUM NASCI, ET SUFFICERE, QUI IN VENTRE EST, LIBERAM MATREM VEL MEDIO TEMPORE HABUISSE

IBID L 7 PAULUS *lib ſingulari de portionibus, quæ liberis damnatorum conceduntur*

QUI IN UTERO EST, PERINDE AC SI IN REBUS HUMANIS ESSET, CUSTODITUR, QUOTIES DE COMMODIS IPSIUS PARTUS QUÆRITUR QUANQUAM ALII, ANTEQUAM NASCATUR, NEQUAQUAM PROSIT

IBID

authorities upon which nine or ten months are thus extended into eighteen or twenty.   I could not easily be reconciled to such a procefs by any number of authorities.   But I am yet
to

IBID. *L* 26 JULIANUS, *l.b* 69 *Digeftorum*

QUI IN UTERO SUNT, IN TOTO PENE JURE CIVILI INTELLIGUNTUR IN RERUM NATURA ESSE   *Nam et legitimæ heredıtates his reftıtuuntur.   Et fi prægnans mulier ab hoftibus capta fit, id, quod natum erit, poftlımınıum habet.   Item patris vel maris condıtıonem fıquitur   Præterea, fi ancilla prægnans fur repta fuerit, quamvıs apud bona fıdei emptorem pepererıt, id quod natum erit, tanquam furtıvum, ufu non capıtur   His confequens eft, ut libertas quoque, quamdıu patronı filius nafcı poffit, eo jure fit, quo funt, qui patronos habent*

VOET's comment upon this part of the Digeft is as follows:

" *Ad hæc ınter homines jam natos et nafcıturos feu* IN UTERO *etiamnum* CONSTITUTOS, *leges diftinguunt   In* UTERO CONSTITUTOS *quod attinet, licet proprie necdum hominıs appellatione venire poffint ob ıncertum natıvıtatıs, fed magıs tales velut* SPEM ANIMANTIS *lex regia confideraverit   L negat. 2 ff de mortuo ınferendo.*   FICTIONE *tamen juris pro* JAM NATIS *habentur*, QUOTIES DE IPSORUM COMMODO AGITUR *L 1 quı ın utero eft 7 & l quı ın utero funt 26 ff h. t   Quâ ratıone poft conceptionem fupervenıens parentıbus calamıtas nocere non folet eı, quı* IN VENTRE *eft: five eum prægnans mater a fervilem deducatur ftatum, vel ultimo damnetur fupplıcıo aut deportetur, partus liber erit et ıngenuus   pr. Inftıt. de ıngenuıs l Imperator 18 ff h t. five ab hoftıbus capta ıllı lem. parıat, partus poftlımınıı jure guadebit, cum alıoquın ad eos, quı penes hoftes et conceptı et natı funt, jus poftlımınıı fe non extendat, parentıbus apud hoftes extınctıs   L. quı ın utero funt 26 ff h t junct l 1 C de poftlımınıo.   Et licet conceptı natıque ex patre, quı fenotu motus eft, fenatorum filiı haud accenfendı fint,* CONCEPTI *tamen antıquam pater ordıne moveatur, licet poft demum natı,* QUASI *fenatoris filiı eadem ratıone ıntelligunt a.   L emancıpatum 7 s. 1 ff de fenatorıbus.   Hereditates quoque legitımæ, ut* JAM NATIS *difeırı folent, ıta et* NASCITURIS IN UTERO CONSTITUTIS *D l 1 quı ın utero funt 26 ff h t qubus et donec natı fuerint, portıones referventur.   L. antıquı 3 & l 4 ff fi pars hered petat.ı.*   QUOD SI NON IPSORUM IN UTERO EXISTENTIUM, SED TERTII ALIUM VERTATUR COMMODUM, CESSAT ILLA JURIS FICTIO, *qâ* PRO JAM NATIS HABERENTUR, NEC ALIIS PROSUNT, NISI NATI *D. l quı ın utero eft 7 ff h t l quod dicın ıs 231 ff. de verb fıgnıf"*

From thefe extracts, and from Jnft. lib 2 t 1 Dig lib 37 tıt 9 de ventre ın poffeffionem mittendo et curatore ejus, l g 1 & tıt 38 tıt 8 leg 1 & l b 5 tıt 2 de ınofficiofo teftamento, leg. 6 and Swınb part 4 f 15 No 14, it appears, that the fiction of the Roman law, treating children *ın the womb as lıving perfons*, was prıncıpally, if not wholly, *for theır own benefit*, and that ın general others could not take advantage of fuch fiction, and that ın general it could not be applied to *theır prejudıce.*

to learn, that before this recent cafe of Long and Blackall, there is to be found any adjudication having fuch an effect; for, as I have already obferved, I muft proteft againft confidering the cafe of Gulliver and Wicket, in 1. Wils. as a judicial decifion in that way.

SECONDLY, I humbly contend, that in this refpect the decifion exceeds the very line it profeffes to adhere to. Lord Kenyon exprefsly ftates the rule with an allowance of only *the fraction of a year* beyond lives in being and the twenty-one years. But the effect of the decifion in favour of the executory devife is, to *double the fraction of a year*, on account of which tendency of the executory devife your Lordfhip feems partly at leaft to have doubted its legality. In other words, nine or ten months are not merely extended into eighteen or twenty; but are fo extended, as if the months were ftill only

In refpect to the law of England, the fame fiction is adopted for *various purpofes*; and more efpecially for the *advantage* and *benefit* of pofthumous children, in cafes, in which *they would be otherwife excluded from provifion, or be otherwife prejudiced* The chief cafes and authorities upon this fubject are collected in Viner's Abridgment, title *Enfant*, H 8 and title *Devife*, I. 9. The chief cafes fince Viner's publication are, Wallis v. Hodfon, 2 Atk. 115. Barnad. Cha Rep 272. Mr. Jodrell's Manufcript Notes, vol 2 and Mr Capper's Manufcript Notes, vol 2. Beale v. Beale, 1. Wms 244 Miller v. Turner, 1. Vef. 85. Lancafhire v Lancafhire, 5. Durnf and Eaft 49. Doe on demife of Clarke, 2 Hen Blackft 399 Long v Blackall, in 7 Durnf. and Eaft; and Whitelock v Heddon, Bofanq. and Pull. Rep. 243.

The point is, whether, according to the cafes and authorities in our law, the *fiction* of treating children *in the womb* as *living* perfons, thus originating for the *benefit* of fuch children, and chiefly at leaft fo applied in our law even on the rule of executory devife, can be properly applied for the *purpofe of protecting executory devife* beyond lives *actually in being for the lives of fuch children when born*; or if the fiction may be fo extended, whether fuch an extenfion fhould be endured, for the purpofe of excluding children *in the womb* from provifion; and of fo making them *living* perfons for their own *exclufion*, merely in order to eke out a fcheme of pofthumous accumulation, profcriptive to the family of the teftator, and at the fame time highly dangerous to the community at large

nine

nine or ten. It is profefsing no extenfion, and yet making a great one. It is doubling the allowance for pofthumous children, without any profefsion to increafe it at all.

THIRDLY, the decifion has the effect of taking the life of a perfon *en ventre fa mere* for a life *in being*, that is, a *future* life for a *prefent* one, a *non-exifting* life for one *exifting*, a *born* child for one *unborn*. This, as I contend and really think, my Lord, operates, though I am fure not intentionally, as imputing to the great Judges who founded and modified executory devife, not merely the moft incorrect, but the moft deceitful language.— It is in effect imputing to them, that, in drawing the boundary of executory devife, they ufed language, which confounds perfons *in the womb*, with perfons *out of it*; perfons *in being*, with perfons *not in being*; perfons *not alive*, with the *living*; *non-entity* with *entity*.——It is in effect, though I am convinced not intentionally, almoft imputing to them, that they verbally, directly, externally, and avowedly, included within the boundary only the lives of born perfons; but fecretly, myftically, internally, and indirectly, intended to fuperadd perfons unborn.——Nay, in effect, it feems imputing to them, though not intentionally I am fure, that, under the pretence and fhew of only adding to exifting lives in being nine or ten months for the birth of pofthumous children to enable their taking under the executory devife, the Judges have contrived impliedly, not only to take that time *twice over*, and fo to include the time for *birth of the pofthumous child of a pofthumous child*, but befides that, as it were imperceptibly, to infinuate the addition of the lives of the pofthumous children in the firft inftance.——It is in effect imputing to them, though I am fure not intentionally, that, inftead of ufing correct, plain, fimple, and intelligible language; fuch as becomes the

Q   dignity,

dignity, the gravity, the fincerity, the integrity, the duty of
judicature; they reforted to the language of difguife, of obfcurity, of fiction, of metaphor, of myftery, of delufion.——
In a word, it is, as it were, imputing to them, that they deliberately and wilfully fpoke one thing and meant another.——
I am fully convinced, my Lord, that thofe reverend judges,
who figned the certificate in Long and Blackall, and to whofe
fuperior and exemplary characters I bow with fubmifsive veneration, are incapable of intending fuch imputations againft
their great predeceffors in office.　Indeed it is impofsible to
harbour the fufpicion of fuch an intention, without fuppo-
fing that they intended to wound themfelves; for they themfelves have defcribed the boundary in fimilar terms.　But I do
humbly fubmit to your Lordfhip, that if the principle, on
which only as I conceive the certificate in Long and Blackall
can be fupported, fhall finally prevail, there will, in point of
effect and confequence, be almoft an invitation fo to accufe,
at leaft thofe who heretofore exercifed the functions of judicatures in Weftminfter-hall.　If too there was nothing more
than the danger of all this aggregate of confequential, though
certainly unintentional, imputation, againft the judicatures
which firft indulged executory devife, and then fixed limits
to circumfcribe it, I fhould humbly contend, that there
would be full enough in the precedent of Long and Blackall
to create alarm amongft thofe zealous for Englifh jurifprudence: nay, fuch an alarm as might well render the beft confidered judgment ever given in any of our Courts a fit fubject
for revifion; and much more the judgment, given as it acci-
dentally and unfortunately was in Long and Blackall, without
argument, in fupport of the claim of the party againft whom
the certificate operated in the nature of a judgment, or in
explanation of the grounds upon which your Lordfhip may be

ple-

presumed to have sent the case as a fit subject for solemn argument.

FOURTHLY, I submit, that construing children *in the womb* as *lives in being* makes the rule of executory devise both *superfluous* and *inconsistent* in its terms. I say *superfluous*; because it by *lives in being* the rule is meant to include the lives of children *in the womb*, it is unnecessary to add any time for their birth. I say *inconsistent*; because allowing the due time for birth of the posthumous child, as the last link of the chain of executory devise, imports, that no time beyond is to be allowed; whereas allowing the lives of children *in the womb* to be *lives in being*, is further allowing the lives of the posthumous persons when born.

FIFTHLY, so considering the lives of persons *in the womb* as lives *in being* would, I submit, involve the judges of England in a great imputation. Here the case of Reve and Long, adjudged about six years after the revolution, becomes material. In that case all the judges concurred, on a devise of land, in refusing to save a contingent remainder for a *posthumous* child; though considering a child *in the womb* as a child *in being* would have clearly produced that effect; and though by not resorting to such fiction the testator's heir and his issue were excluded. Will it be consistent or becoming in our judges to refuse holding a child *in the womb* a child *in being*, to give effect to a contingent remainder in favour of a testator's heir and devisee and his issue, and at the same time to apply that fiction merely to add a further link to executory devise? (*e*)

Should

(1) The case of Reve v Long is reported in 3 Lev 408 4 Mod 282 Skinn 430 1 Salk 227 12 Mod 53 Comberb 252 & Carth. 309 By the decision of the House of Lords, the unanimous judgment, first of the Common Pleas, and then of the King's

Q 2

Bench,

Should this at least feeming inconfiftency be finally adopted, I apprehend, that it will not be excufed by the ftatute of 10. and 11. Wm. 3. which after the cafe of Reve and Long was made in favour of pofthumous children; that ftatute being

Bench, was reverfed in favour of the pofthumous child. But this was done, not only againft the opinion of all the judges, but appears to have been confidered by the whole profeffion as contrary to law. Therefore, notwithftanding the judgment of the lords, doubts prevailed; and to remove them the ftatute of 10. and 11 W 3. chap. 16. in favour of pofthumous children was made. The ftatute even recites the doubts But it is exprefsly confined to the cafe of *remainders*. Judge Levins, who was counfel for the plaintiff in the ejectment in the cafe of Reve and Long, reports the cafe in Law French, of which what follows is a literal tranflation

" *Mich 6. W. and M. in C. B*

" *Reve v Long.*

" In Domo Procerum post clausum hujus Termini.

" Error of a judgment in C. B. affirmed in B. R. where on a fpecial verdict in
" ejectment the cafe was this John Long feized in fee devifes the lands in queftion
" to Henry Long the elder fon of his brother Richard for life; remainder *to his firft*
" *fon in tail*, remainder to all his other fons in the fame manner; remainder to
" *Richard Reve leffor of the plaintiff* for life; remainder to his firft and all his other
" fons in tail, with diverfe remainders over: and dies Henry entered and was feized;
" and *before his having any fon born* dies leaving his wife *grandment enfeint*. Richard
" the leffor enters as in remainder · and *fix months after, the defendant, fon of Henry*
" *was born*, and his guardian enters for him on the leffor, whereupon he brings eject-
" ment. And the cafe being tried before Turton baron of the exchequer, all this
" matter was found fpecially And on argument in C. B. judgment was given for
" the plaintiff by *the whole Court* for two reafons. 1 This being a *contingent remain-*
" *der* to the firft fon of Henry, and he *not being born* at the time of the determination
" of the particular eftate, this becomes void 2. The next in remainder being the
" leffor, and he having entered before the birth of the firft fon. Henry, was in by
" purchafe, and fhall not be put out by an heir born afterwards. 5. E 4. 6. 9. H
" 7 5 &c. Whereupon the defendant brings error in B R. where the judgment was
" *affirmed* by *the whole Court* upon which he brings error in parliament, where the
" judgment was *reverfed* by *almoft all the Lords in parliament*, becaufe being in a will,
" they took it by the intent and equity and meaning, which they faid cannot be *to*
" *difinherit the heir of the name and family of the devifor for fuch nicety* But all the
" Judges were *ftrongly diffatisfied with this judgment of the Lords, and did not change their*
" *opinion upon* it, but ftrongly blamed Baron Turton for permitting it to be found
" fpecially, where the law was fo certain and clear. Levins for the plaintiff in
" the ejectment "

confined:

confined to preferving a *contingent remainder* for them, and not applicable to *executory devife*, efpecially fuch as is to abridge their eftates.

fixtly
~~FIFTHLY~~, It feems no flight objection againft the certificate of the King's Bench in this cafe of Long and Blackall, that the *pofthumous* fon was not confidered as a child *in being*, to *let in* the child to an eftate, the rule of executory devife being fufficient for that purpofe without reforting to that fiction; but was fo confidered to *abridge* the eftate of the pofthumous child, by converting it from an abfolute eftate into a mere life-intereft.

feventhly
~~SIXTHLY~~, I am perfuaded that there is ftill more than all this againft the certificate in Long and Blackall, on the point of objection I am now making againft that cafe, that is, on the point of fuperadding *not the time for birth*, but *the whole life of a pofthumous child*, or rather the whole lives of pofthumous children, to lives in being, *for the mere purpofe of protracting executory devife, and of lengthening its chain of contingency.* Accordingly I beg leave to infift; and *è corde ipfo*, and from a felf-conviction founded on the moft elaborate confideration, and a long experience of this fubject of executory devife, I do humbly infift; that yielding to fuch a latitude in the conftruction of the boundary of execut*ory* devife will lead to an extenfion of that boundary, not only againft the words of thofe great judges by whom the boundary was conftituted, but againft both their real meaning, and in a way extremely novel and at the fame time very mifchievous to the public intereft.—If lives *in being* may be taken for the contingency of executory devife; and if the *lives of children in the womb* are to be confidered *as lives in being*, and are to be taken for
the

the fame purpofe; and if twenty-one years are to be allowed beyond both ; *the boundary becomes in effect extended to the lives of a generation beyond lives in being*. Thus the rule, *of lives in being at the death of the testator* and twenty-one years after the expiration of thofe lives, is enlarged into an allowance of *lives in being at the death of the testator*, of LIVES OF PERSONS IN THE WOMB *at the fame time, and twenty-one years befides*. But I cannot think fuch an interpretation of the boundary of executory devife conformable, either to the authorities by which the rule is fixed or the reafon of the rule. I fay that fuch an interpretation is not according to the authorities. They, in general, including what Lord Kenyon himfelf has repeatedly ftated, mention lives in being and twenty-one years with the *fraction of a year*, as the *ne plus ultra* of executory devife . and I call upon the gentlemen, on the other fide, to cite the books, in which this doctrine of protracting executory devife to the prejudice of *unborn* perfons through confidering them as *actually born*, in order to exclude them, or to abridge their quantity of eftate, that is, by converting an *abfolute eftate* into a mere *life intereft* in favour of a fecond generation of unborn children, is regiftered. I fay, that fuch a latitude of interpretation is *not according to the reafon of the rule*. Under *that*, the boundary is conftituted, with reference, and in analogy, to the entail of inheritance and by fettling or devifing an eftate for life with remainders in tail to the fons and daughters of the tenant for life ; and in order to indulge fettling of property of every fpecies by executory devife, upon the terms of keeping property entailed in that form as long unalienable, as if the entail was in the ftrict and regular way by eftate for life and remainders in tail. For this purpofe the endeavour has been to make the two modes of entail correfpondent in this refpect,

fo

fo far as the difference between an entail barrable by common recovery and an entail not fo barrable will well allow. But if the *lives* of *children in the womb* may be introduced between lives *in being* and the *twenty-one years after,* and may be ufed to enlarge the boundary of executory devife; if the *fiction* of the Roman law, and under the adoption with us of our law alfo, in confidering *children in the womb* as *living* perfons, is to be applied to accomplifh fuch an enlargement; if a legal *fiction,* invented by the Roman law, and adopted by ours for the *advantage of children in the womb* and to enable then taking advantage both of legacies and devifes and in the cafe of inteftacy to enable their fharing in diftribution, is thus to be converted againft both them and others *into an inftrument of extending executory devife,* by adding a new link to the chain; if what our judges avow to be fiction and for the benefit of pofthumous children, is to be confounded with what our judges have gravely and folemnly uttered as no fiction, and is fo to extend a boundary they are pledged not to exceed: then, I humbly beg leave to affirm, my Lord, *that the boafted analogy, between ftrict legal entail by eftates for life with remainders over and the irregular but permitted entail by executory devife, will be difturbed*; and that thus executory devife will be like a fhip without a rudder, and will degenerate from a wife policy into a public grievance. Under fuch an enlargement of lives, the entail by executory devife, which from its nature is unbarrable by recovery, will continue property unalienable for a longer time, than can be effectuated by entail through the medium of remainders. In the latter way, the ultimate point, to which barring by common recovery can be poftponed, is twenty-one years after the death of the tenant for life including the fraction of a year for the birth of pofthumous iffue. But in the former way, if the executory devife

5

be

be fo conftituted, as to keep the executory devifee uncertain till the moment he is to take, as in fact is done by the will of the late Mr. Thelluffon, then the entail will continue un-barred and unbarrable, during lives in being and twenty-one years after and the fraction of a year, *and alfo during the whole lives of the pofthumous children befides.*—In thus ftating, that the neceffary confequence of confounding the *unborn* with thofe *born,* and of converting what was delivered in a plain fenfe of the words into an ingenious fiction, a folemn rule of law into a metaphor, I truft, that I am founded both in *authority* and in *practice.* In *authority,* I hold myfelf to be warranted by the cafe of Humberfton and Humberfton, *(u)* and by other cafes of that clafs, which eftablifh the rule, that *an eftate to an* UNBORN *child for life, with remainder to his firft and other fons in tail, fhall operate as an eftate tail in the* UNBORN *child* for that rule is ever given *without the leaft hint of an exception of* CHILDREN IN THE WOMB. In *practice* I confider myfelf as equally warranted. for I take upon myfelf to fay, from my own perfonal expe-rience afsifted by the experience of thofe I am intimate with, that the habit of conveyancers, in refpect to remainders to unborn children, is againft attempting to make pofthumous children mere tenants for life with limitations to their iffue as purchafers. Yet, if that was thought feafible, a very fhort provifo might be framed to produce that effect in entails by remainder. I do not mean, that there are not fome few inftances of fuch experiments. The cafe of Long and Blackall furnifhes one inftance of an executory devife fo framed, and there may be inftances of remainders to unborn children framed with a like view. But I mean, that the general habit as to remainders is to the contrary. To me perfonally the thing was never fo much as propofed. I have the honor of being intimate with fome of the moft eminent conveyancers both at the bar and other-

(u) In 3 P Willms in Com Rep & in Prec. in Chanc.

2   wife.

wife. But I have not heard, that any of them ever practised
or have been asked to practise in that way. Not even in the
settlements of persons of the first family and fortune, is it
usual so much as to think of such extension of unbariable
entail. Not even in the ambitious will of that very great
general and very profound statesman John Duke of Marlborough, though the first lawyers of the country assisted to
effectuate his wish of perpetuity of entail to the utmost extent
legal acuteness could accomplish, was it attempted to risque
this species of experiment. I humbly conceive, therefore, that
so letting in lives of children *in the womb*, in addition to the
lives of persons in being and the twenty-one years after, and
so protracting the contingency of executory devise beyond
the latest time endured for postponing the barring by common
recovery, is inconsistent with the very rule, which Lord
Kenyon himself lays down in the case of Long and Blackall.
His words in that case are as follow : " The rules respecting
" executory devises have conformed to the rules laid down in
" the construction of legal limitations; *and the Courts have*
" *said, that the estate shall not be unalienable by executory devises*
" *for a longer time than is allowed by the limitations of a common*
" *law conveyance.* In marriage settlements, the estate may
" be limited to the first and other sons of the marriage in
" tail; and until the person, to whom the last remainder is
" limited is of age, the estate is unalienable." Such is the
language of Lord Kenyon in the case of Long *v.* Blackall.
But if I am founded in the explanation I have given, of the
consequence from the extension of executory devise, by including the lives of posthumous children as well as lives in
being, such an addition of persons *in the womb* will enable
making property unalienable longer by executory devise than
can be done by the regular form of entail; nay, will enable

R   it it to the full extent of the difference between the posthumous child's attaining *twenty-one*, and the *whole of his life*. In this view, therefore, the adjudication of Long *v.* Blackall, if it is to be considered as meant to rule the point of adding the lives of posthumous children to lives in being for the purpose of executory devise, a second time infringes the very boundary it professes to observe.

Upon these reasons I humbly conceive, that the certificate of the King's Bench in Long *v.* Blackall, if it is to be considered, as intentionally sanctioning the allowance for a posthumous child in the case of executory devise *twice over*, and as impliedly extending the TIME FOR BIRTH *of the posthumous child' to the* WHOLE LIFE *of him when born,* is not merely an extension of the contingency for executory devise beyond its *ne-plus ultra,* and as such indefensible; but is one of a most dangerous kind; not only adding a new fraction of a year for the birth of a posthumous child to the fraction before allowed for the like purpose, but by the necessary consequence adding *the whole life of a posthumous child,* and so fundamentally subverting the analogy between entail by executory devise and entail in the common form of legal settlement, and granting much more of certain duration to the irregular and barely permitted mode of entail than is permitted even to the regular and strictly legal mode. So also viewing the certificate of Long *v.* Blackall, I humbly beg leave to question the authority of that case. I also humbly beg leave to say, that the case of executory devise, sent by your Lordship for the opinion of that Court, was not sent on light grounds; but was such, as renders it unfortunate to have had decision on the executory devise in question with only an argument on one side; and was such as evinced, that your Lordship looked far

2

beyond

beyond the *furface* of the ordinary learning of executory devife; and that your Lordfhip faw, that there was real danger
of a new extenfion of that boundary, which our Courts both
at law and in equity are *deeply pledged* to defend againft encroachment. Great too, or rather irrepealably fixed, as my
diftance is from judicial fituation, I hazard this free though
refpectful manner of treating the decifion in Long and Blackall, without danger of offence to the learned judges, the
effect of whofe adjudication I thus refift. By that refiftance
for the purpofe of the prefent caufe, I perform a profeffional
duty, in a cafe, of which the vaft value is almoft beyond
example; and I aim to refcue executory devife from that,
which, if endured, would render the indulgence a mifchief
inftead of a convenience. I feel alfo, that your Lordfhip's
fending the cafe for argument in the King's Bench juftifies
me, in doubting the legality of allowing a new fraction of a
year to lengthen executory devife, or rather fuch a new
fraction with the further addition of lives of perfons *in the
womb* to lives *in being*. Nay, I feel, that in fo doing I help
to give an opportunity of recalling a decifion; which, as it
happened, was argued on one fide only; and which, if it be
erroneous, the learned judges, from whom it came, will I
truft be the firft to wifh to have annulled. *The greateft
judge is never fo great, as when he fees his own errors, and is
eager to correct them.* Permit me to add, that there are occafions, upon which a judge, however elevated, however fortunate, however highly endowed, however profperous, may be
affifted in the difcovery of errors, by a profeffional lawyer,
however depreffed, however inferior, however unfortunate,
however difcountenanced, however profcribed, however unprotected.

R 2 BUT,

But, my Lord, though the cafe of Long and Blackall fhould be deemed the moft full, folemn and conclufive precedent of adjudication for extenfion of executory devife, by allowing the fraction of a year for birth of a pofthumous child *twice over*, and *by adding to the time for birth of fuch a child the whole duration of his life*, ftill it would not reach faving the trufts, in the prefent cafe. In Long v. Blackall, *doubling* the allowance for a pofthumous child was to give effect to an executory devife *regulating a feries of provifions for children of the teftator and their iffue.* But in the late Mr. Thelluffon's will the executory devife is conftructed, to deny *all enjoyment* of the devifed property to the teftator's *whole exifting and future family and all the world befides, to the lateft moment, which tampering with the boundary of executory devife could in the firft inftance rifque fuggefting to elude it's real boundary* and for this cruel purpofe, *the pofthumous children are ufed as mere inftruments for excluding both themfelves* and all others. To exprefs this more fhortly, in the cafe of Long and Blackall, the purpofe of the provifions was in fome refpects *laudable* and *meritorious.* but here the purpurpofe is *moft unmeritorious*; is even *cruel* and *unnatural.* In the former cafe, therefore, the judges might feel it a duty to do all in their power to fave the will. But the prefent cafe is fuch, as to make it the duty of judicature, to do all in it's power to difappoint the provifions the will contains: and what might be endurable in the *natural* will of Mr. Blackall, who was the teftator in the other cafe, may properly be confidered as quite intolerable under the circumftances of the unnatural difpofitions made by the will of the late Mr. Thelluffon. Befides *in the cafe of Long and Blackall, the experiment went no further than including the pofthumous children of one perfon.* But *here the experiment em-*

braces

braces the posthumous children of six persons according to the state of the testator's family at the date of his will, and avows comprehending the chance of a much more extensive stock of posthumous lives. What might be endured *for the life* OF ONE POSTHUMOUS *child may be beyond all endurance for* WHOLE CLASSES OF POSTHUMOUS LIVES.

IN these views of this my third charge against the trusts in question, I contend, my Lord,—not only, that the double allowance of the fraction of a year for birth of a posthumous child, that is, first in the commencement of the executory devise and again in the close of it, is an encroachment upon the proper boundary; but is one of a most dangerous nature, in respect of it's opening the door to let in and actually letting in *posthumous lives* in addition to lives *in being*.—not only, that this charge of excess of executory devise is countenanced by your Lordship's sending the case of Long v. Blackall for the opinion of the King's Bench on this point of the double allowance; but that the accident of deciding in the King's Bench, *without hearing any argument in support of the doubts, which influenced your Lordship to send the case,* in effect leaves the point in some degree as if no decision had passed upon it:—and not only, that the real tendency of the case of Long v. Blackall somehow or other seems to have escaped the observation of the King's Bench; but that the court decided, as if the fraction of a year was allowed for the birth of a child in the womb only *once,* when the effect of the decision is to allow it *twice;* and that so, however unintentionally, the court admitted a most extensive inroad upon those very limits of executory devise, which Lord Kenyon himself, at the very moment of deciding, forcibly stated to be it's utmost boundary both in letter and in principle; and therefore that, the reasons of the certifi-

5 cate

cāte in the cafe of Long and Blackall are deftructive of the authority of that ceitificate, and in perfect unifon with your Lordfhip's doubts in fending that cafe out of equity for the opinion of a court of law.

THE refult of this long confideration of my *for excefs of executory devife* third chaige againft the tiufts in queftion, as I fubmit to your Lordfhip, ftands thus.—On the one hand, for me and againft doubling the nine or ten months for birth of pofthumous children and againft comprehending future lives as lives exifting, I have the letter, the fenfe, the fpirit, the principle, the integrity, and the very effence, of the rule for the boundary of executoiy devife, and of the authorities and practice upon which that rule depends.—On the other hand, there is againft me, only the fingle cafe of Long and Blackall : and the decifion in that fingle cafe not only was unfolemn and inftantaneous, and without argument for thofe againft whom the decifion opeated, but profeffes to acknowledge the boundary I contend for ; and fo in this cafe of Long and Blackall I have, as I conceive, the *reafoning* of the Court of King's Bench with me, though not their *certificate.*   Nor is this all : for fuch is the unmeritorioufnefs, fuch is the excefs of the prefent cafe, that even the fulleft application of the certificate in Long and Blackall would not fuffice to fhelter the tiufts in queftion, either againft the objection of doubling the allowance of a pofthumous child in executory devife, or againft the objection of adding to lives in being a new link of continuation through pofthumous lives, and of fo making pofthumous lives inftruments of an ænlarged pofthumous accumulation.

THIRD DAY'S ARGUMENT.

DELIVERED

THE 7th OF DECEMBER, 1798.

MY LORD,

IT was a pain to me yesterday, that I found it necessary to detain the Court for so very long a time,—first in detailing the history of executory devise, and in making the inferences required for the purpose of founding the proper objections to the late Mr. Thelluson's great testamentary trust;—and afterwards in evincing *three* of the *six exceffes*, which I impute to the executory devise his will unfeelingly ambitiously and extravagantly creates.

YET I do not repent of having thus feverely tried the patience of the Court; becaufe I am convinced, that your Lordfhip and the reverend Judges your afsiftants, would not, in a cafe fo deeply involving the character of English jurisprudence, and fo deeply affecting the moft valuable interefts both public and private, wifh for the leaft facrifice to avoid a momentary perfonal inconvenience. If too I have trefpaffed in this refpect, I did not act, without fome degree of fanction, or rather encouragement, from the two eminent advocates, under whom I have the honour to take my fhare in this new battle of executory devife. It was apparent, that in order to

leave

leave a proper opening for the application of my known laborious attention to the fubject of the Thelluffon will, they only glanced at fome of the topicks, for which they knew me to be more particularly prepared.

Thus much I offer in the way of apology for my extraordinary length in the argument of yefterday.

But I have the pleafure to fay, that there is no danger of my again trefpafsing in the like extent on the time of your Lordfhip in thefe caufes.

The points, indeed, which I have ftill to argue, will not I truft, be found fcarce lefs important than thofe I have already difpofed of. But fortunately the compafs of argument upon the remaining points is far more circumfcribed : and I truft, that what I have to offer will be rapidly difpatched.

Yesterday I finifhed with the third of my charges of excefs of executory devife againft the great teftamentary trufts in queftion.

Now therefore I fhall proceed to the fourth of thofe charges.

*Third excefs
of executory
devife, namely, taking a
number of lives,
merely to protract the accumulation, and
the vefting of
the executory
devifes*

The fourth charge, which I alledge againft the trufts in queftion, for excefs of executory devife, is taking a *number of lives, merely to protract the late Mr. Thelluffon's truft of accumulation and the vefting of his executory devifes.*

According to the *letter* of the common manner of ftating, how the extent of executory devife is circumfcribed, the

contingency

contingency as I have more than once had occafion to mention, muft be fuch, that if it happened at all, it muft happen *within a life or lives in being and twenty-one years afterwards, including the fraction of a year for birth of a pofthumous child.*

IT is natural enough, at firft and whilft we look only to the *letter* and *furface* of the boundary to executory devife, to fuppofe, from this manner of expreffing the rule, a *licence* of chufing lives in being, without regard, either to the *number of the lives,* or to *their having connection with the executory devife beyond ferving to extend it's contingency.*

NOR is it in the leaft furprizing, that when a teftator, ardent as the late Mr. Thelluffon was to gratify his unnatural wifh of pofthumous accumulation, was informed of the terms of the rule of executory devife, he fhould interpret it in a way fo chiming with his purpofe ; and then feek to fubftantiate his project, by ftraining to take advantage of the rule of executory devife in it's utmoft *literal* latitude.

BUT in judicature the rule of executory devife muft be infpected in a different manner ; muft be examined with more penetration, and with different views. In a court of juftice, the *reafon* of the rule muft be fcrutinized, as well as the *language* in which it is *ufually* expreffed. There it is a duty to be vigilant, in guarding againft the abufe of executory devife ; and for that purpofe to be even auftere, in refifting all attempts to defeat the *fpirit* of the rule under fhelter of it's letter. There it is a duty, to difcountenance in the ftrongeft manner *all tampering* with the rule ; and fternly to reject *all contrivances, however colourable,* to elude it's real boundary.

Now looking to the *reafon* of the rule, and to it's *fubftantial*

S   limits,

limits, I fay, what I have already endeavoured to fhew, that *executory devife* is an *irregular* mode of entail, *indulged* by the courts, to enable fettling every fpecies of property, in a form not confonant to the ftrictnefs of our law as to particular eftates with expectant remainders and reverfions; and that the *fpirit* of the rule, which our courts have gradually eftablifhed as a boundary to executory devife, is *a qualification of their in-dulgence, to prevent the irregular and barely permitted mode of entail, from exceeding the limits and purpofes of the regular and ftrictly legal mode.*

BUT it is not, I conceive, in the leaft confiftent with the reafon of this *indulgence* of executory devife, or with the *fpirit* of fuch a boundary,—to permit lives in being to be taken *inde-finitely* for *the purpofe of protracting executory devife, to the utmoft poffible extent the duration of an indefinite number of lives can ac-complifh;* or even *to fanction taking any great number of lives, only connected with the executory devife as they are ufed to extend it beyond the duration of the ufual and ordinary mode of keeping pro-perty in an unalienable ftate under a regular entail.*

IT is true, that the *letter* of the rule, as we ufually exprefs it, mentions lives in being generally and without limitation. But even the *letter* of the rule, according to this *common par-lance,* rather imports, that the contingency *muft not exceed lives* in being, than that *any number of lives may be taken.* There is no inconfiftency in faying at the fame time, that lives in being fhall not be exceeded; and that fuch lives fhall be under fome quali-fication as to the number and choice of them. Even upon the *letter* then of the rule in *common parlance,* it is not neceffary to fuppofe lives in being without qualification.

WHATEVER alfo may be the refult of a dry interpretation of
the

the letter of the rule, neither the *spirit* of the rule, nor the *effect* intended by the judges in adopting or rather conftituting it, nor the *practice* upon the rule, accords with an indefinite and unqualified number of lives.

As to the *spirit* of the rule, fuch a conftruction of it would evaporate the true fpirit. The *spirit* is, not to permit executory devife to excurfe beyond the legal and regular mode of entail; not to fuffer an entail to be unbarrable longer by the mode barely permitted, than by the mode ftrictly legal. But entail by executory devife would continue unbarrable longer than entail under a ftrict fettlement by creating eftates for life, with remainders in tail to the fons and daughters born or unborn of the tenant for life, if lives in being of any perfons and *in any number* could be taken for the bafis of executory devife. I fay, that fuch would be the confequence; becaufe then an executory devife might be, upon the contingency of *the death of the furvivor of all the exifting branches of our royal family, of all the exifting peers of Great Britain and Ireland, of all the exifting members of the two houfes of parliament in both iflands, of all the perfons whofe lives are comprized in the feveral exifting tontines;* nay, *if children* IN THE WOMB *are to be counted as perfons* IN BEING, *of all children in the womb to all thefe* CLASSES *of perfons.* Even this is not the utmoft latitude; for if the number of lives is to be quite indefinite, the contingency may be extended, *fo long as any perfon can be found in Europe, or rather in any part of the known world, who was either living or in the womb at the death of the particular teftator.* But if the phrafe of *lives in being* is to be conftrued thus indefinitely, or in a fmall part of fuch an extent, then through executory devife it would become quite facile, to conftitute fuch an entail *as could not fail to continue unbarrable for above a century, or rather for almoft a century and a*

half:

half: for we have not a yearly bill of mortality for London and it's vicinity without fome perfon who has lived feveral years beyond the age of one hundred; and *adding the twenty-one years* and *the double allowance of nine or ten months for pofthumous children,* that is, firft at the beginning of the executory devife, and then at the expiration of the laft of the lives fixed upon, with the chance of a minority when the executory devife commences, there will be a CERTAINTY of about *one hundred and forty years,* and the *chance of twenty-one years more.* Nay, even this is rather underdating the matter: for a minority of nearly twenty-one years after expiration of the lives and twenty-one years beyond might be almoft abfolutely fecured, by fo framing the executory devife, as to require the devifee's being an infant not a year old. But an executory devife CERTAINLY keeping property unalienable for *one hundred and forty* years, and not improbably for above *one hundred and fifty* years, has *no fubftantial analogy* with the ordinary and legal mode of fettlement; for under that there is not a PROBABILITY of keeping an eftate unalienable for above *half of a century,* and the chance is againft it's reaching that time. Confequently to underftand the phrafe of *lives in being* fo extravagantly, will be to proclaim, that executory devife may CERTAINLY accomplifh almoft *thrice as long* a duration for entail, as the regular mode of fettlement can *probably* enfure. This would be *to deftroy the analogy between executory devife and the regular mode of entail,* at the very moment the rule profeffes to eftablifh that analogy; and would go *to the extent of enduring under the difcretionary permiffion almoft treble the time under the ftrictly legal right.*

As to the *effect* intended by the judges in allowing lives in being as a bafis for executory devife, and the *practice* under that allowance, I apprehend, that the idea, of applying an indefinite
number

number of lives, to fpin out executory devife, never fo much as occurred to the minds of thofe, who gradually extended executory devife to the boundary of an unbarrable entail under the legal form of fettlement. Our judges for fome time hefitated about exceeding one life: and this fully appears in the hiftory I have given of the growth of executory devife in the inftance of terms for years. But this hefitation was overcome by the good fenfe of lord chief juftice Hale, lord keeper Bridgman, lord chancellor Nottingham, and other diftinguifhed judges, who faw, that to conftitute the boundary of executory devife with a juft analogy to fettlement by eftates for life and remainders, it was neceffary to allow to the former irregular fpecies of entail the fame proportion of lives, as was of courfe allowed under the latter and regular fpecies, that is, the lives of as many perfons in being, as were the real fubjects of the provifion in the particular will or fettlement. To this ufe of lives in being for the contingency of executory devife it is, that we fhould apply the language of lord Hale, and after him of judge Twifden and others, when they obferved on the allowance of feveral lives, that *all the candles were lighted at once*, and therefore after all it was only the duration of one life. This phrafe, that *the candles were lighted at once* (which however is wholly inapplicable to children *in the womb*, whofe candles of life are not lighted till they are born, and which therefore will not cover the prefent cafe) was originally applied to the truft of a leafe for *one* living perfon for life, and after his deceafe for the life of a *fecond* living perfon in like manner. So applied to the lives of *two* living perfons, the phrafe was natural and fenfible. The difference in point of duration of unbarrable entail between one exifting perfon tenant for life, and having two or three exifting perfons tenants for lives fucceffively, is of flight importance; and in the way of fucceffive provifions for two or even feveral perfons, the extenfion

may

may be well yielded, without danger of going beyond, what belongs to ordinary settlements of inheritance upon succeffive tenants for life with remainders to their respective children. But to infer from there being so slight a difference between one life and two lives, in a cafe so put, as not to make it an object to diftinguish, that there is not any material difference, between taking one life or in the course of settlement two or three lives for the contingency of executory devise, and taking *millions* of lives for the mere purpose of protracting entail by executory devise, seems rather the language of passionate prejudice, than of cool reafoning. Lord Coke, in his Commentary upon Littleton, fol. 260. b. cites and applies the maxim *de minimis non curat lex*. But according to this reafoning from *two lives* to *millions of lives,* it would be justifiable to say, that becaufe our law regards not a *very fmall* difference, therefore it regards not the *greatest poffible* one, and thus the rule, *non curat lex de* MINIMIS, would become *non curat lex de* MAXIMIS. But I apprehend, that fuch great and temperate judges, as lord Hale, could not mean to difregard the difference between two lives and millions of lives. I fubmit, that they merely intended to say, that there was no great matter of difference in duration of time between the fettlement of a term of years on one exifting perfon for life and on two exifting perfons for their lives fucceffively. Accordingly in the beforementioned cafe of Scattergood and Edge, as reported in Salkeld, the court fpoke of *twenty-two or thirty years*, as the *probable* refult of taking lives in being. This way of confidering lives in being is no ill calculation as applied to eftates for life *in the common courfe of family fettlement*; but would, I humbly infift, become moft indefenfible, if applied to taking an *indefinite* number of lives unconnected with the property devifed or fettled, except by being called in aid to defraud the real fpirit of the rule of executory devife and

to

to abuse it's indulgence. Had the attempt at such an abuse been expected by the great judges, to whose wisdom we owe both the permission and boundary of executory devise, it is probable, that whilst they were making out an indulgence to suit general convenience, and for that purpose sanctioning a species of entail which enabled persons to settle every species of property, and indulging those who were meant to be accommodated, our courts would have been more explicit, in guarding against a misconception of the sense, in which they extended executory devise from *one life in being* to *several lives*. But the *practice* under the rules of *lives in being* proves, that the courts were well understood. The step from *one* life to *two* or *more* lives was taken by lord Hale just after the restoration, or, according to lord chancellor Nottingham's manuscript Reports and Prolegomena, a few years before: and I find from lord keeper Bridgeman's manuscript reports, which I have and which are first-rate specimens of judicial argument, that lord Hale was soon followed by the other judges. But though almost a century and a half have since passed, I doubt, whether so much as one instance, of an attempt to act upon the rule, as giving a right to take an *indefinite* or a *very great* number (w) of lives *merely* to

protract

(w) In the course of a very spirited and able argument in support of Mr Thellusson's Will by Mr. Pigott as counsel for the acting trustees, to prove that on the contingency for EXECUTORY DEVISE the number of lives is immaterial, there was a reference to some words of lord Chancellor Talbot in the case of Low and Burron, which arose on the entail of a lease for three lives and is in 3 Wms. 262 The words referred to were as follow " Here can be no danger of a perpe- " tuity, for all these estates will determine on the expiration of the *three* lives. *So if* " *instead of* THREE *there had been* TWENTY *lives*, ALL SPENDING AT THE SAME TIME, " ALL THE CANDLES LIGHTED UP AT ONCE, *it would have been good for in effect it* " *is only one life*, viz *that which shall happen to be the survivor*." This language of Lord Talbot was introduced by the learned counsel for the will of Mr. Thellusson, as an authority to shew, that any number of lives may be taken for the contingency of

executory

protract executory devise; nay, whether, till the prefent cafe, fo much as one inftance, of experiment in that way, can be found.

executory devife, and that all, which the rule of executory devife requires is to have the lives wearing out at the fame time

But this language of Lord Talbot was *not applied by him to* EXECUTORY DEVISE. He applied it to the cafe before him, which was of fuch a kind, as to render the doctrine of executory devife QUITE FOREIGN. The cafe, upon which Lord Talbot thus expreffed himfelf, was, according to the report in Peere Williams, that of a Mr Caffon, who, being feized of lands under a *leafe to him and his heirs during three lives*, devifed the leafe to his daughter for her life, remainder to her iffuemale, remainder to a Mr. Low. The daughter married, but previoufly conveyed the leafe in fettlement by leafe and releafe, to the ufe of her hufband and herfelf and the heirs of their bodies, remainder to the heirs of the hufband and fhe dying without iffue, the points were, whether the devife to Low in remainder was good, and if fo, whether the remainder to Low was *barred* by the conveyance of the teftator's daughter on her marriage Lord Talbot held the remainder to Low, though only in a defcendible freehold, good, but would not allow the daughter's conveyance to be a bar, except to her own iffue, and therefore held it no bar to Low's remainder. From this ftatement it appears, how *foreign to executory devife* this cafe was, and befides this, the cafe in point of authority is objectionable.—1. *Executory devife* was *foreign to the leafe for lives itself* for, whether a leafe for three lives was good or no', if it were poffible to raife a doubt on fuch a point, could not by any ftretch of ingenuity be made to connect with the doctrine of executory devife. On fuch a cafe I fhould fay, that it was quite indifferent in point of legal validity, for what number of lives the leafe was granted, for a leafe for a million of lives is as alienable as a leafe for one life.—2. The *entail*, or *quafi entail*, of the leafe for lives, was equally foreign in Lord Talbot's view of it he holding the entail to be *barrable*, fo far as the iffue of the firft taker was concerned, by conveyance in analogy to the mode of barring the iffue by the anceftor's *alienation* in the cafe of a *conditional fee* before the ftatute de donis; and the remainder over being alienable by him, to whom and to whofe heirs it was devifed, but *executory devife* being quite of another nature and *abfolutely unbarrable* by alienation or otherwife, on which very account it was, that a boundary to the contingency of executory devife became neceffary.—3. The doctrine of Lord Talbot, as to the remainder's not being barred by the alienation of the *quafi* tenant in tail of the leafe for three lives, is moft completely over-ruled by fubfequent adjudications It is now quite fettled, that one, having an intereft in a leafe for lives in nature of an eftate tail, may, by leafe and releafe or any other mode of alienation, or at leaft any other fufficient to pafs a freehold, bar *both his own iffue and* THOSE IN REMAINDER There is a dictum of the court to this effect in a chancery cafe as far back as 1691 (See in 2 Vern 225 the cafe of Baker *v.* Bailey) But the firft abfolute decifion of this point, which occurs

found. Not even the famous teftator Mr. Hopkins (of whom
lord Hardwicke faid, if he could have framed a will that no
one

in our printed books, feems to have been by Lord Chancellor Macclesfield in 1722,
in the cafe of the Duke of Grafton and Hanmer, which decifion is noticed by Lord
Hardwicke in 1 Atk 525 and is given with a fhort ftate of the cafe from the Regif-
ter's book in 3 Wms 266 Probably Lord Talbot was unapprized of this adjudication
by Lord Macclesfield But, be that as it may, there is a feries of adjudications fince
Lord Talbot's time, recognizing the decifion by Lord Macclesfield and founded upon
it. Of thefe cafes there is an enumeration in the 3d ed. of Mr *Fearne's* profound book
on *Remainders and Executory Devife*, p 385 to 391. To them fhould be added, the
cafe of Blake and Blake, which was before the court of Exchequer in 1786, and of
which there is a note in Mr. Cox's edition of Mr. Peere Williams's Reports, p 10. and
the cafe of Blake *v* Luxton in 6 Durnf and Eaft, 289, and alfo the new matter in
Mr. Powell's note in p 390 of his edition of fo much of Mr *Fearne's* book as relates
to executory devife. Therefore the only part of Lord Talbot's words in the cafe of
Low and Burron, which can poffibly be made in the leaft to bear upon executory
devife (if any part can be made fo to bear) appears to contain doctrine now moft
thoroughly exploded.

For the fake of the learned reader, I will add a fhort report of this fame cafe of
Low and Burron from the Manufcript Reports of a deceafed barrifter heretofore of
great practice and eminence, namely, WILLIAM MELMOTH, Efq who was co-editor
with Mr Peere Williams of Vernon's Reports, and as I guefs fole compiler of the
Index of matter to the two volumes, and who was father of the venerable and ele
gant tranflator of Tully's and Pliny's Epiftles.

Mr. Melmoth's report of Low and Burron is in thefe words.

" Low and Burron.

" Lord Chancellor,
" 17 May 1734

" A leafe to A. and his heirs during three lives was devifed to B. and the heirs of his
" body, with remainder to plaintiff.

" B by leafe and releafe, conveys the premifes in confideration of marriage, and
" the defendant claims under that fettlement.

" Among other queftions upon the defendant's plea, one was, whether a leafe for
" lives could be entailed in this manner; and if it could, whether the remainder over
" was not barred by the leafe and releafe

T   " LORD

one fhould take his eftate, it is likely he would have done it)
was advifed to attempt this fpecies of fraud upon the rule of
executory devife (x).   Nor did the frigid and learned apathy of
Mr. Bradley make fuch an attempt on the rule as to *lives in
being*.   But the miferable vice of avarice is not peculiar to the
prefent age, nor to the time of Vulture Hopkins, as he was
called.   All times have been difgraced, by avaricious fordidnefs, and by the longings of pofthumous avarice ; and at all times
it has been open to mifers, to demand profeffional affiftance
to execute fchemes of ftopping the ufe of property.   This
latenefs of the attempt, then, to ftrain the rule of *lives in being*

" LORD CHANCELLOR of opinion, a leafe for lives might be fo entailed, and the
" iffue, if any, or if none, the remainder man, took as fpecial occupants, and there
" was no danger of a perpetuity, for the eftates depended upon *three* lives, which were
" all in being   And though this cafe is not within the ftatute *de donis*, which re-
" fpects only eftates of inheritance , yet a leafe for three lives might be limited to one
" in tail with remainders over, for it is only an appointment who fhall be the fpecial
" occupant.

" As to the leafe and releafe, he was of opinion, that the remainder to the plain-
" tiff was not barred thereby.   Nothing paffed by that conveyance, but what B. had
" a power to grant

" However the defendant's plea was *overruled* upon fome other circumftances,
" which were in the cafe "

With refpect to the latter part of this report, probably the word *overruled* is a
miftake , for according to Mr. Peere Williams the court *allowed* the plea, and the
circumftances he ftates appear to confirm his account; and if he is right in this,
Lord Talbot's opinion, that the remainder over to Low was not barred, was in a
manner *extrajudicial.*

(*x*) See the cafe of Hopkins *v.* Hopkins in 1. Atk. 581. Lord Hardwicke's words
are in p 589 of that book.   In a manufcript note I have of Hopkins and Hopkins
from papers of the late Sir Thomas Sewell, mafter of the rolls, the words of Lord Hardwicke were. " I muft own, that I believe, that if the teftator could have framed a
" will fo as no perfon fhould take the immediate profits, he would have done fo "

into

into a right to take *lives in being* INDEFINITELY, proves, that the rule was not underftood in any fuch latitude, even by thofe, who were feeking to take the fulleft advantage of the rule in every poffible manner.

UNDER a reliance upon thefe reafons, againft conftruing the rule of *lives in being*, as giving a right to affume lives *indefinitely* for extending the contingency of executory devife, I claim to infift, that neither *an unlimited affumption*, nor *any approach to it*, is endurable even for the *moft meritorious* executory devife ever yet generated; and much lefs is endurable for as *cruel and unnatural* a purpofe, as ever contaminated the verieft mifer yet heard of.

HERE, therefore, it only remains to confider, whether *tampering* with the rule of *lives in being*, as it is practifed in the formation of the trufts in queftion, is fufficient to conftitute an excefs of the rule.

THAT the late Mr. Thelluffon's will amounts to *tampering* with the rule of *lives in being*, is grofsly apparent. He takes feven claffes of lives to work upon. Through thefe lives, the teftator gains the lives of three fons of the teftator and of three grandfons; not to provide for and make them happy; but, *to exclude them from provifion*, and fo far as their grandfather's unfeeling difpofitions can operate, to make them miferable, and at the fame time *to exclude all others* from enjoyment of the property: and then in the way of frefh fupply of faggots to feed the fire for his hot-bed of accumulation, he grafps the lives of *all fuch iffue, as fhould be born to his three fons and his three grandfons and to the iffue of his future grandfons, between his will and his death, or fhould at his death be in the womb.*

T 2   There

There is such a stretch in this selection of lives, as shews, that at least he was not without hope to live long enough to see great grandchildren married and having issue, and that in his view, his six faggot lives for protraction of his executory devise coupled with accumulation would probably before his death be encreased to twenty or even thirty lives. Nor was there any thing very extravagant in such an expectation. When he made his will, he was little more than sixty years of age, and from his perfect health and seemingly strong constitution, it was probable, that he might live at least about twelve years longer; and as his three sons were married to ladies bearing children, the prospect of adding sixteen or even above twenty new lives, and so encreasing the stock to two and twenty or almost thirty, was by no means remote. Indeed this prospect was not realised; because, in consequence of a sudden failure in his health and constitution, he lived scarce more than a year after his will. But even in that short time there has been a gain of three additional lives: for his third son's lady was brought to bed of a son between the will and the death of the testator, and his eldest son's lady has been brought to bed of twins, which were in the womb at the death of the testator, and are therefore just born time enough to extend the executory devise, and if the will shall prevail, to be excluded from all benefit under the dispositions of their unnatural grandfather, and to live sacrifices to his inordinate selfishness and avaricious vanity.

THE short state of this part of the case, then, amounts to this, that the late Mr. Thellusson took *six existing lives* to experiment upon, adding such an *expectancy of further lives*, as fairly promised fifteen new lives, and might have produced twenty more, or even a greater number; and such as, notwithstanding the unexpected shortness of his life after his will, has

actually

actually encreafed the fix lives to *nine*. But if taking fix prefent lives and *a good chance of twenty or thirty lives more*,
MERELY *to extend executory devife*, and enterprizing this great
extenfion *to exclude all beneficial enjoyment* of his immenfe mafs of
devifed property, are not fufficient overt acts of tampering with
executory devife to elude it's limits, and to abufe it's indulgence, I know not, what fort of evidence of grofs abufe of the
rule of *lives in being*, fhort of fome fuch monftrous experiment,
as taking all the lives of all the royal family and of all the exifting members of both houfes of parliament, both in Great
Britain and Ireland, or of all the lives in the feveral exifting
tontines within the two iflands, can be adequate to convince the
underftanding, that the intent was to defraud the law, under
which the teftator's ambitious avarice takes fhelter. His own
fcope would probably have gone even fuch vaft lengths, and
have attempted fome fuch vaft ftrides, as I thus mention. But
his profeffional advifers were not fo blind, as not to fee, that
fuch extremities would have completely betrayed the defign of
the teftator. It may well be imagined, that their fagacity
ftopped the teftator in his career ; and that he became deterred
by them from rifquing himfelf fo deep in *experimental accumulation and experimental executory devife*. His not going further
only fhews, that he was fufficiently inftructed to be afraid ;
and fo became reconciled to being content with taking lives
enough to give a *probable chance* of accumulation for almoft a
century, inftead of attempting a *certainty* in that way. But it
may be hence collected, that he was made confcious of his
aiming at fomething irregular, fomething exceffive ; and fo
was prevailed upon by his advifers, to abftain from unmafking
himfelf entirely. If he had not yielded fomething to their influence, the outrage upon the boundary of the rule of *lives in
being* would have been too vifible and grofs to bear argument.

But

But I contend, that if he really meant to tranfgrefs in any degree, the penalty is incurred; and that his truft of accumulation and executory devife muft pay the forfeit, as much as if the teftator had trefpaffed more avowedly and more largely; and that it is no excufe, that he has veiled and abridged his purpofe, in order to trefpafs more fecurely.

FROM thefe views of the rule of lives in being, and of the cunning of the teftator in endeavouring to fhelter his fcheme under that rule, it will, I truft, appear,—that the rule of executory devife is far from allowing lives of any perfons and in *any number*, without limitation or difcrimination.—that whatever may be the extent of the *letter* of the rule, it's *real fpirit*, it's analogy to *ordinary family fettlements*, the *monftrous confequence* of taking *lives indefinitely*, and the *practice* upon the rule, all confpire to fhew a boundary inherent:—and that the will of the late Mr. Thelluffon, not only tampers with this part of the boundary of executory devife; but, notwithftanding all the cunning employed to veil his purpofe and all his fear of trefpaffing fo as to be difcovered, ftands convicted of a real encroachment.

FIFTH charge of excefs of executory devife, namely, *protracting the executory devife, after expiration of the lives, till completion of all the purchafes of land.*

I NOW come to my FIFTH charge againft the trufts in queftion, fo far as excefs of the limits of executory devife is concerned.

BUT few words may be fufficient for the purpofe of this charge. It fpeaks for itfelf. The fhort amount of it is, that though the will of the late Mr. Thelluffon permits his beneficial

cial devifees to be individually afcertained, when all the claffes
of lives, which he conftitutes to build accumulation upon, are
exhaufted : yet the will feems ftill to harp upon accumulation ;
and for the fake of adding a further link to the chain of his project, ftill to exclude actual enjoyment of the devifed property.
At leaft there appears an opening for fo underftanding the provifion : for it directs, that until convenient purchafes of land
can be found, or until a fufficient fum of money fhall be accumulated to make proper purchafes of lands, the intereft dividends and proceed of the ftocks and fecurities conftituting the
teftator's refiduary perfonal eftate, and it's encreafe from the
feveral fources of accumulation appointed by the teftator, fhall
accumulate in the fame manner and for the fame purpofes,
as the rents and profits of the lands to be purchafed under the
will are directed to accumulate. This provifion feems to be
aiming *at all events* to continue the accumulation of the perfonal eftate and it's encreafe both from itfelf and the accumulating profits of the lands purchafed and to be purchafed, until
purchafes of land fhall be actually effectuated ; that is, without
regarding, whether all the lives poftponing the executory devife are or are not expired. In general, where money is to be
laid out in the purchafe of land for fettlements, there is a provifion, that till the lands fhall be purchafed, the intereft of the
money fhall belong to the fame perfons as the rents and profits
of the lands if purchafed would belong to. But in the late Mr.
Thelluffon's will, the provifion is againft fuch an application of
the intereft of the perfonal eftate and it's encreafe, and for it
fubftitutes a truft of accumulation. The effect of this provifion
then, unlefs there fhall be found room *conftructively* to make it
determinable with the laft of the various lives, which are made
fubfervient to protracting the executory devifes, will be to give
the

the chance of a further and uncertain poftponement of any enjoyment under them. In this view of the provifion, if the
whole of the perfonal eftate and it's encreafe from it's own accumulations and thofe of the real eftate fhould be uninvefted in
land, when the laft of the various lives drops, the accumulation
will continue for *the whole* of that fund during a new and uncertain period of protraction, that is, till proper purchafes of
land fhall be found and completed; and the executory devifees,
though become afcertained, will be forced to wait for enjoyment accordingly. If a *part* only of the fame perfonal property and accumulations fhall remain uninvefted, when all the
claffes of lives are exhaufted, then the enjoyment of only fuch
part will be further poftponed. But, from the nature of the
cafe, every part of the immenfe perfonal property and it's ad-
herent accumulations is equally liable to be affected by this
new protraction of the executory devife in point of enjoyment.
Therefore if this new link of protraction be an excefs of executory devife; if, from it's fucceeding fuch a feries of exifting
and expectant lives, and from the uncertainty of it's duration,
this further poftponement be fufficient to make it a trefpafs on
the eftablifhed boundary; I contend, that it will at leaft infect
the trufts for all parts of the refiduary perfonal eftate and it's ad-
herent accumulations as well from the devifed real eftates as
from it's own proper fund, and confequently make the trufts
illegal for almoft half a million of the property in queftion.
Nay, perhaps, the court may feel itfelf juftified to confider the
whole of the devifed property as implicated in this charge of
excefs of executory devife, in refpect that in point of actual enjoyment the whole of the refiduary devife is affected by this further attempt at protraction.

My

My sixth and last charge againſt Mr. Thelluſſon's will *for excess of executory deviſe is,* that not content with protracting his executory deviſes both in point of veſting and in point of enjoyment till expiration of all his claſſes of lives, and not content with farther protracting his executory deviſes in point of actual enjoyment till completion of all the purchaſes of lands he directs to be made with his vaſt funds of accumulation, the teſtator attempts the ſtill farther protraction as well for veſting as for actual enjoyment, by making it uncertain, who ſhall be the lineal male deſcendants to take beneficially, till the very moment of actual partition amongſt them, or rather till actual conveyance of the ſeveral allotments of lands in execution of ſuch partition.

Sixth and laſt charge of exceſs of executory deviſe, namely, *protracting it till actual conveyance for partition amongſt the firſt beneficial takers.*

Upon this charge, I ſhall ſay very few words.

It depends upon the conſtruction of the word *then* in the clauſe which appoints how partition ſhall be made. That clauſe directs, that after the deceaſe of the laſt of the lives for protracting the executory deviſes and the concomitant accumulation, an equal partition ſhall be made by the truſtees, by dividing all the lands into lots of equal value : -to effectuate which, in the caſe of ſuch vaſt eſtates as muſt in any event be the ſubject of the valuation and diviſion, much time muſt neceſſarily be conſumed. This direction to divide the eſtates into 3 lots is followed, with ordering, that the premiſes in one allotment *ſhall be conveyed* to the uſe of the eldeſt male lineal deſcendant *then living* of the teſtator's eldeſt ſon : and the like phraſeology is made uſe of as to the two other allotments for his two other ſons.

Now I contend, my Lord, that by the words *then living* the teſtator means living at *the time of the conveyance of the allotments :*

U

ments : and if this be fo, I conceive, that it amounts to protracting the executory devifes accordingly. I fubmit alfo, that
thus extending, the contingency of the enjoyment and vefting,
for a time fo uncertain beyond the duration of all his claffes of
lives, is a clear excefs of the boundary of executory devife.

HERE the queftion is, whether the teftator actually intended
fuch a farther protraction. The literal conftruction, on the
rule of relation to the laft antecedent, is, I apprehend, clearly
for fo underftanding the teftator. His fcheme, of ftretching executory devife to it's utmoft limits, is alfo for the fame conftruction. Nor are the grofs and mifchievous purpofes, for which
the teftator conftitutes his executory devifes, fmall temptations,
to confider his words according to literal conftruction, and to
take advantage of them.

IT is for the other fide to fhew, and for the Court to judge,
whether there is enough to encounter this head of charge againft
the trufts in queftion.

I WILL not now prefs this charge further. But I think it
juft to add, that it doth not originate with me, but comes from
the gentlemen, who are concerned *as folicitors* for the Thelluffon family
and againft the will, and who have I am convinced difcharged
their duty in that refpect with exemplary zeal, and who have
had no fmall fhare in encouraging my exertions in the prefent
cafe, fuch as they are. I beg leave alfo to fay, that the charge
thus fuggefted by others appears to me to deferve very ferious
attention, and that I therefore fubmit it to the difpofal of your
Lordfhip.

I HAVE

I HAVE now travelled over all the fix charges I make, againft the will of the late Mr. Thelluffon, for exceeding the boundary of executory devife. All of the charges appear to me to deferve confideration.

EVEN the imputation, of his meaning covertly to comprehend the twenty-one years after his deceafe for the generation and birth of new lives to protract his executory devifes, which is the fubject of the SECOND charge,—the imputation of his intending to protract his executory devife in point of enjoyment, under the chance of it's remaining to purchafe lands when all the lives fhall be expired, which conftitutes the FIFTH charge,—and the imputation of intending a ftill further protraction, under fhelter of the direction to make partition, which conftitutes the SIXTH and laft charge,—appear to me charges very far from being fuch as to juftify me in paffing them over.

As to the FIRST of the fix charges; which imputes to the will having left the third fourth fifth and fixth claffes of the lives for accumulation, or at leaft the third clafs, unguarded by the reftrictive words at the clofe of the feventh and concluding clafs; and which, in refpect of the confequential letting in various future lives in fome degree indefinitely, will, if well founded, fhew a clear encroachment of the rule limiting the contingency of executory devife to lives in being and twenty one years after :—I have great confidence, that, the grofs unmeritorioufnefs of the trufts being confidered, there will be found fully fufficient on this head alone to invalidate the trufts in queftion.

BUT as to the THIRD charge, which imputes to the will,

U 2   taking

taking the 9 or 10 months twice over, and at the fame time
fuperadding collectively the lives of iffue in the womb at the
death of the teftator, and born to his fons and grandfons and
even to great grandchildren in due time afterwards; I conceive,
that I have not only with me your Lordfhip's doubts and the
reafoning of the King's Bench in the cafe of Long and Blackall
which thofe doubts produced, but that the charge is in it's nature unanfwerable.

Nor, as to the FOURTH charge, which depends upon the
confideration, whether it is allowable, under the rule of lives in
being, to take the lives of all or any perfons indefinitely; and
whether if it is a fraud upon the rule to conftitute a large collection of lives to enfure fpinning out executory devifes beyond
a century, the late Mr. Thelluffon has not fufficiently tampered
with the rule in that way, to convict the will of that fraud, and
to annul it's cruel and unnatural trufts upon that ground only:—
have I the leaft idea, how the reafoning adducible to fupport it
can be thoroughly anfwered, either on the fpirit of the rule of
lives in being; or on the fenfe in which our courts have underftood it; or on the practice under the rule from it's firft eftablifhment till the prefent moment, except in the fingle and recent inftance of the eccentric and experimental will now in
queftion.

Second ge-
neral head of
objection to
the trufts,
namely, the
charge of
*excefs of trufts
of* ACCUMU-
LATION

Having explained and argued all the feveral charges againft
the grand truft of the will of the late Mr. Thelluffon, which are
comprehended in my firft general head, and have their foundation in the line or boundary prefcribed by our courts of juftice
to executory devife, I fhall next proceed to my fecond general
head of argument againft the fame trufts.

HITHERTO

HITHERTO I have impeached the trufts, *for exceeding the limits of the rule of* EXECUTORY DEVISE, and as being therefore invalid, on account of no lefs than fix feveral trefpaffes upon that rule.

BUT now I am to impeach the fame trufts for a vice independent of excefs of the boundary, by which the wifdom of our Courts gradually circumfcribed executory devife, as they gradually indulged it.

HERE the vice, which I impute to the trufts, is pofthumous accumulation, in fuch a *monftrous excefs* and for fuch a *monftrous purpofe*; as not only to be unworthy of fhelter, either under the law of executory devife, or under any defcription of exifting law whatever; but even to require being difdainfully rejected, as amounting to a precedent of teftamentary difpofition, which it would be equally a dangerous fhock to the interefts of the country at large and a reproach to it's law and judicature to tolerate.

IT is a circumftance very material to this fecond general head of attack upon the trufts in queftion, that the will cannot be extricated from all the imputed exceffes of executory devife; except under the terms of adminiftering vaft affiftance to the argument againft the trufts upon the fingle and independent ground of exceffive accumulation, by reafon of the confequences, which overruling fome of my chief objections of trefpaffing upon the limits of executory devife, and difregarding the principles upon which I have endeavoured to enforce thofe objections, would produce.

IF the will of the late Mr. Thelluffon fhould be acquitted of all trefpafs upon executory devife, it will follow, I conceive,—

that

that executory devife may depend upon the contingency of *any number of exifting lives at the death of the teftator, without limitation of any kind whatever* ;—that the contingency may be further extended to *the lives of an unlimited number of perfons* IN THE WOMB of their refpective mothers at the fame time ;—and that ftill further to enlarge the ftock of lives, the contingency may include twenty-one years, from the death of the furvivor of fuch unlimited number of lives of fuch *exifting* perfons and of fuch perfons *in the womb.*

BUT if thefe confequences are to be the refult of overruling my objections to the legality of the late Mr. Thelluffon's executory devife, it tells ftrongly indeed againft **the** accumulating truft, with which his executory devife is coupled. It will elevate and extend executory devife. But it tends to deprefs and abridge truft of accumulation; for it will go far, I fhould think, towards proving, that executory devife and truft of accumulation fhould not be fuffered to confubftantiate, fhould not be fuffered to be made co-equal and co-extenfive; or in other words that truft of accumulation ought not to find fhelter in executory devife by being incorporated into it. Upon the doctrine and principles, which I have refifted, but which muft be adopted, if the late Mr. Thelluffon's executory devife be adjudged within the due boundary, it will be poffible, that by tontining upon fuch an expanfe of contingency from an unlimited number of lives of perfons exifting and perfons in the womb and 21 years beyond, as I have defcribed and in the manner I have exemplified under my firft general head of argument, a fkilful doctor in the art of executory devife may apply it, fo as *with certainty to keep property unalienable for a century and twenty-one years at leaft.* Nay, by fhaping the executory devife, fo as to let in no perfon

under

under it, but such as shall be of the age of a few months when it shall take effect, there will be a further gain of above twenty years to the period for keeping property *unalienable*; and *so property may be made unalienable to a certainty during more than one hundred and forty years*. If too trust of accumulation should be allowed to couple with executory devise, and to be made commensurate in duration, the same effect will be produced as to keeping property unusable. Thus executory devise may with certainty be applied *to prevent* ALL ALIENATION *of property for almost* 150 *years*, and with the adjunct of accumulation *may be made with equal certainty to prevent* ALL BENEFICIAL ENJOYMENT *during the same great length of time*. Thus assisted also by accumulation, executory devise——which our courts professedly indulged merely for the *general convenience* of a species of entail applicable *to all kinds of property*, and in *analogy* to the unbarrable duration of the regular kind of settlement by estates for life and remainders over in tail,——and which therefore our judges have considered as not probably calculated to render property unalienable for more than half a century,——would become manufactured into an engine, for laying such an embargo on *the use of property both real and personal throughout the kingdom, as to make it possible to prohibit all beneficial enjoyment for* 120 *or even* 140 *years*, with as much CERTAINTY, as if such long term of years was expressly assumed for the purpose.

FROM this view of the effect, which would result from grafting trust of accumulation upon executory devise, under the principles and extensions, upon the terms of which only can the late Mr. Thellusson's executory devise escape (if it can escape on any terms) the being condemned for excess of the prescribed boundary; it is apparent, that such a combination

of

of truſt of accumulation with executory deviſe could not be endured, without the moſt glaring and dangerous miſchiefs to the community. It would enable every miſerly perſon, every unfeeling peiſon, every reſentful perſon, every capiicious or humourous perſon, every perſon philoſophically though not legally inſane; if he poſſeſſed any thing, however great in va- lue, which could be made the ſubject of ſettlement taking effect on his death; to ſtagnate the uſe and enjoyment of the wealth of the kingdom at his pleaſure for a centuiy and almoſt 50 years beyond; and ſo to erect a mauſoleum of property, for the almoſt boundleſs gratification of private vanity and private aggrandiſement. It would enable this, at the expence of the commerce, the circulation, the revenue, the ſtrength, the re- ſources, the hoſpitality, the comforts, the literature, the ſcience, the morality, the government, the conſtitution, nay, the very exiſtence of the kingdom: for how can all theſe things con- tinue, if every individual is to be at liberty, by teſtamentary diſpoſition, to interdict the uſe and enjoyment of his property, by a truſteeſhip of accumulation for a century and more after his own death?

The deſtructive conſequences, to be expected from allow- ing ſuch an extravagant indulgence of poſthumous avarice, may be well exemplified, by reference to the vaſt property, deſtined by the will of the late Mr. Thelluſſon to build a monument to his avaricious and unnatural project of ſoidid fame. The fortune, which his will appropriates to accumulation, may be taken at the capital ſum of £. 600,000. which is about the real value; and if continually employed by the year *at* compound intereſt at £. 5 per cent, it would double the ca- pital in 14 years, and ſo progreſſively afterwaids. But even

upon

upon a calculation of 15 years for fo doubling the capital, the effect would be as follows:

The capital would be, in

15 years	£ 1,200,000.
30	2,400,000.
45	4,800,000.
60	9,600,000.
75	19,200,000.
80	25,600,000.
90	38,400,000.
105	76,800,000.
120	153,600,000.

ACCORDING to this calculation, therefore, if the principles, on the terms of which only, as I have before obferved, the trufts in queftion can be extricated from excefs of the limits of executory devife, are to be allowed, the accumulation, under that fhelter, would at the end of ninety years, which is at leaft 30 years fhort of the full extent of the duration pofsible to be enfured on the full extent of thofe principles, conftitute a fortune of nearly 13 millions a-piece for fuch of the three male defcendants of the late Mr. Thelluffon's three fons, as at the expiration of that term fhould fall under the defcription of his will; and if there was only one fuch defcendant, it would be £ 38,400,000. Confequently if there were three defcendants to take, each, at an intereft of five per cent, would have an income of about £ 650,000. a year; and if there was only one fuch male defcendant, he at the fame rate of intereft would have a yearly income of above £ 1,900,000. that is, more than double his Majefty's civil lift revenue. Even at 75 years,

X each

each of tho three male defcendants would, on the fame rate of calculation, have a capital of above fix millions a-piece, and from that capital a revenue of above £ 300,000. a year; and if there was only one fuch defcendant a capital of £ 19,200,000. and from it a revenue of above £ 900,000. a year, that is, a greater income than is allowed by parliament to the King of Great Britain, according to the civil lift in it's prefent and higheft ftate of advancement.

THIS ftatement prefents fuch an enormity of effect from accumulation made commenfurate with executory devife, as feemingly to make it a wafte of words, to defcribe the ruinous confequences of fo indulging pofthumous avarice. Indulged to the will of Mr. Thelluffon only, the public mifchief from the ftagnation of £ 600,000. would be of an alarming magnitude in every point of view. On the one hand, there would be erected a monument, to commemorate his rapid acquifition of a vaft fortune, and his abufe of the teftamentary power; by facrificing that fortune and the interefts of all his living and deareft relations and his and their iffue for two or three generations, to a felfifh and unfeeling vanity; and for that purpofe by his locking up his immenfe property in the cheft of accumulation *irrevocably* for many years above a century, and fo accomplifhing, what no mifer ever before accomplifhed, a plan, by which the *income* of property may be locked up from expenditure as well as the *capital* for feveral generations after his own death. On the other hand, during the fame long period of pofthumous accumulation, there would be a continual injury of a moft extenfive operation, ftarving the commerce, fhrinking the revenue, and choaking the circulation of the wealth of the country, by denying to it at the beginning all expenditure of almoft a million of

money;

money; and this mifchief would be progreffively encreafing at a ratio, which, after comprizing millions and tens of millions, would, before the end of the period of accumulation and non-enjoyment, amount to above 150 millions of property in value. Nay, if lands were purchafed from time to time, as the will of the late Mr. Thelluffon directs, this monftrous evil would be aggravated, by *monopolifing* the landed eftates of the kingdom to the value of millions and tens of millions, into the condition of property without even the *poffibility* of any expenditure, till the century or rather the 125 years of non-enjoyment fhall be completely expired. Such an indulgence, in the fingle inftance of the late Mr. Thelluffon's fortune, would be the caufe of public mifchiefs of a vaft and alarming magnitude. But thefe mifchiefs would not ftop there. What is indulged to his will or teftamentary fettlement, if fuch inftruments are to be called by fuch a name, muft be indulged to the wills and fettlements of others: and fo all kinds of property, in all parts of the kingdom, would be liable to the fame embargo upon and proscription of all beneficial enjoyment; and in proportion as pofthumous avarice fhould become fafhionable, the landed eftates and the perfonal property of the whole country might be brought into *a condition of pofthumous and therefore irrevocable non-ufer and non-enjoyment for any beneficial purpofe whatever, during as long a fpace of time as executory devife can be wire-drawn to include.*

ACCORDING to thefe views of the pernicious confequences, which would be incident, to allowing truft of accumulation to be confolidated with executory devife, to the extent of the latitude, neceffary to be conceded to the latter, if the will of the late Mr. Thelluffon is to be fupported; to fanction the

truft in queftion would be eftablifhing, not merely a precedent againft *public good* in a *common way*, and upon common
probability, but a precedent fo much againft public good as to
engender a CERTAIN *public calamity.*

INDEED the late Mr. Thelluffon has not ventured to go all
the lengths of accumulation, which executory devife, in the latitude of principle requifite to fuftain his trufts, would allow.
But if thofe principles fhould be judicially fanctioned, a future Mr. Thelluffon will be encouraged to *tontine* upon the
conjunction of truft of accumulation and executory devife to
the utmoft ftretch of fuch latitude. Even the prefent time
will probably furnifh fome Thelluffons in extent of fortune,
and very many in extent of avaricious vanity and unfeeling-
nefs; and fhould a decree be made to execute Mr. Thelluffon's fcheme of pofthumous accumulation, there will be no
room for thofe apprehenfions, which alarmed him; and what
he tampered with, others may execute unhefitatingly, and in
the fulleft latitude the principles of fuch an adjudication
would admit, and fo openly refine the practice of executory
devife and truft of accumulation combined, into the moft
extended tontine of accumulation fuch a conjunction will
allow.

BUT for the purpofe of the prefent argument there is no
occafion to refort to that extremity of public mifchief, which
might refult from combining executory devife with truft of
accumulation, to the extent of the principles, upon which
only the late Mr. Thelluffon's executory devife can be fuf-
tained. The incidental public mifchief, even upon the rule
of executory devife under the limitations as I underftand
them, is I conceive, far greater than is neceffary to exclude
                                                      fuch

fuch a combination. I allow, that fo confining executory devife to it's proper limits, as I fee the boundary, greatly reduces the quantum of the evil. Though it denies to pofthumous accumulation the means of extending it with *certainty* to a century and a quarter; yet it leaves very probable means of protracting accumulation for half a century, that is, during a life in being, or feveral lives, not being mere faggots to feed the avaricious fire of executory devife, and twenty-one years beyond, with nine or ten months more; or at leaft leaves the compafs of one life however foreign to the provifions, if any life can be ufed for the mere purpofe of protracting executory devife. But under this reduction, the public evil would be monftroufly great. Still there would be a monftrous fcope for pofthumous accumulation. With every man having a capital of £ 600,000. the computed amount of the late Mr. Thelluffon's beginning fund of accumulation, there would be an opening, through accumulation and executory devife, to keep millions out of circulation, and to profcribe all beneficial enjoyment of fuch millions, till a fortune of feven or eight millions fhould be faved, and, in cafe of the accident of a minority of twenty-one years at the end of the executory devife, a fortune of about 17 or 18 millions.

Thus, under the moft ftrict interpretation of the boundary of executory devife, it will be impoffible to permit truft of accumulation and executory devife to be co-durable, without an opening for the moft dangerous mifchiefs to the country at large, at the pleafure of every teftator, whofe hard-heartednefs fhall prefer the unnatural gratification of pofthumous avarice to the natural proper and becoming difpofition of his fortune.

IN thefe views, therefore, of the unavoidable confequences of allowing truft of accumulation to be grafted upon executory devife, there arife fome very potent objections to the validity of the trufts in queftion.

IF the trufts in queftion are fuftainable, it muft be under an exercife of various powers, all of which are conferred by the law or indulged by the judicature of the country; namely,—the *general and ftrictly legal teftamentary power*,—the *particular* and *indulged power of executory devife*,—and the *permitted power of creating trufts*.

BUT every one of thefe powers exifts under limitations wholly inconfiftent with fheltering truft of accumulation under executory devife.

THE *general teftamentary power* was given, in order to enable thofe, who have acquired property, to appoint, who fhall fucceed them in the ufe and enjoyment, and under certain limitations to conftitute entails. But it is the aim of trufts of accumulations, fuch as the trufts in queftion, not to regulate ufe and enjoyment, but abfolutely to ftop and prevent them; nay, under the combined fhelter of truft and executory devife, to do fo during fuch a number of lives, as in *poffibility* gives a chance of continuing the prohibition of beneficial enjoyment for a century, and even in the events which have happened leaves a great probability of duration beyond fixty years. In other words a power entrufted for general convenience is applied to produce a general mifchief.

THE

THE *particular power of executory devise* emanated from an exercise of discretion by the courts both of law and equity. Executory devise was their joint production. Though it was against the genius of our law, and almost against its precepts, our courts indulged it. However the indulgence was expressly meted out for general accommodation. But by the trusts in question, it is attempted to make executory devise an instrument of general injury.

LIKE executory devise, *trust* was almost a stranger to our common law; and it long existed only at the mercy of the conscience of the party entrusted. At length our courts of equity for the sake of general convenience adopted trust, under the implied reserve of a discretion not to allow it for any unmeritorious purposes or against public good. But the trusts in question aim to gratify the fanciful avarice and the ambitious vanity of the individual testator, in an extensive scheme of posthumous accumulation; not only in breach of his duty as a parent and husband, and in despite of his dying professions to a numerous unoffending and attached family; but even to the danger of inflicting calamity upon the community at large.

UPON these grounds, then, I insist, that the pernicious scheme of accumulation, which it is the project of the late Mr. Thellusson's will to substantiate, so infects the trusts in question, as to place them wholly out of the reach of all shelter; either from the testamentary power; or from executory devise; or from that jurisdiction over trusts, which is the peculiar province of our courts of equity. So probed, and contrasted, the trust of accumulation, with its dependent executory devises, is so monstrously against public good,

as

as to threaten public calamity, if the precedent fhould be
eftablifhed ; and is therefore equally out of the compafs of
general teftamentary power, and out of the fhelter of executory devife and of the jurifdiction over trufts.

BOTH our courts of law and equity have been often called
upon to condemn upon the principles of public good and
public inconvenience. Upon thofe principles, they reject
cuftoms, they reject conditions, they reject covenants and
agreements. But if the view I have exhibited of the
trufts in queftion, in refpect of the confequence of mount-
ing truft of accumulation upon executory devife to accomplifh purpofes of the moft unmeritorious defcription, be in
any moderate degree founded ; there is more than a common call upon a court of equity, to reprobate the trufts
in queftion ; and to condemn them, not merely as privately
cruel and unnatural, but becaufe they are alfo fo pregnant
with the moft dangerous mifchiefs to the public intereft, as
to be wholly out of the fhelter both of excutory devife and
of truft. There is even fuch a peremptory call, as to render it
an indifpenfable duty to prevent their being carried into execution.

TRUST of pofthumous accumulation in any extent I take
to be rather a novel practice. I doubt, whether it can be
traced much earlier than the commencement of Lord Hardwicke's adminiftration of equity. I take it to have been
unknown long after Lord Chancellor Nottingham's time.
Had it been early attempted to make it an adjunct to
executory devife in the fmalleft degree, probably it would
have checked the eftablifhment of executory devife itfelf.
But my prefent conjecture is, that pofthumous accumulation was an *after thought*. In ftrictnefs, I fhould even fay,

that fuch pofthumous trufts, for aggrandifing families pro-fpectively by fufpending all beneficial enjoyment, ought not to have been in any degree countenanced by courts of equity, without whofe aid all pofthumous accumulation would be wholly impracticable.

THERE is a fort of invincible necefsity in permitting the owners of property to be mifers, that is, to be poor and miferable to the utmoft extreme during their own lives. Whilft they live, there is a *pofsibility* of expenditure. But if they were to be enabled by a court of equity to entail their fordid fyftem to the extent of truft in the nature of executory devife, an alleviation of the mifchiefs of avarice would be-come impofsible: for after the mifer's death there would be no perfon authorifed to relax from the accumulation; and it is not in any degree requifite, that a court of equity fhould pander to the continuation of avarice after the mifer's death.

HOWEVER, fomehow or other, the practice of pofthumous accumulation has, I confefs, infinuated itfelf. During *in-fancy* and *infanity,* fuch a truft is fcarce more than a re-ftraint upon expenditure almoft neceffarily incident to the fituation. Hence perhaps a truft for the fame purpofe efcaped obfervation. Pafsing this over might lead to at-tempting the thing, for a fhort time after, and in a way in-dependent both of minority and mental incapacity. Thus I conceive, that infenfibly, as it were, truft of accumula-tion obtained fome fort of footing. At length, I believe, that even refpectable lawyers have been led to fuppofe it al-lowable to annex truft of accumulation to executory devife, as if they were of the fame nature. And this notion may have been encouraged by the cafes, which have fettled, that, on an executory devife of *perfonal* eftate, the profits between

Y   the

the death of the teftator and the vefting of the executory
devife, fhall accumulate for the benefit of the executory devifee, wheie the will is without any other difpofition of them;
and that even for *real* eftate, if the devife be of a *refidue,* the
force of that word is fufficient to produce the fame effect. *(z)*
But the point of allowing the fame latitude to truft of accumulation as to executory devife, as far as I know at prefent,
has never been regularly debated. *(a).*

INDEED, in the cafe of Mr. Bradley's will, to which I
have before adverted more than once, there was an opening
for arguing the point on behalf of his next of kin.   But it
became unneceffary to debate any thing on their behalf :
Lord Thurlow inftantaneoufly queftioning the whole truft
of the will; and, aftei hearing the then Attorney Geneial in
fupport of the tiuft, decreeing for the next of kin, without
calling for any argument in their favour.   Had he decided
againft them, or called for aigument on their fide, it might have
led to difcufsing the point, whether truft of accumulation may
not be made co-extenfive with executory devife : for the will of
Mr. Bradley feems to have been framed, with a view to experiment
in that way, by directing a truft of accumulation from the
moiety of the yearly income of a capital of about £30,000.
in value, for 30 yeais, and then a truft of accumulation for
a fmaller portion of the fame yearly income for fixty years

(z) The doctrine and chief cafes on this fubject are collected in Mr FEARNE's Effiy
on CONTINGENT REMAINDERS and EXECUTORY DEVISES. See pages 434 to 439,
of that excellent work.   There are fome additional cafes in Mr. Powell's late edition
of the part on EXECUTORY DEVISES.

(a) The ftrongeft cafe of this kind, I have met with, is Lord Camden's decree
in Phipps *v* Kelynge, as ftated in Mr. POWELL's edition of Mr. FEARNE's book on
EXECUTORY DEVISES. See page 83, and in the note.   But no account is given of
any argument on the point, whether ACCUMULATION may be carried as far as EXE-
CUTORY DEVISE can be extended.

more.

more. By thus qualifying and dividing his truft of accumulation; and by making the accumulation fubfervient to a truft, to buy fuch books as might have a tendency to promote the interefts of virtue and religion and the happinefs of mankind, and to diftribute fuch books in Great Britain and the Britifh dominions; and further by referring it to the wifdom of the Court of Chancery to carry this charity, as Mr. Bradley called it, into execution; the learned and acute apathift, who made this experiment, on the combination of accumulation with executory devife one of the lateft acts of a long life in the line of a provincial conveyancing counfel, probably thought, that he fhould fucceed in thus difgracing truft and executory devife under the color of religion and morality; or at leaft that he fhould carry his point to the extent of his firft ftage of accumulation, namely the thirty years. But Lord Thurlow required to know, what could be urged in favour of fo ftrange and vague a truft; and having heard what duty extorted in its behalf from an amiable and able advocate the then Attorney General, his Lordfhip briefly and indignantly annulled the truft as unfit to be executed, and decreed the property to the next of kin to Mr. Bradley. Whether Lord Thurlow meant to include an opinion againft making truft of accumulation and executory devife commenfurate, I dare not undertake to fay. But I fhould not wonder, that an underftanding, fo mafculine and fo endowed, fhould have reached the point without the procefs of argument. At all events this cafe on Mr. Bradley's will cannot pofsibly be ufed, in favor of conftituting the fame extenfive boundary for truft of accumulation as is eftablifhed for executory devife. Much lefs can that cafe be fo ufed for truft of accumulation under fuch principles of latitude, as thofe, upon which only the trufts in queftion, even confidered as mere executory devife, can be fupported.

Y 2   THE

THE truth, I believe is, that *it remains to adjust the boundary of trust of accumulation*; and however in future that boundary may be adjusted in other respects, I should hope, that both the public interest and the honor of the law of the country will prove amply sufficient, to prevent applying the latitude of executory devise to trust of accumulation. Executory devise is the mixed progeny of our courts of law and our courts of equity. Trust is the child of our courts of equity. Both courts are deeply pledged to defend the public against all abuse of executory devise; and our courts of equity are as much bound to guard the public against injury from the abuse of trust. But I conceive, that the most insufferable abuses and the most injurious effects must be the result, if ever the time shall arrive, when executory devise and trust of accumulation shall be confounded, by an adjudication allotting the same large boundary to the former, as is settled for the latter, even under the limitations for which I have contended to prevent its excess. It is one thing to allow a period for the duration of an entail keeping property *unalienable*. It is another thing to allow a period for a trust making property *unusable* and unenjoyable. Lives in being and twenty one years beyond may be a reasonable and proper allowance, as a period for enduring the unbarrableness of entail; and yet be an allowance quite intolerable for enduring prohibition to use or enjoy property. I hope, that I shall never see judicial sanction given to such an abuse of executory devise, as shall bring trust of accumulation within the same latitude of limits. At least I trust, that if such an adjudication shall pass, it will not be in a case like the present one; for it will not, I apprehend, be found possible in the present case to annex executory devise to trust of accumulation, without a dangerous extension in point of principle to the latitude of executory devise,

                                                                and

and at the fame time making that extenfion to fuftain a teftamentary difpofition fo unmeritorious, that to countenance it, may caufe reproach both to Englifh law and Englifh judicature.

———————————————

I NOW come, my Lord, to my *third and laft general head of objection* to the teftamentary trufts in queftion.

Third and laft general Head of Objection to the Trufts, namely, *uncertainty in the defcription of the primary beneficial devifees, and of the fucceffion to and after them*

HERE my objection is, that the beneficial trufts, conftituted by the will of the late Mr. Thelluffon to commence when his ambitious profcriptive truft of accumulation is made to ceafe, are fo vague and obfcure as to be rejectable for uncertainty.

THE objection, I have to offer in this refpect, appears to me to deferve a very ferious confideration. But from the nature of it, I hope to be able to explain myfelf on this part of the cafe in a very brief manner.

THE objection arifes from the particular language, in which the teftator has thought fit to defcribe the beneficial devifees appointed to take under the partition he directs to be made, when the truft of accumulation fhall be determined.

THE truft for this purpofe orders a divifion of the eftates into three lots of equal value, and that one of the lots fhall be conveyed to the ufe of the *eldeft male lineal defcendant then living* of his eldeft fon in tail male: and the direction for the firft limitation of ufe of the two other lots in favor of the male defcendants of the two other fons of the teftator is in the fame language.

BUT I beg leave to infift, that this very outfet of the beneficial trufts is a chef d'œuvre of obfcurity.

THE

THE teſtator, by *eldeſt male lineal deſcendant*, may mean the eldeſt of that deſcription *in point of age*, without in any degree regarding heirſhip to his eldeſt or other ſon. This indeed ſeems to be the moſt literal interpretation. Yet that he ſhould diſregard heirſhip, and thus wholly look to age, is not very probable.

BUT he may mean by *eldeſt lineal male deſcendant*, ſuch deſcendant, as ſhould be *heir male* of the body of each ſon, and be both *very* heir, or heir *general*, and *male*.

HE may alſo mean, by *eldeſt male lineal deſcendant*, an *heir male*, as uſually oppoſed to an *heir general*.

HERE then are *three* uncertainties, of ſuch a nature, that the will becomes very like a deviſe to A. B. or C. But if the deviſe was literally ſo framed, would the Court undertake to gueſs, what the teſtator intended? Would not the Court rather ſay, that the deviſe was too uncertain to be interpreted; and that if teſtators will exerciſe the teſtamentary power enigmatically, it is fit, that the will which the law makes for them, where they die inteſtate, ſhould prevail?

BUT this *triple* uncertainty, who is meant by *eldeſt male lineal deſcendant*, is not the only uncertainty of the deſcription. This ſhews the uncertainty as to *perſon*, when the time of taking comes. But there is another uncertainty, namely, of *time*, when the deſcription ſhall attach. In this reſpect the uncertainty is even *quintuple*. The teſtator might mean the *eldeſt male lineal deſcendant* at *the very moment the truſt of accumulation ſhall ceaſe*. But his words are ſo equivocal, that he might mean any one of *four other times more diſtant*, that is,—*when all the accumulated monies ſhall be in-*
veſted

vefted in lands,—or when thofe lands fhall be valued,—or when they fhall be allotted for partition,—or when the conveyance of partition fhall be executed.

THUS, from the teftator's anxiety to continue the fecret, who were to take beneficially, to the very laft moment; and fo to make his executory devife fecure againft all alienation till the moment of actual enjoyment fhall arrive; he was tempted to exprefs himfelf fo darkly, and fo to wrap up his meaning, that only *four* words are open to *eight* uncertainties. In fhort, it feems as if, after excluding *every body* for a time, which may be feventy or even an hundred years, he was determined at laft to leave his eftate to *nobody.*

NOR is this complication of uncertainty, in the outfet of the beneficial trufts, the whole extent of the obfcurity which pervades them. Both in the remainders in tail male to the fecond and every other male lineal defcendant of each of the fons, and in the crofs-remainders of entail as between the uncertain male defcendants of the teftator's three fons, the fame ftrain of ambiguity, or rather of unintelligibility, prevails. It is uncertainty upon uncertainty, or rather one aggregate of uncertainties upon another. Indeed it could not be well otherwife; for the *octuple* uncertainty in the *defcriptio perfonæ,* with which the defcription begins, is necefferily continued, to make the feveral branches of the enigma confiftent, and to make the myftery all of a piece. Accordingly there is an uniform repetition of or reference to the vague words *eldeft male lineal defcendant,* with a continuation of the vague words *then living,* to the end of the chapter of this enigmatical part of the will. In other words, it is the will of *octuple* uncertainty at leaft *three times three.*

2   THE

THE queſtion then is, whether this accumulation of ob-ſcurity and equivocalneſs will not juſtify the court, in treating the beneficial truſts for the eldeſt male lineal deſcendants of the three ſons, as too *uncertain* to be properly carried into execution, and therefore as void.

I AM perfectly aware, that it is the duty of judicature to do its utmoſt, to give effect, to laſt wills, and to conveyances of every deſcription; and that it both is and ought to be an arduous thing, to prevail in an attempt to nullify inſtruments for uncertainty.

BUT our courts do ſometimes go the length of rejecting, not only *wills,* but even *deeds* and *agreements* for uncertainty. There are precedents of this both at law and in equity.

IN Viner's Abridgment, title *Deviſe,* letter *D.* there is a large collection of cafes of this deſcription on *wills*; and in many of them deviſes and legacies appear to have been con-demned for uncertainty.

THE Abridgment of Equity Cafes, under the fame title, fur-niſhes ſome precedents of deviſes, void for uncertainty either in the deſcription of the thing or of the perſon of the devi-fee or legatee; and the fame ſubject is taken up, with ſome additions, in the title *Legacies and Deviſes,* in the new edition of Bacon's Abridgment, which well deſerves to be entitled an improved edition of that uſeful and in ſome parts very able work.

IN Viner's Abridgment, title *Grant,* letter *R.* there is a collection of cafes of *grants* void for the uncertainty of the
5   thing

thing granted; and fome other branches of the fame title furnifh matter of a like kind: and Bacon's Abridgment, under the fame title, letters *C.* and *F.* contains much matter explaining where a grant fhall be void for uncertainty.

IN Coke upon Littleton, fol. 20. b. there is the cafe of the gift to A. for life, remainder to B. in tail, remainder to C. *in formá prædictá*; in which this laft remainder was held void for uncertainty.

IN Corbet's cafe, 1. Co. 84. b. and 85. a. Lord Anderfon, after citing a cafe, in which a condition enlarging a leafe for life to a fee was held utterly void for uncertainty, accounts for it, by obferving, that judges ought to know the intent of the parties by certain and fenfible words, fuch as are agreeable and confonant to the rules of law; and then he puts a further cafe of grant, which was adjudged void for the uncertainty and infenfibility.

LORD Vaughan, in his Reports 176, concludes his judgment in Crowley and Swindley, for rejecting a claufe of diftrefs, by faying, that words being infenfible ought to be rejected.

IN Bromley and Jefferies and others, 2. Vern. 415, Lord Chancellor Somers refufed to decree fpecific performance of an agreement, partly becaufe it was uncertain.

THERE are alfo recent precedents of rejection for uncertainty.

IN the cafe of Leflie and the Duke of Devonfhire, 2. Bro Cha. Cas. 188. Lord Kenyon, whilft Mafter of the Rolls, held

Z   a bequeft

a bequeſt of ſome mortgages, which were ſo deviſed, as to refer to two ſets of limitations of two other eſtates, without ſpecifying which ſet was meant, too uncertain to have effect; and obſerved, that where the Court cannot ſee it's way, the property ſhould be conſidered as undiſpoſed of.

In Thomas againſt Thomas in 6. Durnford and Eaſt 67. a deviſe was held void by the Court of King's Bench for uncertainty in the deſcription of the deviſee.

In the third volume of Mr. Veſey's Reports, there is your Lordſhip's judgment in the great caſe on the *mutual wills* of the late Horace Lord Walpole and his great nephew the Earl of Orford; and I collect from it, that your Lordſhip refuſed to enforce the alledged contract of mutual will between the two teſtators, very much under the impreſſion of the contract's being too vague and uncertain.

In the caſe on the will of the famous conveyancing counſel of the North the late Mr. Bradley, your Lordſhip's great predeceſſor Lord Thurlow, as I have always underſtood, conſidered the object of Mr. Bradley's experiment of a truſt of accumulation, as too vague: and though the teſtator, not only cunningly referred himſelf to the diſcretion of the Court to aſſiſt the mode of executing his truſt; but cunningly divided it into parts, ſo as to give the better opportunity of having the benefit of the *cy près* doctrine of this Court; yet Lord Thurlow refuſed to modify the truſt and ſo to purge it of it's vague properties; and refuſed to execute the truſt even in the ſmalleſt degree.

FROM

FROM thefe precedents it is plain, that contracts, deeds, wills, and inftruments of every fort, may be rejected both at law and in equity for uncertainty.

HERE then the point is, whether the uncertainties I impute to the trufts in the prefent cafe are deficient either in *quantity* or in *quality*.

UPON this point, we afk the judgment of your Lordfhip; not in the cafe of a will of honourable intention; but on a will of profcription, a will againft nature, a will againft the publick good in a monftrous degree; on a teftament, not only *inofficiofum* to the family of the teftator, but *inofficiofum* to the public at large; on a will contrary both to private duties and to public intereft.

I TRUST, that fuch a teftamentary difpofition will not be affifted by this Court, without a neceffity the moft invincible.

I TRUST, alfo, that the confequence of thus refufing to ftamp the beneficial trufts for the male defcendants of the three fons of the teftator, will not be, to let in the truft towards paying off the *national debt*; and fo to convert a victory over the teftator's executory devifes and trufts of accumulation for remote male defcendants, into a complete difinherifon of his whole family, both prefent and future. There are indeed, cafes, both of remainders *(b)* and executory devifes, *(c)* which have been held to operate immediately, where the preceding eftates have failed taking effect. But

(b) See Fearne on Conting Rem. and Exec. Dev. 3d ed. 163 and 234 and the additional cafes in thofe parts of 4th ed

(c) See Fearne on Conting Rem and Exec Devife, 3d ed. 399 and the further matter in that part of 4th ed. in the volume edited in 1795, with additions by Mr. Powell.

Z 2   I fubmit,

I fubmit, that there is not any room for applying fuch cafes to the will in queftion.   In this refpect the will of the late Mr. Thelluffon is particularly conftituted.   According to the fettlement, his will directs of the vaft landed eftates, which it was his project to accumulate for remote lineal male defcendants of his three fons, there is to be inferted, after the remainder in tail male to an only male defcendant of the three fons, in cafe of there being but one, a *remainder* to the ufe of the truftees in fee.   But this ultimate remainder is not *immediately* and *fimply* upon a truft to fell the lands for the ufe of the finking fund.   On the contrary, by the will, the truft for the finking fund is made the fubject of a fubfequent and diftinct claufe, and in that is *expreſsly* and *pointedly* directed to take place UPON FAILURE OF MALE LINEAL DESCENDANTS of the teftator's three fons AS AFORESAID.   Therefore to let in the truft for the finking fund, whilft any fuch male lineal defcendants are to be found, would be, againft the moft expreſs language of the teftator : and would be to conftrue a *diftinct* and *fubftantive* truft for the finking fund upon the contingency of *failure of lineal male defcendants* of the three fons, as if the truft was conftituted without any fuch contingency annexed ; and fo to deprive the heir and next of kin of the benefit of the only cafe, in which the will omits to exclude them.   The teftator cannot be fuppofed to have forefeen, that the fettlement, he directs to be made upon the lineal male defcendants of his three fons, would be difappointed by the uncertainty of his own language.   The cafe, then, in this refpect is left unprovided for by the teftator.   Unlefs, therefore, the Court fhould undertake to fupply the omifsion for him, the truft for the finking fund becomes in effect the fame, as if it was fimply and unconnectedly on a *general failure of iſſue male* of the three fons, and fo under the rule of executory devife

                                                            abfolutely

abfolutely void. But will the Court undertake fuch an office for the teftator againft his heir widow and children; merely becaufe the unnatural fpirit of the will may juftify conjecturing, how the teftator, if he was living to fupply the omiffion, probably would have arranged the matter between the finking fund and his family *(d)* ?

———————————————————

AT length I reach the conclufion of my arguments againft the laft will of the late Mr. Thelluffon, fo far as it affects the grand bulk of his vaft fortune, and fo far as it is now under confideration; that is, fo far as the will excludes all his exifting unoffending family from his general real property and from his refiduary perfonal eftate.

Conclufion of the Argument.

THE refult of the whole, as I fee the cafe, ftands nearly thus.—The trufts of the will are impeachable for various *dangerous exceffes of the boundary of* EXECUTORY DEVISE.—Of the exceffes imputed, thofe the moft clearly proveable are fuch, as make the *irregular and barely permitted* entail by EXECUTORY DEVISE a CERTAIN mode of keeping property of every kind *unalienable* for nearly *a century and a half* · and if this be permitted, a mode of entail, the permiffion of which originates from the *difcretion* of the courts of Weftminfter Hall, will in duration be greatly elevated above and greatly extended beyond the *ordinary and ftrictly legal mode of entailing inheritance*; that is, in the proportion, which the

(d) See in 3 Vef Jun 317 the cafe of Holmes and Craddock, which is a late decifion of his Honour the prefent Mafter of the Rolls, againft fpeculating to abridge the contingency of a legacy to the prejudice of an *heir* and fee feveral other cafes of a like kind there cited.

5 *certainty*

certainty of almoft *a century and a half* bears above an *uncertainty* not in *probability* reaching above *fifty or fixty years and never free from inftantaneous determination.*—If *any one* of the imputed excefles be proved againft the trufts, it will be fufficient to invalidate them.—Independent of all excefs of the limits of executory devife, the trufts in queftion are impeachable *for conjoining with executory devife a truft of* ACCUMULATION, fo conftituted in principle, as to make the *whole income* of property, of every defcription and in every extent, *unenjoyable* and *unexpendible* for as long a time, as, by our law, entail, thus greatly extended, as I have defcribed, by the artificial ftretching of *executory devife,* can make property *unalienable.*— If fuch a truft of *executory devife and accumulation combined,* fhall prevail, it will be a precedent, enabling teftators to carry *pofthumous accumulation to the full extent of pofthumous entail,* thus cunningly protracted through executory devife ; and fo will authorize putting all kinds of property throughout the kingdom, into a ftate of *non-ufer, non-enjoyment,* and *non-expenditure,* with *certainty* for almoft a century and a half ; and, even in the prefent cafe of beginning experiment, fuch an effect will moft probably be produced to the extent of about fixty or feventy years.—Throughout alfo this project of pofthumous avarice, there is an apparent *tampering* with executory devife and truft of accumulation, to abufe a mere indulgence, and to elude and defraud the real boundaries.—Further, in all this, the fcheme of the teftator is of the moft *unmeritorious kind* ; is to abufe teftamentary power ; is to abufe executory devife ; and is to abufe truft ; for purpofes as dangerous to the public intereft, as they are cruel and unnatural towards the family of the teftator ; for purpofes facrificing public welfare, private duties, and private affections, at the fhrine of avaritious vanity.—From an eagernefs,

eagernefs, alfo, to keep all fuccefsion to his fortune *out of fight*, the teftator has fallen into fuch an obfcurity of defcription of the heirs and fuccefsion he meant to appoint, as feemingly to give the opportunity of invalidating the will for *uncertainty* of exprefsion.

EVEN on the ground of *uncertainty*, I fhould hope, that when that objection fhall be thoroughly invefligated ; and the inftances I have generally referred to, of rejecting devifes and legacies for that defect, fhall be fully confidered ; there will be found, in a cafe *not merely unmeritorious*, but *monftrous* in all views of it public as well as private, more than fufficient to juftify a court of equity, in the moft unqualified condemnation of the trufts in queftion.

BUT at all events I truft, that at leaft fome of the charges againft the trufts, on the ground of *excefsive executory devife* and *excefsive pofthumous accumulation*, are invincible. Upon the mere fuperficies of executory devife, I can conceive, that *momentarily* the moft refpectable underftanding might not become fufficiently imprefsed to detect the illegality of the trufts. But when the rule of executory devife is traced to its real origin ; when the reafons of indulging executory devife are examined ; when the *fpirit* of the boundary is fought for ; nay, in fome refpects when the *letter itfelf* is accurately attended to, and when all this is contrafted, with the *grofs tampering* of the late Mr. Thellufon's will to pervert an indulgence for general convenience into a fource of public mifchief as well as private profcription ; then, as I at leaft feel the fubject of this cafe, there will be found feveral clear grounds for declaring the trufts a complicated excefs of the

2   boun

boundary of executory devise, and therefore illegal, without
so much as entering upon further confideration of the cafe.
But fhould the cafe be purged of all the imputed exceffes of
executory devife, ftill, exclufive of the objection of the
vague and uncertain language ufed in conftructing the beneficial part of the trufts, there would remain againft them the
monftrous attempt to render *entail of property and the non-
enjoyment of its income co-extenfive in duration*; and the monftrous attempt, to effectuate this, by making the rule of
executory devife fubfervient to truft of accumulation. So
confolidating executory devife and truft of accumulation,
I confider as conjoining, what their feveral natures require
to be kept diftinct and feparate. But the late Mr. Thelluffon
has thought fit to conjoin them: and if the conjunction be
irregular, then on the part of his injured and deceived wife
children and grandchildren, I infift, that the juft forfeit for
that irregularity is a total failure of all effect from the illegal
connection, and confequently not merely a failure of the
truft of accumulation, but a failure of the fubfequent and
dependent executory devifes. The teftator prefumptuoufly
confolidates them. If he is irregular as well as prefumptu-
ous, and was living, he could not complain of a court of
equity, for refufing to feparate what he has confolidated, and
for fo condemning his truft of accumulation and his executory devifes to the fame difappointment.

THUS, as I fee the prefent cafe after a long and anxious
ftudy, it involves, not only the valuable interefts of the family,
on whofe behalf I have argued, but the credit of the law of
England. If it is adjudged againft the will, at the fame
time the Thelluffon family fhall be relieved from the effect
                                                    of

of an unnatural teftamentary difpofition, the law of England and the courts of Weftminfter Hall will be fafe from all imputation of improperly enduring executory devife and trufts of the fame nature. The victory over the will of the late Mr. Thelluffon will be gained for Englifh jurifprudence, even in a greater degree than for the Thelluffon family. Notwithftanding the immenfe deprivations to the family of the late Mr. Thelluffon from his abforbing and felfifh truft of accumulation, they are fo far happily fituate, as to be able to bear the injury, under which in that event they muft fubmit to fuffer. But fhould your Lordfhip, in your character of firft Judge of Englifh Equity find yourfelf under an invincible necefsity of enforcing fuch a will, I am at a lofs to conceive, how Englifh Law and Englifh Judicature can efcape at leaft the liability to reproach, for being ancillary to pofthumous avarice, at the rifque of gradually merging all the property of the kingdom in *mere trufteefhip*, and of fo gradually depriving the *people of England* of all *beneficial enjoyment*.

THEREFORE againft a decree confirming the late Mr. Thelluffon's profcriptive will,—I deprecate to your Lordfhip; not merely, on behalf of the interefts of the Thelluffon family; but on the behalf alfo of the character of the law of England, which I fear will be highly degraded, if the will of Mr. Thelluffon fhall be fuffered to prevail:—and I deprecate to your Lordfhip, on behalf of the characters of thofe venerable Judges; by whom the law of executory devife, and the law of truft of accumulation, were under an exercife of judicial difcretion founded for general utility, and whofe fame is thereby become refponfible for the confequences:—and I

A a

alfo

also deprecate to your Lordship, on behalf of the people of England, whose most essential interests may be deeply wounded, should executory devise and trust of accumulation be suffered to degenerate into public mischiefs.

If your Lordship shall annul the monstrous executory devise and the monstrous trust of accumulation, against a decree for which I thus solemnly deprecate, you will prove, that a great mind is above prejudices, however seducing, and however generally prevalent; and you will, I am persuaded, entitle yourself to the thanks of the people of England.

It so happens also, that the task of annulling the will is far more easy, than that of confirming. The objections, against the will of Mr Thelluson, are numerous. Any one of them, if well founded, will be sufficient to overturn the will. But if the will is to be sustained, all those numerous objections will be to be disposed of; and this I conceive will at least be a work of immense labour, even to your Lordship's mental powers, great as they are. In this view of the case, then, to overturn the will is the course, not only most honourable, but most easy.

In hearing the arguments against the will, very much of the valuable time, of your Lordship and the reverend judges your assistants, hath been occupied; and I feel, almost with repentance, that I have been more particularly the cause of so long an intrusion. But perhaps this great cause may now take a short turn in the hearing. It is a cause in many respects very singular. One, amongst other singularities, which I at least impute to it, is, that it is a cause against a last will with *every body* interested to overturn it, with *nobody* really interested to

preserve

preferve it from deftruction. It is the caufe of a will excluding every perfon now living; and every perfon who fhall be
born for many, very many, years to come, probably for
about feventy years, pofsibly for even more than a century.
It is a will alfo againft public intereft. This may lead to a
great abbreviation of the caufe in its fubfequent progrefs.
Perhaps, in this view of it, the law officers of the crown may
not think it a duty to prefs for a decree in favour of the
will. Perhaps, even the counfel of the truftees may not feel
themfelves bound, to be exceedingly anxious, to eftablifh a
will againft public good for the fake of fome future and diftant generation of the name of Thelluffon *(e)*.

Upon the whole, I fubmit to your Lordfhip, that the trufts
in queftion, in every view of them, ought to be declared invalid
and inoperative. and confequently that, as to the grand bulk
of Mr. Thelluffon's immenfe fortune, this court ought to
treat the cafe as an inteftacy, and accordingly to declare a
refulting truft for the widow and children of the teftator;
that is; as to the general real eftate for the eldeft fon
and heir; and as to the refiduary perfonal eftate for the widow
and fix children of the teftator, according to the ftatute of
diftribution.

Should fuch a decree be the refult of thefe caufes, your
Lordfhip will refcue the law of England, or rather its judicatures, from the imputation of introducing fuch an extended
pofthumous accumulation; as was never endured by the law
or judicatures of any other country; and as cannot be endured

---

(e) It is here proper to take notice, that neither the counfel for the truftees
in the will, nor the counfel for the crown, acted, as if they confidered themfelves at liberty to decline making their beft exertions. They argued the cafe
for the will, very much at length, with very great and able exertion, and with
very great learning.

in this, without public mischiefs of a kind the most threaten-ing and alarming.

Of such a decree, Lord Chancellor Nottingham, were he living, might be induced to speak in terms of the highest eulogium. In justice to your Lordship as the author of such a decree, he might naturally and properly say to you,

" I was the great patron of executory devise and of trusts
" of the same nature. Lord Coke and the judges of his
" time, for the sake of public convenience, permitted entail
" by executory devise both for inheritance and terms of
" years in lands, to the extent of a life in being, and upon
" a principle which included personal chattels. Lord Hale
" and the other judges of my time extended the permission,
" to two or more co-existing persons, where they were named
" to take in a course of settlement, as in the case of succes-
" sive remainders to various existing persons for their lives.
" After Lord Hale's death a new alarm took place amongst
" some of the judges; least, under shelter of executory devise,
" the law against perpetuity of entail should be gradually
" undermined: and so impressed, they strove to deny to a
" term of years, what was too clearly confirmed to be avowedly
" denied to inheritance; and had they succeeded, probably
" it would have been attempted to repeal executory devise
" for the latter also. But I was successful in resisting this
" attempt against executory devise; and so gradually every
" species of property after my time became in substance
" equally the subject of entail and settlement. I was not,
" however, blind, to the possibility of abuses of entail by
" executory devise and by trusts of the same nature. Fore-
" seeing such abuses, I pledged this Court, that the dif-

2   " cretion

" cretion over executory devifes and over trufts fhould be
" effectually exerted to prevent public inconvenience. It
" was referved for you, to decide, whether the pledge thus
" coming from me fhould be made good. You have had an
" arduous duty to perform ; and the ftrong prejudices in fa-
" vour of a literal adherence to the boundary of executory
" devife have encreafed a difficulty otherwife fufficiently
" great. Many judges of a very high clafs might have been
" very unequal to fuch a conteft with fraud upon executory
" devife. But you have fhewn yourfelf fully equal to the
" fituation. You have unmafked the fraud attempted by
" the will of Mr. Thelluffon. You have prevented entail by
" executory devife, from being artificially and irregularly
" extended beyond entail by the ordinary legal mode of
" fettlement. You have exemplified the true principle of
" the boundary of executory devife. You have prevented
" truft, from being made an inftrument for effecting the
" double mifchief of excefsive entail and excefsive accumu-
" lation. You have fhewn, that the boundary of entail and
" the boundary of pofthumous accumulation are diftinct ;
" and that what may be properly allowed for the former
" may be intolerable for the latter. You have proclaimed,
" that neither executory devife, nor truft, can be made
" fubfervient to plans of ftopping both the alienation and
" ufe of Englifh property for almoft a century and an half.
" You have evinced, that Englifh judicature is too watchful
" of pofthumous avarice to minifter to it's monftrous excefses.
" By all this, you have done juftice, not only to the cha-
" racters of the founders and patrons of executory devife ;
" but to the law of England itfelf ; and to that principle of
" public utility, which is the only legitimate father of
" executory

" executory devife and truft of the fame nature and of then
" refpective boundaries."

[In the Appendix, the Reader will find two papers connected with
the preceding THREE ARGUMENTS. No. I. of the Appendix is
a ftatement of the cafe, which is the fubject of the Arguments;
and though it is part of a paper prepared by the Author of them
for the ufe of the other Counfel againft the Will of the late Mr.
Thelluffon, before inftitution of the two Caufes, in which the three
Arguments were delivered, it doth not materially differ from the
cafe as it appears on the Bills and Anfwers   No. II. of the Appendix is introduced for the fake of fhewing, how far the remarks,
in the courfe of the *Three Arguments*, as to the probable confequences of giving effect to the late Mr Thelluffon's teftamentary
trufts of accumulation, may be relied upon.]

APPENDIX.

A P P E N D I X.

No. I.

EXTRACT *from a* CASE *and* ARGUMENT *on the* LAST WILL *of the late* PETER THELLUSSON, ESQUIRE, *by the Author of the Three Arguments against that Will now printed;—consisting of the* INTRODUCTION *and the* CASE STATED.

INTRODUCTION.

THE laft will of the late Mr. Thelluffon prefents a very fingular fubject for the confideration and decifion of Englifh judicature. Our courts of juftice have often been called upon to refift and counteract fchemes for unduly preventing the alienation of property, and for introducing a perpetuity of entail But the ambition of interdicting all expenditure, even of the income, from an overgrown fortune, till it fhall have accumulated into a landed fortune of millions, and of making the devifees of fuch accumulated wealth uncertain till the very moment the accumulation is appointed to ceafe, feems to have been in great meafure referved to diftinguifh the afpiring and ingenious avarice of Mr. Thelluffon and from the fate of his grand teftamentary arrangement for this vain and oftentatious purpofe, it will probably be afcertained, whether the policy of the law of England is not as adequate to difappoint monftrous projects of accumulation, as it has hitherto proved to limit the excefs of entails, and to obftruct the eftablifhment of perpetuities.

When

When I was first consulted on the extraordinary trusts, to which Mr The luffon's last will devotes his very immense refiduary fortune, I was struck with the novelty of the case in some points of view, and I forefaw the great difadvantage, under which his family would be, in contesting those trusts, from the confequential want of direct precedents to affist judicial decision.   It therefore became me to be extremely cautious in forming my opinion.   Those of the Thelluffon family, who are deeply interested against the grand trust of accumulation, and who honoured me with their confidence, had a right to expect great anxiety to affist them professionally in a business of such magnitude of value.   Exclufive also of the just demands upon me as one of their counfel, I was so difgusted with the testator's unfeeling exclufion of all his children and grand-children, without sparing even issue in the womb at his death, as to feel zealous to extricate his family from the effects of his unnatural project   But then on this very account it was proper, that I should be the more on my guard in expressing my fentiments; least my prejudices, against the grand refiduary bequest, for its extreme harfhness, should make me blind to the arguments in favour of its legality, and so betray me into encouraging an ill-founded hope of victory, over a testamentary difpofition, which, however odious, might not fall within any principle of judicial condemnation.

However, notwithstanding these checks upon me, I avowed my doubts—whether the trusts, which Mr. Thelluffon's will creates of his refiduary estate, that is, of the great bulk of his princely fortune, were not a nullity,—and whether, from this failure of the trusts, his refiduary estate, both real and personal, is not in effect devolved upon his family, in the same way, as if he had died intestate.

In thus questioning the legality of the late Mr. Thelluffon's great refiduary bequest, I stated various grounds upon which the trusts of it appeared to me attackable.   But I endeavoured to be as brief and general in the statement, as was confistent with being intelligible, and with that view I repressed my ardour to fubdue an odious precedent of testamentary difpofition.   Sometimes anxious length of opinion generates ungracious comments instead of thankful acknowledgments. Sometimes, the more zealous a professional person is in his first services, the more unnecessary he is deemed afterwards.   There was a time when I would not have listened to such truths   But too frequent experience of their importance at length forces me to be somewhat mindful of them; and under their influence, I was become fearful of erring by being over explicit, and I was prudentially careful to avoid the imputation of doing more than was either expected or wished for.

But

But though I ſtudied ſhortneſs of expreſſion in anſwering the caſe upon the will of the late Mr. Thelluſſon, there was enough ſtated, to lead to all or moſt of the topicks, which influenced my ſentiments againſt the great reſiduary truſt. Therefore I had the ſatisfaction of knowing, that ſomewhat like an outline of my impreſſions was communicated, and that ſo the immediate object of conſulting me was as ſufficiently accompliſhed, as could be expected in the form of opinion from my means of information.

In this ſtate of the buſineſs there was an opportunity of ceaſing to claim my profeſſional aſſiſtance in the buſineſs, and I am not unaware, that from the talents and learning of the other counſel conſulted, my further ſervices might have been ſafely diſpenſed with.

But it was not thought fit ſo to treat my firſt efforts againſt the will in queſtion. On the contrary, thoſe intereſted to ſet aſide the great reſiduary truſt of the will, and their ſolicitors, not only in the moſt handſome terms evinced a deſire of continuing confidence in me, but anxiouſly ſolicited the fulleſt expreſſion of my ideas in the form of a written argument

Accordingly I have adventured upon ſuch an undertaking, under the impreſſion and hope, that my labours in the firſt inſtance, however unſucceſsful they ſhall be, may, when the buſineſs ſhall be ripe for diſcuſſion in the proper forum, prove in ſome degree ſubſidiary to thoſe capable of far ſuperior exertion. If I ſhall adminiſter uſeful matter to be worked upon by their higher energies, I ſhall conſider myſelf as having fulfilled the purpoſe expected from me.

Thus engaged in this buſineſs, I ſhall proceed to ſtate and argue the caſe without any further introduction.

THE CASE STATED.

The caſe on the laſt will of the late Mr. Thelluſſon, under the impreſſion, that the purpoſe, of arguing the validity of the truſts created of his reſiduary eſtate real and perſonal, renders it convenient to include ſome ſhort account of his ſituation and character, and to give the outline of the whole will, may be thus ſtated.

The late Mr Thelluſſon was born at Paris in the year 1735; but may be conſidered legally as born a ſubject of the republic of Geneva,

his

his father being at the time Minister from that republic to the court of France   He came over to England about the year 17 , when he was in his   year.   He settled in London as a merchant, and was naturalized by Act of Parliament in 17 .   He began here with a fortune supposed to be about £.10,000.   Many things concurred, to distinguish him as a commercial person, and to insure his acquisition of great wealth   He had an understanding of compass, acuteness, quickness, and discrimination.   His knowledge of commerce was deemed extensive and profound.   His industry in the application of his talents and information to mercantile affairs was continual.   He possessed and exhibited a spirit of enterprize in his undertakings: but it was corrected by a penetrative caution and a solid judgment.   His thirst for money was unquenchable, and appeared so to absorb his feelings, as to render them in great measure subservient to the acquisition of it. His œconomy therefore was severe and unceasing.   But with all his avarice he did not quite answer the description of one, *qui non possedit divitias, sed divitiis possessus est.* for, though he was for many purposes rather a slave to wealth than the possessor of it, yet neither in his stile of living, nor in the management of his family and domestic concerns, did he usually condescend to that coarse vulgar and ungentlemanly sordidness, which some misers practise.   In truth his avarice for the most part was of the higher order, and in some respects assumed a dignified mein.   His constitution of body was naturally robust; and he was too temperate to injure it by any excess. The result of all this was a prosperity in the commercial line almost unexampled.

At the time of making his last will, which was in April 1796, the state of his family and fortune was to this effect.

Some time after having settled in England, he married Miss Ann Woodford.   This Lady, of whose merits his will with all its faults bears ample testimony, was living.   By her he had living three sons and three daughters.   The three sons were settled together in partnership as merchants in the house in London, from which their father had recently retired; and were prosecuting the same extensive commerce.   All three of the sons had married most respectably with the full approbation of their father   The eldest and second sons had issue, the former three sons and two daughters; the latter two daughters; and both had a prospect of more issue.   The third son was but recently married   All three of the sons, a little before the date of Mr. Thelluson's will, were become Members of the British House of Commons, and there was reason to presume, that his pride was not a little gratified at a circumstance remarkable for any father, and much more so for a father of foreign birth and of a foreign family,

and

and only become a full subject of Great-Britain by an act of naturalization. Of the three daughters of Mr. Thelluſſon, two were of age, and the eldeſt was married to the Honourable Mr. Auguſtus Phipps, a younger brother of Lord Mulgrave.

In reſpect to the fortune of Mr. Thelluſſon, it may be ſufficient here to mention, that notwithſtanding very conſiderable proviſions advanced for his three ſons, amounting according to the ſtatement of his will to nearly £.16,000. a piece, and notwithſtanding the portion he had advanced to his eldeſt daughter on her marriage with Lord Mulgrave's brother, the aggregate of Mr. Thelluſſon's real and perſonal eſtate probably amounted in value to ſome ſum about ſeven hundred thouſand pounds. I ſay probably: becauſe ſo it hath been eſtimated ſince his death; and no circumſtance appears to have occurred to cauſe any material encreaſe between the date of his will and the time of his death, which was little more than the interval of a year.

Thus ſituate in family and fortune, and being above the age of ſixty, and in the moſt perfect health, and at leaſt ſeeming to be on terms of the moſt affectionate amity with all the near relatives I have deſcribed, the late Mr. Thelluſſon made the eccentric laſt will, which is now in queſtion.

THE will bears date the ſecond of April 1796.

The firſt part is chiefly taken up with making proviſion for his Lady.—For this purpoſe he firſt gives to her 300 guineas payable in ten days after his death. He then bequeaths to her all the wines and liquors at his capital meſſuage at Plaiſtow near Bromley in Kent, and all the corn, hay and ſtraw, in the buildings and ſtack-yards, and all the jewels, watches and trinkets, in her poſſeſſion and cuſtody. Theſe bequeſts to his wife are followed by a legacy of 300 guineas a-piece, to three gentlemen, who are made truſtees throughout the will, namely, his brother-in-law the Reverend Matthew Woodford Archdeacon of Wincheſter, James Stanley Eſquire Barriſter at Law, and Emperor John Alexander Woodford Eſquire. but this is explained to be an acknowledgment for their trouble.—Next, he gives 25 guineas a-piece for a ring to Mr. Lear and Mr. Handaſyde, with whom, after retiring from his general mercantile buſineſs, the teſtator continued to have a ſugar concern: but theſe rings were given conditionally;

ditionally; that is, if, they were in partnership with him at his death.
—Then, after giving half a year's wages to all his servants; the teftator refumes the confideration of his wife, by devifing his capital
meffuage at Plaiftow, with its lands, gardens, and appurtenances; and
with the linen, houfehold furniture, glafs, china, pictures (except
fome family pictures afterwards fpecifically bequeathed) books,
horfes, cattle, carriages, harnefs, carts, waggons, ploughs and im-
plements of hufbandry, or belonging to his gardens and hot-houfes,
which fhould be in or upon the premifes at Plaiftow, to Meffrs.
Matthew Woodford, James Stanley and Emperor John Alexander
Woodford, their heirs and affigns upon various trufts for Mrs.
Thelluffon and other purpofes. The firft truft is to permit his wife
Mrs. Thelluffon to enjoy during fuch part of her life as fhe fhall
continue his widow: and this is mixed with a direction, that fhe fhall
have the ufe of 1,400 ounces of plate, which in a fubfequent part
of the will are given amongft his three fons upon her death or fecond
marriage, and with a declaration that the provifions for her by this
will are to be in bar of dower. But upon her death or marrying
again, the will directs the truftees, to fell all the property at Plaiftow
fo devifed in truft, and to carry the money from the fale to the
account of his refiduary perfonal eftate.—Then the will gives directions, for fecuring out of the dividends of £ 22,000, Bank Stock and
by £ 600 a year Long Annuities, a neat yearly income of £ 2,140,
for Mrs. Thelluffon during her life.—But this income is made re-
ducible to £ 300 Long Annuities and the intereft of £ 5,500 Bank
Stock in cafe of her marrying again.

These provifions for the wife of Mr. Thelluffon, which conftitute
all the bequefts in her favour, except an annuity of 100 livres for her
life in the French Funds, are accompanied, with a bequeft of £22,000.
Bank Stock and £ 600 a year Long Annuities, fubject to her life income out of thofe funds, amongft his three fons and his three
daughters. It is a complication of bequefts in the arrangement.
But the fubftance is, that the fum of £ 4000. a piece is given out
of the Bank Stock to his three fons; that the 600. a year Long
Annuities and £ 4,500. of the Bank Stock are equally appropriated
amongft his three daughters; and that the fum of £ 5,500. refidue of
the £ 22,000. Bank Stock is made appointable by the will of Mrs.
Thelluffon amongft the fons and daughters and their iffue, and in
default of appointment equally amongft fuch of them as fhould fur-
vive her and the iffue of fuch as fhould be dead.

Having thus provided for his wife, and difpofed of the property
at Plaiftow and fettled the £ 22,000. Bank Stock and £ 600. a year
Long Annuities upon her and the fix children, the teftator proceeds

2   to.

to give other legacies to his three fons.—Thefe are £ 7,600. to Mr. Peter Ifaac Thelluffon his eldeft fon, to make the money already advanced to him £ 23,000. with a fmall annuity on his life in the French Funds : £ 7,600 to Mr. George Woodford Thelluffon the fecond fon, to make up £ 23,000. to him in the fame manner, with a fmall annuity in the French Funds on his life : and £ 7,600. to Mr. Charles Thelluffon the youngeft fon, to make up £ 23,000. to him, with £ 100. on his life in an Irifh Tontine.

Thefe legacies to the three fons are followed by long provifions arranging a fettlement of the before-mentioned £ 4,500 Bank Stock and £ 600 a year Long Annuities in three equal proportions upon his three daughters and their iffue, and by a legacy of £ 12,000. a piece in truft for the two unmarried daughters, with various reftrictions, and limitations to prevent their marriage without confent of his wife and executors, and to fecure a fettlement of the legacies of £ 12,000. and alfo in the cafe of fome events to carry over great part of thefe provifions for the daughters to the great fweeping fund of the teftator's refiduary perfonal eftate.

Then the will bequeathes £ 100. Irifh Tontine to the eldeft daughter, and various life annuities in the French funds amongft her and her two fifters; and it appropriates other life annuities in the fame funds, for his grandfon, the eldeft fon of Mr. Peter Ifaac Thelluffon, and for two nephews-in-law, fons of Colonel Woodford by the Duke of Gordon's fifter, the Countefs Dowager of Weftmoreland.

The teftator's next bequeft is of his houfe and warehoufes in Philpot-lane, London, where he had long carried on his bufinefs as a merchant, and where at the time of his will his three fons were carrying on the fame bufinefs in partnerfhip. It is a property of confiderable value ; and he gives it to the three truftees before mentioned, on truft to permit his three fons to carry on their bufinefs for fix years from his death. If they continue in bufinefs to the end of that time, the property is in effect given amongft them abfolutely If they fhould all quit bufinefs before the expiration of fix years, the truft is to fell the property, and the money from the fale is added to his refiduary perfonal eftate. His anxiety, that his fons fhould never quit bufinefs, is expreffed with a pathos almoft ludicioufly extravagant . for in adverting to fuch an event within the fix years, he adds in a parenthefis " which I moft earneftly hope and pray to God will *never* be the cafe."

From his Philpot-lane property, the teftator paffes over to the making fome arrangement, as to the income of two eftates in Montferrat and Grenada, which he and the reprefentatives of a Mr Cofsart held in partnership, and of which the teftator's share was fifteen-fixteenths; and and alfo as to £ 250. Long Annuities belonging to the fame partnerfhip.

Having advanced thus far in his difpofitions, the teftator makes a paufe; and fo forgets the feelings of a parent, as to introduce a moralizing fneer at the expence of his three fons, and fo to prepare them as it were for the fhock of the fucceeding difinherifon of them and their children from the great body of his vaft fortune. It is in thefe words. " The provifion, which I have made for my faid three " fons, and the very great fuccefs they have met with, will be fuf-" ficient to procure them comfort, and it is my earneft wifh and " defire, that they will avoid oftentation vanity and pompous fhew, " as that will be the beft fortune they can poffefs "

This unbecoming infinuation againft his three fons is followed with petty legacies of £ 105. a piece for the benefit of his two nephews-in-law, fons of Col. Woodford and Lady Weftmoreland, and fo fettered by a piovifion of accumulation, and fo contingently carried into the gulph of his refiduary truft, as to lofe great part of their little value.

There next follow various legacies of rings, particularly rings each of the value of £ 50. to his three daughters-in-law the ladies of his three fons, and to his fon-in-law Mr. Auguftus Phipps. Thefe are juft fufficient to fhew, that the teftator thought thefe relatives intitled to fome remembrances. Confidered alfo as legacies in that form, they are, it muft be confeffed, handfome: indeed much more fo than could be fpared by the fordidnefs of the vulgar fpecies of avarice.

Then there is a legacy of £ 1000. to his executors in truft for a brother of the teftator in Switzerland for his life, and afterwards for fome nieces there; but ftill with an eye to the favourite fund of the teftator; for if all the nieces fhould die in his brother's life time, the legacy is made to fink into the teftator's refiduary perfonal eftate

After this fparing remembrance of his foreign relatives, the teftator introduces fome legacies to his three fons, and his eldeft giandfon; fuch as, though nothing in a pecuniary point of view, are yet otherwife not wholly inexpieffive of parental amity and family affection. Thofe to Mr. Peter Ifaac Thelluffon the eldeft fon are,—the large picture of the teftator's father by Rigaud,—the large picture of the teftator's mother by Largillere,—all other his family pictures except what are afterwards mentioned,—his father's buft in marble,—his gold feal with the family arms,—the gold fnuff-box; which Lewis the Fifteenth gave to the teftator, containing the portrait of his fon the Dauphin father of Lewis the Sixteenth,—the filver medal copy of the gold one given to the teftator's father by the city of Geneva,—and the filver coffee-pot and

                                                                    falver

salver given to him by that city with the Geneva arms upon them The articles given to the three others are,—a picture of the father of the testator at his seat at Brodsworth to the second son Mr George Woodford Thellusson,—a gold watch by Mudge with three seals to Mr Charles Thellusson the third son,—and the testator's small gold watch to his eldest grandson John Thellusson.

But these little mementos of parental affection are immediately followed, with a further preparation for the grand blow the testator meditated against all his family. This second notice of the projected harshness towards them is conveyed through a bequest, which is chiefly of articles at the testator's seat at Brodsworth in Yorkshire, where his principal real estate was situate for he bequeaths the remainder of his plate, with his books, china, linen, wines, and the remainder of his pictures, and all the furniture at Brodsworth, to be sold, and the money from the sale to be carried to the grand reservoir of his ambitious avarice, his residuary estate ; but qualifies the bequest with the significant exception of such part of the things so given, as his trustees should " think necessary to be " kept for the purpose of receiving any of them or *of his sons who* " *should chuse to spend a little time there occasionally.*"

Having thus the second time broadly hinted at some extraordinary unkindness towards his family, the testator at length fully discloses his vain and ungenerous purpose in the following manner

He begins with devising all the manors lands and hereditaments in Yorkshire which he had purchased of Lord Kinnoul and others, and all his manors lands and hereditaments for the purchase of which he had contracted in writing, and all other his real estates whatsoever and wheresoever, to the three trustees already named, so as to vest the legal fee simple in them upon the trusts after mentioned. The devise is thus expressed

" I give and devise all my manors or lordships messuages lands tene-
" ments and hereditaments, situate at Brodsworth Marr and Ham-
" pole in the county of York, purchased by me from the Right Hon.
" the Earl of Kinnoul, and also my other freehold manor messuages
" lands tenements and hereditaments, purchased by me from William
" Crowther Thomas Bradford and the widow Ducket, situate near
" Hampole and in the several parishes Adwick Thorp and Owston
" near Doncaster in the said county of York : and also the advowson
" right of patronage and presentation of and to the church of Marr
" in the said county, and all the messuages or tenements lands
" hereditaments and premises, for the purchase whereof respectively
" I have made and entered into any contract or contracts in writing,
" together with the benefit and advantage of such contract and
" contracts respectively ; and all other my real estate whatsoever and

B 2   " where-

" wherefoever, unto and to the ufe of the faid Matthew Woodford
" James Stanley and Emperor John Alexander Woodford their heirs
" and affigns for ever, upon the trufts and to and for the intents
" and purpofes herein after mentioned of and concerning the fame."

It is obfervable, that this devife of the teftator's real eftate is expreffed without any exception whatever. But without doubt it
muft be underftood to be fubject, to the previous fpecific arrangements of the teftator's eftate at Plaiftow near Bromley and his houfe
in Philpot-lane London, and his plantations in Montferrat and
Grenada.

Immediately after the devife of the fee of the real eftates, there is
the following bequeft of all the refidue of the teftator's perfonal eftate
to the fame truftees, under a direction to convert the whole into
money, and to inveft fuch money in the purchafe of freehold lands
and hereditaments in fee fimple in England, and of copyholds of
inheritance there not exceeding the proportion of one-fourth of the
whole.

" And as to for and concerning all the reft refidue and remainder
" of my perfonal eftate of whatever kind and condition the fame be,
" as well that which I may be poffeffed of at the time of my de-
" ceafe, as alfo fuch of the faid feveral fums as are in the events and
" on the conditions herein before-mentioned expreffed ordered and
" directed to fink into fuch refiduum, I give and bequeath the fame
" and every part thereof with the appurtenances, unto the faid Matthew
" Woodford James Stanley and Emperor John Alexander Woodford
" their executors adminiftrators and affigns, upon truft and to the
" intent and purpofe, that they the faid Matthew Woodford, James
" Stanley and Emperor John Alexander Woodford and the furvivors
" and furvivor of them and the executors adminiftrators and affigns
" of fuch furvivor, do and fhall as foon as conveniently may be
" after my deceafe, lay out and inveft the fame, converting fuch
" parts thereof into money as fhall not confift of money, and calling
" in fuch money as fhall be placed out on fecurities, in their or his
" own names or name, in the purchafe of freehold lands tenements
" or hereditaments of inheritance in fee fimple, or of copyhold
" eftates of inheritance in that part of Great Britain called England,
" fo that fuch copyhold eftates do not exceed one-fourth in pro-
" portion of the whole of the premifes fo directed to be purchafed
" as aforefaid, but upon the truft and for the intents and purpofes
" herein after-mentioned expreffed and declared of and concerning
" the fame."

Having thus vefted the legal fee of all his Yorkfhire manors and
eftates and his refiduary real eftate and his refiduary perfonal eftate

in the three truftees, and directed them to inveft all his refiduary
perfonal eftate in the purchafe of lands in England, the teftator proceeds to unfold his fcheme, to be an exclufion of all his exifting
iffue, for the fake of accumulating three fortunes, each of unexampled
magnitude, to aggrandize three future and remote male defcendants,
or in cafe of there being only one of the given defcription when the
period of accumulation fhould ceafe and the time of enjoyment
fhould commence, to concentre the whole of the immeafurable
accumulation in fuch fingle individual

The teftator opens this his grand project, with eftablifhing a truft
preventive of all expenditure whatever during a number of lives,
which, on the moft reftrictive conftruction of the language, promife
a period of accumulation for fixty years or more, and leave a poffibility of its lafting for above a century. This part of the plan is thus
expreffed.

" And I declare and direct that the faid Matthew Woodford,
" James Stanley and Emperor John Alexander Woodford, their heirs
" and affigns, fhall ftand and be feized of my faid manors or lord-
" fhips meffuages lands tenements and hereditaments and real eftate
" herein before to them devifed, and of and in the faid freehold
" and copyhold eftates herein before by me directed to be purchafed
" as aforefaid, upon the trufts and to and for the intents and pur-
" pofes herein after-mentioned expreffed and declared of and con-
" cerning the fame, (that is to fay,) upon truft that they the faid
" Matthew Woodford James Stanley and Emperor John Alexander
" Woodford, and the furvivors and furvivor of them, and the heirs
" and affigns of fuch furvivor, do and fhall *(from time to time*
" *during the natural lives, of my faid fons Peter Ifaac Thelluffon,*
" *George Woodford Thelluffon, and Charles Thelluffon, and of*
" *my grandfon John Thelluffon fon of my faid fon Peter*
" *Ifaac Thelluffon; and of fuch other fons as my faid fon*
" *Peter Ifaac Thelluffon now has or may have, and of fuch iffue,*
" *as my faid grandfon John Thelluffon may have, and of fuch iffue,*
" *as any other fons of my faid fon Peter Ifaac Thelluffon may*
" *have, and of fuch fons as my faid fons George Woodford Thel-*
" *luffon and Charles Thelluffon may have, and of fuch iffue, as fuch*
" *fons may have,* AS SHALL BE LIVING AT THE TIME OF MY
" DECEASE OR BORN IN DUE TIME AFTERWARDS, *and during*
" *the natural lives and life of the furvivors and furvivor of the*
" *feveral perfons aforefaid) collect and receive the rents and profits*
" *of the manors or lordfhips meffuages lands tenements and here-*
" *ditaments herein before by me devifed and fo to be purchafed as*
" *aforefaid : and do and fhall from time to time lay out and inveft*
" *the money arifing from fuch rents and profits, in fuch purchafes*
" *as*

" *as I have herein before directed to be made with my said personal*
" *estate: and so from time to time do and shall collect and receive*
" *and lay out and invest the rents and profits of the manors or lord-*
" *ships messuages lands tenements and hereditaments herein before*
" *by me devised and to be purchased as last aforesaid, in the man-*
" *ner herein before directed with respect to the rents and profits of*
" *the manors or lordships messuages lands tenements and heredita-*
" *ments herein before by me devised and to be originally purchased*
" *as aforesaid.*"

After this ACCUMULATING appropriation of the rents and profits
from the testator's general real estate, and the lands to be purchased
with his residuary personal estate, there immediately follows a direction to the trustees, from time to time to cut down the timber fit for
felling, and to sell such timber, and to apply the money from the sale
for the same purpose of purchasing lands · and then the testator
empowers the trustees to make leases of the landed property, and to
act in the management of it, as if the estates were their own

Thus having fixed how long the accumulation should continue,
and such a manner of conducting it, as most completely excludes the
least application of the income from the devised property for any
other purpose, the testator proceeds to describe, what persons should
primarily enjoy the excessive mass of landed property he aimed to
constitute, and what should be the order and manner of succession to
them. His object in this respect is, to divide the accumulated landed
estates into three equal lots, and to settle one lot on the male descendants of his eldest son, another lot on his second son's male descendants, and the remaining lot on his third son's male descendants;
and so to erect three landed fortunes of a magnitude hitherto unknown in England for three distinct branches of the Thellusson
family. His object also is, if there should be a failure of male descendants from one of the sons, to augment with the lot of his branch,
the loss of the branches of the two other sons; or if there should be
a failure of male descendants from two of the three sons, to consoli-
date the three lots into one huge mass of landed property exceeding
the largest territorial private fortune yet known in Europe But in
the execution of this vain project the testator shews more of cunning
than clearness and precision The cunning appears, from his securing
against all possibility of alienating these accumulating expectances,
by making it uncertain who should be the devisees till the very moment the accumulation should cease, and from his attempting to
win Judicature and even Parliament into a support of his project,
by appropriating the accumulated fortune to lessen the national
debt on the remote contingency of an entire failure of male issue of
his three sons But either because his scheme of future entail was

too whimfical to be clearly defcribed , or becaufe he had not a com-
mand of our language adequate to convey a full idea of his meaning
to thofe who affifted him in the will profeffionally, there is fuch an obfcurity, as at leaft makes it very uncertain, both who was the male
defcendant of each fon intended to take in the fift inftance, and
who on the determination of fuch male defcendant's eftate in tail
male were intended to take fucceffively as male defcendants afterwards.

The direction of the teftator, for ceffer of the accumulation, and
for partition and entail of the accumulated property on the male
defcendants of his three fons when that time fhall arrive, is given to
his truftees in the following manner   It begins thus

" And I do hereby direct that AFTER THE DECEASE OF THE
" SURVIVOR OF THE SAID SEVERAL PERSONS, DURING WHOSE
" LIVES THE RENTS AND PROFITS *of the manors or lordfhips*
" *meffuages lands tenements and hereditaments herein before by*
" *me devifed and to be purchafed as aforefaid* ARE HEREBY DI-
" RECTED TO ACCUMULATE *as aforefaid, an equal partition fhall*
" *be made by my faid truftees,* or the furvivors or furvivor of them
" and the truftees to be appointed as hereafter mentioned, *of the*
" *manors or lordfhips meffuages lands tenements and hereditaments*
" *herein before devifed and fo to be purchafed* from time to time
" as aforefaid, *and the whole thereof divided into* THREE *lots of*
" *equal value,* or as near thereto as poffible "

This direction for a divifion into three lots is immediately followed
with an inftruction, how to fettle the FIRST lot, and for that purpofe the will proceeds thus .

" *And that the premifes contained in* ONE SUCH LOT *fhall be*
" *conveyed to the ufe of the* ELDEST MALE LINEAL DESCENDANT
" THEN LIVING *(and who fhall be entitled to the choice of fuch*
" *allotments) of my faid fon Peter Ifaac Thellvffon in tail male* ,
" *with remainder to the* SECOND, THIRD, FOURTH, AND ALL AND
" EVERY OTHER MALE LINEAL DESCENDANT OR DESCENDANTS,
" THEN LIVING, WHO SHALL BE INCAPABLE OF TAKING AS
" HEIR IN TAIL MALL OF ANY OF THE PERSONS TO WHOM A
" PRIOR ESTATE IS HEREBY DIRECTED TO BE LIMITED, OR
" MY SAID SON PETER ISAAC THELLUSSON SUCCESSIVELY IN
" TAIL MALL   *with remainder in equal moieties,* TO THE ELDEST
" AND EVERY OTHER MALE LINEAL DESCENDANT OR DESCEN-
" DANTS THEN LIVING OF MY SAID SONS GEORGE WOODFORD
" THELLUSSON AND CHARLES THELLUSSON, *as tenants in com-*
" *mon in tail male, in the fame manner as herein before directed*
" WITH RESPECT TO THE ELDEST AND EVERY OTHER MALE
                                            " LINEAL

" LINEAL DESCENDANT AND DESCENDANTS OF MY SAID SON
" PETER ISAAC THELLUSSON; *with cross remainders between or*
" *among such male lineal descendants as aforesaid of my said sons*
" *George Woodford Thelluson and Charles Thellusson in tail male,*
" *or in case there shall be but* ONE SUCH MALE LINEAL DESCEN-
" DANT, *then* TO SUCH ONE *in tail male, with remainder to the use of*
" *them the said Matthew Woodford James Stanley and Emperor John*
" *Alexander Woodford their heirs and assigns for ever, upon the*
" *trusts and for the intents and purposes herein after-mentioned*
" *expressed and delared of and concerning the same* "

Having directed this settlement of one of the three lots, in favour
primarily of future male descendants of Mr. Peter Isaac Thellusson
the *eldest son*, but with limitations over in moieties to the future
male descendants of the two younger sons respectively, and with cross
remainders; the testator goes on to direct a settlement of the two
other lots on a like plan. That is the testator, in the same obscure
way, first orders one of the two remaining lots to be entailed on his
second son's future male descendants, with limitations over in moieties
to his eldest son's and his third son's future male descendants and
cross remainders between them; and the third and remaining lot to
be in like manner limited to the third son's future male descendants,
with remainders over to the future male descendants of the eldest
and second sons, and with cross remainder between them also. This
further disposition is in the words following :

" And that the premises included *in one other of such allotments*
" and which shall compose the same, shall be conveyed *to the use of*
" *the* ELDEST MALE LINEAL DESCENDANT THEN LIVING *(who*
" *shall likewise be intitled to the second choice of such allotments)of*
" *my said son George Woodford Thellusson in tail male, with remain-*
" *ders to the* SECOND THIRD FOURTH AND ALL AND EVERY OTHER
" MALE LINEAL DESCENDANT OR DESCENDANTS THEN LIVING,
" WHO SHALL BE INCAPABLE OF TAKING AS HEIR IN TAIL
" MALE OF ANY OF THE PERSONS TO WHOM A PRIOR ESTATE
" IS HEREBY DIRECTED TO BE LIMITED OF MY SAID SON
" GEORGE WOODFORD THELLUSSON SUCCESSIVELY IN TAIL
" MALE, WITH REMAINDERS IN EQUAL MOIETIES TO THE
" ELDEST AND EVERY OTHER MALE LINEAL DESCENDANT OR
" DESCENDANTS THEN LIVING OF MY SAID SONS PETER ISAAC
" THELLUSSON AND CHARLES THELLUSSON AS TENANTS IN
" COMMON IN TAIL MALE, *in the same manner as is herein before*
" *directed with respect to the eldest and every other male lineal*
" *descendant or descendants of my said son George Woodford Thel-*
" *lusson, with cross remainders between or among such male lineal*

5

" *descen*

" *descendants as aforesaid of my said sons Peter Isaac Thellusson*
" *and Charles Thellusson in tail male, or in case there shall be but*
" *one such male lineal descendant then to such one in tail male;*
" *with remainder to the use of the said Matthew Woodford James*
" *Stanley and Emperor John Alexander Woodford their heirs and*
" *assigns for ever, upon the trusts and to and for the intents and*
" *purposes herein after-mentioned expressed and declared of and*
" *concerning the same.*"

" And that the premises included in the *remaining lot*, which
" shall compose the same, shall be conveyed *to the use* OF THE
" ELDEST MALE LINEAL DESCENDANT THEN LIVING *of my*
" *said son Charles Thellusson in tail male, with remainder to the*
" SECOND THIRD FOURTH AND ALL AND EVERY OTHER MALE
" LINEAL DESCENDANT OR DESCENDANTS THEN LIVING, WHO
" SHALL BE INCAPABLE OF TAKING AS HEIR IN TAIL MALE
" OF ANY OF THE PERSONS TO WHOM A PRIOR ESTATE IS
" HEREBY DIRECTED TO BE LIMITED, OF MY SAID SON CHARLES
" THELLUSSON SUCCESSIVELY IN TAIL MALE, *with remainders*
" *in equal moieties to the eldest and every other male* LINEAL DE-
" SCENDANT OR DESCENDANTS THEN LIVING OF MY SAID SONS
" PETER ISAAC THELLUSSON AND GEORGE WOODFORD THEL-
" LUSSON, AS TENANTS IN COMMON IN TAIL MALE, *in the same*
" *way as herein before directed with respect to the eldest and every*
" *other male lineal descendant or descendants as aforesaid of my*
" *said son Charles Thellusson, with cross remainders between or*
" *among such male lineal descendants as aforesaid of my said sons*
" *Peter Isaac Thellusson and George Woodford Thellusson in tail*
" *male, or in case there shall be but one such male lineal descendant*
" *then to such one in tail male, with remainder to the use of the*
" *said Matthew Woodford James Stanley and Emperor John*
" *Alexander Woodford their heirs and assigns for ever, upon the*
" *trusts and to and for the intents and purposes herein after-mentioned*
" *expressed and declared of and concerning the same.*"

These dispositions of the three allotments of the landed fortune, into
which the testator divides his vast general and residuary estate and the
expectant uncountable accumulation from it, are succeeded by a further blow to his children and grandchildren. It is observable, that
the entail of each allotment concludes with a remainder in fee upon
trusts referred to as declared by a subsequent part of the will. After
such pains peremptorily to exclude all his existing issue, and contingently to exclude all future issue, till the long trust of accumulation should expire, there could not be any reason to expect, that the
testator would shew any kindness to his family in the further and
ultimate disposition. Accordingly even the remote reversionary interest is denied to them; and under the appearances of an extraor-

c   dinary

dinary devotion to the interest of the country, into which the testator was naturalized, he gives the finish to the disinherison of his existing issue of every description, by creating a trust, on determination of his entail on the future male descendants of his three sons, for selling the whole of the accumulated property, and for applying the money from the sale to the use of the SINKING FUND towards paying off the NATIONAL DEBT. The manner of this ostentatious disposition is thus.—First there is the following clause directing the trustees to sell.

" And I declare and direct, that the said Matthew Woodford,
" James Stanley and Emperor John Alexander Woodford, their heirs
" and assigns, shall stand and be seized of the manors or lordships,
" advowson, right of patronage and presentation, messuages, lands,
" tenements and hereditaments, and real estate herein before by me
" devised and so to be purchased as aforesaid, UPON FAILURE OF
" MALE LINEAL DESCENDANTS *of my said sons Peter Isaac*
" *Thellusson, George Woodford Thellusson and Charles Thellusson*
" *as aforesaid, in trust to make sale* and dispose of all the said
" manors or lordships advowson right of patronage and presenta-
" tion, messuages, lands tenements and hereditaments and real
" estate, either together or in parcels, unto any person or persons
" whomsoever, for the best price or prices in money that can be
" reasonably had or gotten for the same."—After this direction
to sell the accumulated property, there is a provision authorizing the trustees to give receipts to purchasers.—Then comes a bequest of the money from the sale, ordering it to be paid to the Crown for the use of the SINKING FUND in these words.

" And I declare and direct, that the said Matthew Woodford
" James Stanley and Emperor John Alexander Woodford their heirs
" executors administrators and assigns, *do and shall pay the money,*
" *to arise and be produced from the sale* or sales of my said manors
" or lordships advowson, right of patronage and presentation, mes-
" suages lands tenements and hereditaments and real estate herein
" before devised and so to be purchased as aforesaid, *unto his Majesty.*
" *his heirs and successors Kings and Queens of England to be ap-*
" *plied to the use of the* SINKING FUND *in such manner as shall*
" *be directed by act of Parliament.*"

This ultimate destination of the money from sale of the accumulated landed estate to the public use, upon the remote contingency of *failure of male lineal descendants* of the testator's sons and grandsons, is accompanied with a bequest of rents and profits to the same public purpose in the mean time till sale.

The will next contains power to the trustees to place out the testator's personal estate, and the accumulating monies from it and from the purchased lands, upon security, till convenient purchases shall

shall be found; and this power * is so expressed as seemingly at least *to continue the accumulation* till purchases of land shall actually be made; and if this be so, it adds an uncertain protraction of the accumulation and consequently of all enjoyment under the executory devises or trusts, beyond the various lives selected to postpone the commencement of them.

After this come the usual provisions for indemnity of the trustees, with power for the trustees for the time being to appoint new trustees, if the three named by the testator, or any of them, should decline to act or die before completion of the trusts of the will.

Then the will gives a direction as to the devised advowson and as to any advowsons which should be purchased, appointing, that when the livings should become void the trustees should present to them, as his three sons in rotation and after them their respective *eldest male lineal descendants* should nominate.

The next provision of the will is a very anxious one, for confining the enjoyment of the accumulated fortune to the name of THELLUSSON. To secure this primary object of his ambitious project of erecting three huge landed fortunes, the testator not only

---

* The clause is in the following words

" And whereas my said trustees may not be able immediately to find a convenient
" purchase or convenient purchases, wherein to lay out my said personal estate;
" and the money, which shall arise from time to time by the rents and profits of any
" lands to be purchased as aforesaid or by the sale of timber from such estates, may
" not, as the same shall from time to time, accrue, amount to a sufficient sum to
" make proper purchases. Now I do hereby authorise and empower my said trust-
" tees and the survivors and survivor of them his executors administrators and assigns,
" in the mean time and until a convenient purchase or convenient purchases can
" be made, to permit such part of my said personal estate as is now invested in the
" Funds or consists of securities for money to remain in such Funds or upon such
" securities, and to invest or place out the money to arise from such part of my
" said personal estate as shall not at my decease consist of money and from the rents
" and profits of the lands tenements and hereditaments to be purchased pursuant to
" the directions of this my will or from the sale of timber upon such estates, in any
" of the public Stocks or Funds or on any Government or real security or secu-
" rities; and from time to time to sell all or any of the Stocks or Funds wherein
" any of the said trust money is or may be invested, and to call in all or any part
" of the said trust monies, which is or may be placed out on any security or secu-
" rities, and again to invest the money to arise from such sale or sales and to be
" called in as aforesaid, in any other of the public Stocks or Funds or upon any
" other Government or real securities, when and so often as my said trustees or the
" survivors or survivor of them his heirs executors or administrators shall think
" proper, UNTIL A CONVENIENT PURCHASE OR CONVENIENT PURCHASES CAN
" BE FOUND OR UNTIL A SUFFICIENT SUM OF MONEY SHALL BE ACCUMULATED
" TO MAKE A PROPER PURCHASE OR PROPER PURCHASES And I do hereby declare,
" that THE INTEREST DIVIDENDS AND ANNUAL PRODUCE OF THE SAID STOCKS
" FUNDS AND SECURITIES SHALL ACCUMULATE, IN THE SAME MANNER, AND
" FOR THE SAME PURPOSES AS THE RENTS AND PROFITS OF THE LANDS TO BE
" PURCHASED AS AFORESAID ARE HEREIN BEFORE DIRECTED TO ACCUMULATE "

requires.

requires, that all perfons, becoming intitled to the accumulated property or any fhare of it, fhould at all times afterwards ufe the SURNAME of THELLUSSON ONLY, but, in default of their fo doing, directs the truftees to fell the eftates, and to pay the money from the fale of them to the King to the ufe of the SINKING FUND

Having thus nearly concluded his provifions for facrificing the moft valuable interefts of his children and grandchildren at the altar of vanity, the teftator, as if doubtful, whether the monftroufnefs of his unfeeling difinherifon of his exifting family might not tempt Parliament to refcind the chief difpofition of his vaft fortune, folemnly adds a kind of earneft fupplication to the legiflature not to interpofe His words are, " As I have earned the fortune, which " I now poffefs, with induftry and honefty, *I truft and hope that* " *the* LEGISLATURE *will not in any manner alter my will*, or the " limitations thereby created, but permit my property to go in the " manner in which I hereby difpofe of it."

After this folemn invocation of Parliament not to difturb his will, the teftator directs the rent of his houfe in Philpot-lane, till the end of the fix years after which under a prior part of the will his three fons, if they continued together in bufinefs, were to have it, to be carried to the great fund of his refiduary eftate, and in favour of the fame fund, he revokes the before-mentioned legacies of £ 12,000. to his two younger daughters, if they fhould marry in his life time.

Here alfo, in order ftill further to guard againft all deduction from the grand fund of his refiduary eftate, and for that purpofe to go the utmoft length in excluding his heirs at law, whoever they might be, from all poffible benefit in that character, the teftator even attempts to devife away his future purchafes of land. He had already included in his favourite refiduary fund the lands which he had contracted to buy. But his acutenefs led him to forefee what really happened, namely, that after his will he might contract for other purchafes. And as it may be prefumed, being informed, that all fuch contracts would intitle his heir to have them completed for his benefit out of the perfonal eftate of the teftator, he aims to exclude his heir, whoever he fhould be, even from fuch a cafualty. With that view the teftator inferts the following claufe :

" In cafe I fhall in my life time enter into any contracts for the " purchafe of any lands tenements or hereditaments, and I fhall " happen to die before the neceffary conveyances thereof are execut- " ed, I order and direct, that all and every fuch contract or con- " tracts, fo entered into by me as aforefaid, fhall be completed and " carried into execution by my faid truftees after my death, and

2   " that

" that the purchafe monies for fuch refpective eftates and premifes
" fhall be paid by them, by with and out of my perfonal eftate and
" effects, and that the deeds and conveyances thereto refpectively
" fhall be made to them their heirs and affigns ; and that they and
" every of them fhall ftand remain and be feized and poffeffed of all
" and fingular the premifes fo to be conveyed, upon under and fub-
" ject to fuch and the fame ufes trufts limitations provifoes and con-
" ditions, as are in and by this my will created of and concerning
" the eftates hereby directed to be purchafed by and with the afore-
" faid refiduum of my eftates and effects in the manner herein before-
" mentioned "

With this laft provifion, for thus profpectively abforbing even his
future purchafes into the mafs of the fund of accumulation, the teftator haftens to the conclufion of his will. for the fmall remainder
of it is confined, to fubftituting Mr George Hibbert the merchant
as a truftee with a legacy of 300 guineas, in cafe of the death in the
teftator's life time of either of the three truftees Mr. Matthew
Woodford Mr. Stanley and Mr. Emperor John Alexander Woodford, to appointing the three latter gentlemen and his wife Mrs.
Thelluffon his executors and executrix, and to revoking all his
former wills.

———————

Such is the *unnatural* laft will of the late Mr. Thelluffon ; and
fuch are the proud and vain trufts, for the fake of which he has
thought fit to devote the grand mafs of his vaft fortune, in breach
of the ties of natural affection, and in defiance of the powerful claims
of his numerous exifting family.

The object of the prefent confideration of his will, being fingly
to argue and controvert the validity of the trufts it creates of his
general real property and of his refiduary perfonal eftate, it may
feem, as if a fhorter and more limited ftatement might have fufficed,
and as if all notice of any parts of the will, beyond the grand difpofition now meant to be controverted, might have been fpared   But
there are points of view, in which, neither can the objections, againft
the aggrandizing truft of accumulation, and againft the trufts appointed to take effect when that is permitted by the teftator to ceafe,
be underftood in their full force ; nor can the demands upon judicature to condemn all thofe trufts be preffed in their full extent,
without occafionally adverting to the bearings of the will and its de-
pendencies and connections in other refpects.   At leaft this is my
feeling of the cafe.   Therefore I have undergone the labour of
travelling over every part of the will, and I have fo ftated and explained its various arrangements, as to give the largeft poffible fcope
for remark and the wideft range for argument.

With

With refpect to the facts fubfequent to the will, they lie in a narrow compafs, being only to the following effect

Some fhort time after the making of the will, there was a great change in the late Mr. Thelluffon's conftitution; and from being feemingly in the beft ftate of health and likely to live to a very extended age, he fell into a decay; and the refult was his death the *21st* fecond of laft *May* April*, which was about a year and four months after the date of his will, leaving Mrs Thelluffon his widow, Mr. Peter Ifaac Thelluffon his eldeft fon and heir, and him and his younger brothers Mr. George Woodford Thelluffon and Mr. Charles Thelluffon and their three fifters Mrs Phipps, Mifs Maria Thelluffon, and Mifs Augufta Charlotte Thelluffon, his fix children and only next of kin.

At the time of his death, the ftate of his family was nearly the fame as when his will was executed. The difference was, that about five months before his deceafe the Lady of his fon Mr. Charles Thelluffon was brought to bed of a fon who is ftill living; and that the Lady of Mr. Peter Ifaac Thelluffon the teftator's eldeft fon was pregnant, the refult of which pregnancy is not yet afcertained †. Including therefore Mrs Thelluffon the teftator's widow who is ftill living, and the grandfon fo born between the teftator's will and his deceafe, and the child or children with which his eldeft fon's Lady was and ftill is pregnant, the teftator's family ftood thus. It confifted of his widow, three fons all married, one married daughter, two daughters unmarried, four grandfons, four grand-daughters, and one grand-child or more or grand-children *en ventre fa mere*, and that is the prefent ftate of the family concerning which the table annexed to the prefent cafe and argument will give fome other explanations more efpecially as to the ages of the children and grand-children

As to the teftator's fortune at his death, it appears from a ftatement, which has been fince made, that, exclufive of fome plantation property in Grenada and Montferrat, his real eftate confifted of the manor of Broadfworth and other manors and freehold eftates of inheritance in Yorkfhire, of the value of about £ 4000 a year, and computed with the furniture of Broadfworth Houfe to have coft £ 140,000 — an houfe and eftate at Plaiftow, which including furniture is valued at £ 25,000.—and his freehold houfe and warehoufe in Philpot-lane, London, valued at £ 10,000 more. According alfo to the fame ftatement, the teftator's perfonal fortune confifted of three per cent Stock, which including £ 113,388 . 9 10. three per cent Imperial Annuities amounted to £ 396,458 8 . 7 in

* April *July* 1797

† She was, foon after the writing of the cafe and arguments from which this extract is made, brought to bed of twins, namely, two fons.

three

three per cents—£ 21,000. Bank Stock—£ 14,125 India Stock—£ 36,005 : 11 · 1 four per cents—£ 2,500 in South-Sea Stock—£ 3000 five per cents Loyalty Loan—£ 1500. Irifh five per cents—£ 712 Irifh Annuity—£ 900 Long Annuity—to the value of £ 2,500. in Hudfon's Bay Stock—£ 49000 payable by inftalments and fecured by the Bond of a firm of undoubted credit—various other debts valued at £ 56,000.—£ 24,000 in bills on the Eaft-India Company—and £ 5,500. cafh at his banker's

Put together the teftator's property real and perfonal has been eftimated at the vaft fum of £ 721,000 Even, notwithftanding the prefent low ftate of the Public Funds, the great bulk of the fortune,—that, which his will cruelly wrefts from his exifting family, and appropriates as a facrifice to pride and to gratify vanity,—that, which the will conftitutes as a fund for accumulation, till all his fons and exifting grandfons fhall have ceafed to exift,—is thought to be equal to about £ 600,000. in value.

No. II.

Copy of Mr. MORGAN's *Calculation of the Accumulation under the Trufts of the late Mr.* THELLUSSON's *Will*

FROM the annexed claufe of of Mr. Thelluffon's will it is obvious, that the final diftribution of his property cannot be determined before the extinction of the nine lives of his male defcendants now aged 37, 33, 29, 13, 6, 5, 1, 1, and 2 years, and confequently that the fame muft be fuffered to accumulate during the whole continuance of a term, which fhall be equal to the duration, of the laft furvivor of thofe lives.

From the moft correct tables of the probabilities of human life, it appears to be *more* than an equal chance, that one or other of nine fuch lives will continue in exiftence to the full term of 70 years, and therefore that it is *more* than an equal chance, that Mr Thelluffon's property will be fuffered to accumulate to the end of this term. Affuming, however, this period for the whole time in which the property is to accumulate, it will follow, if the money being improved at five per cent, that each £ 100,000. of which Mr. Thelluffon died poffeffed, will, when it comes to be finally difpofed of amount to £ 3,042,642. fo that if he died poffeffed of £ 600,000 it will amount to £ 18,255,852, if of £ 650,000 it will amount to £ 19,777,173; and if of £ 700,000. it will amount to £ 21,298,494. At prefent, indeed, money is capable of being improved at a much

higher

higher interest than five per cent; and were it to continue at the same rate, as it is now, the accumulation would be *twice* as much as I have stated it. But it is not probable, that for so long a period circumstances will remain so favourable to the improvement of property and therefore it would be improper to compute on such principles. It must however be observed, that the preceding calculations, by limiting their continuance to 70 years, are founded on the supposition, that all the lives will *certainly* become extinct in that period, although it is *more* than an equal chance, that the contrary will prove so Were we allowed to argue from a *possible*, and not from a probable event, the term might be extended to the utmost limit of human life, which, as the two youngest children are only one year old, would equal 95 years During such a period, each £ 100,000 improved at five per cent, would amount to more than ten millions, and at the present rate of interest to more than 25 millions. But this, though a *possible*, is an *extreme* case, and therefore not to be adopted Nevertheless, it cannot be denied, that there is an essential difference between a *possible* and the *probable* event, however remote that probability may be; and in consequence that it cannot be unsafe to extend the term of the accumulation rather further than that, for the continuance of which the probabilities are more than equal, considering the possibility of a minor being alive at the death of the last survivor, which of course would postpone the final distribution a few years, and as the chances are nearly equal, that the last survivor does not die before the end of 75 years, I do not think that the term of this accumulation ought to be taken much if at all below 80 years, during which period the property, if £ 600,000. will amount at five per cent, to £ 29,736,865, if £ 650,000. it will amount to £ 32,214,937, and if £ 700,000. it will amount to £ 34,693,009. Should it however be thought more reasonable to limit the accumulation to 75 years, these several sums will in that case amount even to £ 23,299,611. £ 25,241,245 and £ 27,182,880. respectively, which are indeed sufficiently immense, but perhaps considerably inferior to the sum, to which they will hereafter be found to have accumulated, as well from the improvement of money at a higher rate, as from the lengthened duration of the last survivor's existence.

November 30, 1798.

WILL MORGAN.
Equitable Assurance Office.

FH
MVSEVM
BRITANNICVM

Lightning Source UK Ltd.
Milton Keynes UK
UKHW050823130123
415295UK00010B/945